# The Learning Differences Sourcebook

Also by Nancy Boyles and Darlene Contadino:

*Parenting a Child with*
*Attention Deficit/Hyperactivity Disorder*

# The Learning Differences Sourcebook

*by*

Nancy S. Boyles, M.Ed.

*and*

Darlene Contadino, M.S.W.

LOWELL HOUSE

LOS ANGELES

*NTC/Contemporary Publishing Group*

**Library of Congress Cataloging in Publication Data**

Boyles, Nancy S.
    The learning differences sourcebook / by Nancy S. Boyles, Darlene
Contadino
    Includes bibliographical references and index.
    ISBN 1-56565-795-0
    ISBN 0-7373-0024-8 (paperback)
    1. Learning disabled children—Education—United States—Handbooks,
manuals, etc. 2. Learning disabilities—United States—Handbooks, manuals, etc.
3. Cognitive learning styles in children— United States—Handbooks, manuals,
etc. 4. Learning—Handbooks, manuals, etc. I. Contadino, Darlene. II. Title.
LC4705.B69 1997                                                            97-37654
370.15′23—dc21                                                                  CIP

Requests for such permissions should be addressed to:
Lowell House
2020 Avenue of the Stars, Suite 300
Los Angeles, CA  90067

Published by Lowell House, a division of NTC/Contemporary Publishing Group, Inc.
4255 West Touhy Avenue, Lincolnwood, Illinois 60646-1975 U.S.A.

Text design: Dello & Associates, Inc.

Printed and bound in the United States of America
International Standard Book Number: 0-7373-0024-8
    7890 DOC DOC 01987654

*"There is no loneliness greater than the loneliness of failure."*
—Eric Hoffer

For all the children who learn differently
and whose struggles have inspired us.

# Acknowledgments

A special thanks to Barbara Easter for her computer skills, expertise, and patience as she assisted with formatting the manuscript; Janice Fuller for carrying the load during Nancy's family crisis so that she could continue to write; Rosemarie Smith for moral support and finding sanity in chaos; to everyone who supported us and patiently put their priorities on hold so that this book could be written in a timely manner; most especially, my (Nancy's) forever, patient, supportive, and loving soul mate, David, and our equally encouraging son, Christian.

We also wish to thank the following agencies and individuals who shared resources and provided support for this project. Agencies: Obsessive Compulsive Foundation; National Council for Learning Disabilities; Cincinnati Occupational Therapy Institute; Autism Services Center; Special Educational Regional Resource Center of Southwestern Ohio; U.S. Department of Education; American Speech-Language-Hearing Association; Brain Injury Association, Inc.; Cincinnati Association for the Blind; American Foundation for the Blind; St. Rita's School for the Deaf; Tourette Syndrome Association, Inc.; ARC, Board of Mental Retardation & Developmental Disabilities; Division of Audiology, University of Cincinnati Medical Center; Public Library of Hamilton County and Cincinnati; Spina Bifida Association of America; United Cerebral Palsy Association, Inc. Individuals: Karin Riley, attorney for Ohio Department of Education; Melvin D. Levine, M.D., University of North Carolina at Chapel Hill; Neil Matkin, Ph.D., University of Arizona; Nancy McIwain, New City Schools; Sandra Tattershall, Ph.D., C.C.C., speech pathologist.

An extra special thanks to the following individuals who read portions of the manuscript and shared their insights. Joan Dostal, OTR, Cincinnati Occupational Therapy Institute; Anne M. Bauer, Ed.D., head of Early Childhood Education, University of Cincinnati; Peggy Riegal, director of Special Education Regional Resource Center of Southwestern Ohio; Susan Kerscher, M.S., C.C.C., speech pathologist; Laura Griffin, ARC, M.R.D.D.; Robert Keith, Ph.D., and Rebekah Fallis, M.S., Department of Audiology, University of Cincinnati Medical Center; Gina Carroll, L.I.S.W., Cincinnati Association for the Blind; Sue Levi-Pearl, Tourette Syndrome Association.

# Contents

# Foreword

A colleague eyed me skeptically when I related my latest undertaking. "A sourcebook discussing the myriad of disabilities in *one* volume?" she questioned, glancing at her floor-to-ceiling bookshelf, which contained books primarily on reading disabilities, her area of expertise. This was a common reaction among our colleagues.

We rose to the challenge, however, to prepare a sourcebook with a very comprehensive look at the children who are seated in classrooms each day. The purpose of this manual is not to give readers a detailed description of every disability, but to introduce them to the topic. Provided with thorough, basic information, our readers can become familiar with the specific areas of concern to them. More specific and inclusive information can be attained through the resources we have noted throughout the book.

The amount of information available on each topic amazed and often overwhelmed us. We were very impressed by the willingness of national organizations to share large quantities of information and then refer us to state and local agencies for additional resources.

Both authors are parents of children with learning disabilities. Darlene's children were diagnosed with attention-deficit/hyperactivity disorder (AD/HD) and have specific learning disabilities. Nancy's children have also been diagnosed with AD/HD and have learning disabilities and language disorders.

When our children were diagnosed with AD/HD, very little information was available to us, and few support agencies were in place. We experienced firsthand the feelings of grief, isolation, and guilt. We struggled with educators to get accommodations for our children before the laws made it mandatory.

Our children, however, are survivors with promising futures. Both of Nancy's children have college degrees. Darlene's older son is working toward his college degree, her younger son is in high school looking toward college, and her daughter is married and has a young son. We have shared our personal experiences in our collaborative effort *Parenting a Child With Attention Deficit/Hyperactivity Disorder*.

In this book, we share our professional expertise in working with children with learning differences and their families. As a social worker, Darlene addresses family issues, grief, and clinical management techniques. She is part of a collaborative system that finds ways to help individuals and their families manage their concerns and get the appropriate supports.

As an educator and a learning specialist, Nancy guides parents and teachers through the identification, evaluation, and intervention planning phases to meet the needs of the learner. In classrooms every day, she works collaboratively with school personnel, community professionals, and parents to make learning successful for the child.

Through our personal and professional experiences, we have come to recognize that learning is shaped by a multitude of experiences. Environment, genetic makeup, and early learning experiences are just a few pieces of the puzzle that shape the child and set the stage for learning. However, we realize that all stages are not created equal. This does not mean some are less valuable than others, just that they are different. If a child with a learning difference is to be successful, it may be necessary to fill that stage with sturdier props, stronger supporting characters, and a more focused direction. This job usually falls to the parents and to the school.

Over a hundred years ago, Walt Whitman wrote a poem called *Song of Myself*. It is a celebration of human diversity. He wrote that we are "learners and teachers all." That is how we can fulfill our jobs as parents and teachers. We learn first of all by watching the child. He is the best teacher of his song. Then we must educate ourselves about learning differences. It is not enough just to recognize a learning difference; we must also understand the child's needs and how all the factors influence the child in the academic, social, and family systems.

After we have learned, we must teach. We teach by advocating for the child whenever obstacles are tossed in his path. We also must teach the child by demystifying the differences with which he struggles. Then he can understand how to advocate for himself and find new ways of learning. This protects his spirit and helps him and us cope with the bad reviews.

These have been our goals in writing this sourcebook. We are providing the basic information needed to begin the process of learning about the child who is striving for success. From here, there are generous and knowledgeable individuals available to support you along your journey. They are waiting with information to share, as well as the time and patience to answer your questions and point you in a specific direction. You do not have to travel this road alone.

This sourcebook can help you formulate the right questions. Once you know the questions, you can determine which resources will supply the answers. To effectively use this manual, it may help to visualize it as organized in the shape of an hourglass: The information goes from very general to specific to general again.

We begin by looking at the total child. It is our strong belief that children are much more than the labels we place on them. It is our hope that by developing an awareness of all the components influencing how a child learns, the reader will gain an appreciation of the complexity of the process.

After presenting a multifaceted perspective of the child and learning, we address the guidelines described in the federal legislation that protects the rights of a child with disabilities. How the specific needs of the learners protected by these laws are evaluated and identified is divided into two parts. The school and clinical evaluations are examined separately. Inclusion, the new buzz word for the least restrictive placement of children, is also explored. We include many technical terms and the jargon that parents need to know and understand so they can effectively advocate for their child.

The middle section of the book is the narrow waist of the hourglass. It is very specific, in that each disability, disorder, and condition that can interfere with learning is discussed in a separate chapter. Each chapter begins by defining the disability and ends with effective suggestions that can be used to support the learner. This section begins with those disabilities for which the school most frequently evaluates, and progresses to neurological and physical disorders requiring a clinical diagnosis.

As the hourglass fans out at the base, our topics again become more general. The focus in the last section of the book is on supporting the child and the family. A chapter on the grieving process begins this section. Then we discuss some of the more commonly used clinical therapies and management approaches available for parents, schools, and the child. We conclude with a look to the future. Developing study and test-taking skills is discussed, along with alternatives to the traditional classroom. The selection of a college or vocational placement concludes this sourcebook.

Just as the sand slips back and forth through an hourglass, so the chapters in this sourcebook overlap. It is impossible to separate many of the issues involving learning. We would be naive to try to oversimplify such a complex function. With every part of our lives interrelated, we cannot look at learning through only one lens. We must consider the environment, culture, family values, genetic composition, developmental maturation, life experiences, and available support systems as integrated parts of the learning process.

Life is not static. Just when we think we have it all together, someone turns the hourglass over, and the sands of our lives shift once again. A new teacher enters the picture, and the process of educating him or her about your child's needs begins anew. Semester exams or thirty-page term papers rock the equilibrium of the student barely keeping up with daily assignments. A traumatic change within the family, such as a death, divorce, or major illness, sends everyone reeling.

For these reasons, we prefer to think in terms of learning differences rather than disabilities. Within the context of this book, it may appear we are contradicting ourselves. At the top and bottom of our hourglass, we are referring to learners in general. Everyone learns differently, for all the reasons mentioned. Many students struggle in school with differences not severe enough to be identified or to qualify the students for support services. Unless the factors that influence how they learn are identified and addressed, these children with differences in how they learn fall through the cracks in the educational system.

When we are referring to disabilities affecting learning, our focus becomes more specific and narrows, as does the neck of our hourglass. In addition to all the learning differences, the child also demonstrates specific characteristics, physical and/or neurological, that classify as a disability. At one time, such children were excluded from the right to a free appropriate public education, but naming the specific disability now guarantees the child an education under federal law.

Unfortunately, the reality is that unless the disability is named, no support services can be given to make learning more conducive. Therefore children get labeled. Personally, we dislike labels. Terms such as "LD child", "ADDer," and "blind children" send shivers down our spines. As parents of children who have struggled with learning disabilities, we know how frustrating it is when others only see the disorder and miss the child.

We acknowledge the necessity of a label to obtain services for the child. However, the focus should never remain on the child's disabilities. Once these are identified, focusing on the strengths and talents of the child will direct the path to successful intervention. For this reason, we have used "person first" language in this book. This means that we refer first to the individual instead of the disability. For example, we reference "children with ADD" or "children with traumatic brain injury," rather than "the mentally retarded child."

The theme of putting the child first permeates this book. In using this manual as a starting place, you can find good basic information and resources to discover the child before you. Yes, we admit that entire books have been written about each of the topics we address, but their purpose is not that of a sourcebook. This handbook is designed to relate information in an abbreviated form. Though condensed, every topic in this writing has been well researched and documented to give you the most current and pertinent information available as you search for answers. Through the kindness and generosity of expert readers (see Acknowledgments), we can ensure that our research has been accurately consolidated and that we have honored the child with the disability.

To assist you as you strive to better understand the child and the learning process, we have provided food for thought and a variety of perspectives to broaden your scope. We have attempted to provide different lenses through which to view the learner. Children are curious about their world. They are eager to learn and even more eager to please. When learning becomes an unpleasant experience, we need to find out why. This book will assist as you explore the possibilities in your search for answers.

# 1

# The Whole Child

We don't do rap. At least not very often. Yet when we hear a truth, we acknowledge it, and the artist Coolio has expressed a truth in the song "Gangsta Paradise": "If they don't understand, how can they reach me." Indeed we cannot reach and teach a child if we don't understand him. This is especially true for the child with a disability or one who learns differently.

For the most part, school curricula are designed to have each student achieve certain academic milestones along a predetermined timetable, such as cursive and multiplication tables by the third grade. The problem? Not every child is on this developmental schedule.

Still, schools and sometimes parents continue to demand uniformity in skill development, achievement, and performance. The stakes and the risks are raised by placing roadblocks to success through rigid curriculum development, which does not acknowledge developmental variations. Children who are not able to meet these demands are often seen as lazy, dumb, or oppositional. Perhaps it is only that they learn differently.

If we are to reach the child with a disability, we must learn to understand with our heads and our hearts. Only when we discover the whole child will we begin to understand how to reach him.

Many things go into creating the child we see before us. Learning styles, life experiences, developmental stages, environment, culture, and support systems are just a few components of the puzzle that influences a child's success. These pieces of the puzzle in Figure 1.1 may have both negative and positive effects on the child.

**Fig. 1.1. Components that Influence Learning**

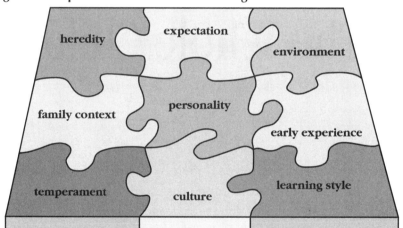

# Development

Much of this book is devoted to describing disabilities and symptoms of learning problems. That makes sense. This is a book about learning differences. Still, all this information needs to be kept in perspective. The yardstick and time lines we use to measure a child's development are merely flexible guidelines, not the Ten Commandments of Achievement. The guidelines simply acknowledge the variations in development as each child reaches the developmental milestones at his own pace. Therefore, attaining a skill later than peers or siblings is not necessarily cause for alarm.

Just as a child's motor skills and language skills vary in development, so does cognitive ability. Recognizing this, we must carefully evaluate the pressure placed on the child and make sure the tasks we are demanding are developmentally appropriate. How do we do that? We can begin by learning a little about how children learn and what is normal development. The following theories provide some insight into how children learn and what they need. If you are concerned about your child's developmental progress, discuss it with your doctor. She can ease your concerns or make a referral for assessment.

Why does it help to understand the course of development in children? Understanding can lead to intervention. Understanding helps identify areas for remediation and prevents adding to the child's frustrations by making developmentally inappropriate demands on the child.

## Jean Piaget's Theory

Jean Piaget is one of the most influential theorists in the area of childhood cognition. While his descriptions of cognitive development are not universally accepted, his ideals provide a framework and foundation for understanding the child's thought process.

Piaget's theory of cognitive development states that there is a developmental sequence to intellectual growth. Piaget believed there are four major stages of cognitive development. Each stage is age related and has features that refer to certain kinds of thinking.

1. **Sensorimotor stage**. Birth to two years. Infants think through their senses and motor abilities. The major acquisition of this stage is understanding that an object still exists when it is out of sight (object permanence) and remembering and imagining experiences (mental representation).

2. **Preoperations stage.** Ages two to six years. Children use symbolic thinking, including language, to understand the world. Symbols are things that stand for something else. Words are the

**Fig. 1.2. The Six Stages of Sensorimotor Development**

I.  Birth to 1 month. Reflexes: sucking, grabbing, staring, listening.

II.  One to 4 months. The first acquired adaptations. Grabbing a bottle to suck it, sucking a pacifier differently from a nipple.

III.  Four to 8 months. The child learns to make interesting sights last and becomes more aware of objects and other people.

IV.  New adaptations and anticipations. The child develops the understanding that an object continues to exist when it cannot be seen (object permanence). When Dad plays peekaboo behind a blanket, Baby knows Dad hasn't really gone away.

V.  New means through active experimentation (12 to 18 months). The little-scientist stage. Children learn through trial and error. It was during this fun stage that Darlene discovered her gym shoes did not leak pancake syrup. A pair of shoes mistakenly left by the back door, right under the cupboard that contained the pancake syrup. Hmm, what is this sticky stuff for?

VI.  New means through mental combinations (19 to 24 months). One sign that a child has achieved this stage is that he begins planning his activities. The child also develops the ability to pretend and to use his imagination.

most common symbols. All languages have spoken and written symbols for concepts. Children may only understand the world from their own perspective. The major acquisition for this stage is to begin to look beyond themselves and understand other points of view. Some common features of preoperational thought are:

- *Centration* is the tendency to think about only one thing at a time. Children may think in black-and-white terms and have trouble understanding cause and effect.

- *Conservation* refers to the idea that amount is unaffected by changes in shape or placement. This is not always obvious to children at this stage. A child may quarrel that her brother has more milk because she believes a tall, slender glass holds more than the short, wide glass. Children may think that a long rope of clay is more clay than a round ball or that six toy cars strung across the table are more than six cars placed close together. A child may understand different forms of conservation at different times. Five-year-old Steven would argue the entire day that his brother, who got the tall, slender glass, had more milk. But presented with six cars close together and six spread apart, he at first thought the longest row had the most cars. Then he stopped to count them and exclaimed, "Hey, you're trying to trick me. They are the same."

3. **Concrete operational.** Ages seven to eleven years. The child understands and applies logical operations or principles to help understand and interpret specific experiences. A major acquisition of this stage is the use of logic in understanding the basic ideas of conservation, number classifications, and other concrete ideas. According to Piaget, until the child reaches this stage he learns mostly by rote and doesn't really understand. Features of concrete operational thought are:

   - *Identity and reversibility.* Understanding that 50 is 50, whether it is shown as 30 + 20 = 50 or 25 + 25 = 50.

   - *Classification.* The concept that objects can be thought of in terms of categories.

   - *Seriation.* This concept may be necessary for the understanding of number lines, arranging items by height, arranging items into series, and understanding greater and less. School activities usually focus on practical, visible experiences. In English, the focus may be on rules of grammar and spelling and mechanics of reading and writing. Social studies may cover the review of historic events, using maps, and understanding graphs.

4. **Formal operational.** Ages twelve and up. The adolescent or adult is able to think about abstract ideas and hypothetical concepts and is able to move from the real to the possible. The

major acquisition of this stage is the ability to take a broader and more theoretical approach to experiences. One example of formal operational thought is the development of scientific reasoning. This ability to think abstractly means that students can grasp advance concepts in science and math. They also understand more complicated concepts in literature, such as metaphor, sarcasm, and irony. The study of social sciences may expand to include discussions of what might have happened and an analysis of current events. But as children enter adolescence and begin to develop formal operational thought, education should not exclude the use of more concrete examples and personal experiences. Development of cognitive abilities varies from child to child. Children, especially those with learning differences, may continue to experience difficulty applying what they know.

## Erikson Psychosocial Theory of Human Development

Erik Erikson theorized that there are eight stages of psychosocial development. Each stage revolves around a particular crisis or conflict that must be resolved. These stages are centered on each person's relationship to the social environment. Erikson describes two extreme resolutions to each crisis. Most individuals will reach a solution to these conflicts somewhere in the middle ground between the two.

These are important ideas to consider when working with a child who is not achieving in school. If a child's attempts to explore have been constantly thwarted, he may need to resolve issues of doubt before he can trust in his own abilities. The same applies to the stage of industry versus inferiority. Imagine you are a child with learning disabilities, who, despite herculean efforts, fails to be successful in school. Will you be confident in your role or place in the world? Or imagine the child with fetal alcohol syndrome who is passed from one foster home to another. How would this experience be an additional roadblock to success? See Figure 1.3.

**Fig. 1.3. Erikson's Psychosocial Stages of Human Development**

I.   Trust versus mistrust (birth to 1 year)
     Babies learn to trust or mistrust that others will meet their basic needs, including warmth, food, sucking, cleanliness, and physical contact.

II.  Autonomy versus shame and doubt (1 to 3 years)
     Children learn to be self-sufficient or double their own abilities in activities such as feeding, walking, talking, and toilet training.

III. Initiative versus guilt (3 to 6 years)
     Children want to take initiative but may overstep limits set by parents and feel guilt.

IV.  Industry versus inferiority (7 to 11 years)
     Children learn to be competent and productive or feel inferior and unable to do anything well.

V.   Identify versus role confusion (adolescence)
     Teens try to figure out who they are. They establish identities or are confused about what future roles to play.

VI.  Intimacy versus isolation (adulthood)
     Young adults seek companionship and love with another person or become isolated.

VII. Generatively versus stagnation
     Middle-age adults engage in productive meaningful work and raising a family or become stagnant and inactive.

VIII. Integrity versus despair
     Older adults try to make sense of their lives and either find life meaningful or despair of ever reaching their goals.

# The Social Competence of the Learner

Unless we are good detectives, we may draw false assumptions about a child's abilities, difficulties, and supports. It is important to beware of stereotypical thinking. Not every child in poverty will drop out of school nor every middle-class child go on to college. A child may live in poverty but have a large support system of neighbors, church members, and extended family. A child from an upper-middle-income neighborhood may have material advantages but have a family where

---

**Fig. 1.4. Psychosocial and Environmental Problems**

**Primary support group** may include the death of a family member, health problems in family, disruptions of family by separation, divorce, or estrangement, removal from the home, remarriage of parent, sexual or physical abuse, parental overprotection or neglect of child, inadequate discipline, discord with siblings, or the birth of a sibling.

**Problems related to the social environment** include the death or loss of friend, inadequate social support, living alone, difficulty with acculturation, discrimination, or adjustment to life-cycle transition (such as retirement).

**Education problems** may include illiteracy, academic problems, discord with teachers or classmates, or an inadequate school environment.

**Occupational problems** include unemployment, threat of job loss, stressful work schedule, difficult work conditions, job satisfaction, job change, or discord with boss or co-workers.

**Housing problems** address hopelessness, inadequate housing, unsafe neighborhood, or discord with neighbors or landlord.

**Economic problems** could be extreme poverty, inadequate finances, or insufficient welfare support.

**Problems with access of health care services** may be inadequate health care services, transportation to health care facilities unavailable, or inadequate health insurance.

**Problem related to interaction with the legal system/crime** including arrest, incarceration, litigation, or a victim of crime.

**Other psychosocial and environmental problems** may include exposure to disasters, war, other hostilities, discord with non-family care givers such as counselors, social workers, or physicians, or the unavailability of social service agencies.

Source: *American Psychiatric Association: Diagnostic and Statistical Manual of Mental Disorders*, Fourth Edition. Washington, DC, American Psychiatric Association, 1994.

---

both parents work and have moved often, thus limiting the support system for the family and child. There may be a crisis or an illness in the family that detracts from supports ordinarily available to the child. Figure 1.4, from the *Diagnostic and Statistical Manual of Mental Disorders*, 4th ed. (*DSM-IV*), describes many psychosocial and environmental problems that may affect the child's ability to perform in school and the family's ability to provide necessary support.

As you review this list, don't focus only on areas in which your child and/or his family has problems. Search for areas of strengths. This information will help when designing interventions.

# Cultural Issues Influencing Learning

Culture must be taken into consideration if appropriate assessment and interventions are to be made. Culture can strengthen the child by providing support and guiding through cross-generational learning. The strengths that culture provides may be overlooked by the clinician who misunderstands the role culture plays in a child's life.

Culture itself is certainly not a negative. However, problems may arise when we judge all children and their families by the values of the majority. Culture differences may result in cultural bias, especially in standardized testing. The following are types of bias identified in instruments designed to assess intelligence.

**Direction bias:** the phrasing of questions and instructions in a complex manner that seems to discriminate against minority groups.

**Linguistic bias:** the assessing of a child's knowledge of a particular language or dialect rather than the child's general linguistic development.

**Value bias:** the designing of tests so that answers reflect the responses acceptable to the dominant culture.

**Situational bias:** a mismatch between examiner and child. Mismatches can occur in expectations and testing environment. For example, a clinician may expect a child to guess when he doesn't know the answer to a question, whereas the child, afraid of answering wrong, instead avoids completing statements.

## Most Truths Depend On Your Point of View

Alan's answer surprised his friend: "Everybody knows what's most important. It's helping your family and doing chores."

"Not in my house," Jesse sputtered. "I better study and get my homework done before anything else."

"Homework and chores will have to wait," explained Stu. "There's a game this weekend, and I've got to get to practice."

Three friends from the same neighborhood with very different priorities. No one family is necessarily right or better in setting priorities. Perhaps Alan's primary care giver is a single parent and he has to help care for siblings after school. Maybe Stu's family prizes athletic achievement and hopes for a college sports scholarship.

Acknowledging intragroup differences is important. Each culture includes members who hold a wide variety of beliefs, values, and experiences. Physicians Ian A. Canino and Jeanne Spurlock, in their book *Culturally Diverse Children and Adolescents*, write that it is essential to determine how families "identify themselves rather than assume, for example, that English-speaking persons with dark skin and kinky hair are African-American, or that those with olive skin, straight hair, and a Spanish surname are Latino."

The old adage about not judging a person until you've walked a mile in their moccasins should always be kept in mind. Each child and family experiences the world differently. Those experiences form each individual's truth. That truth defines the path they take to become a whole person.

# Self-esteem

Any parent of a toddler can tell you a child is born curious and with a desire to be independent. As he grows, he needs to feel competent and able to handle himself in his environment, be that school, home, or neighborhood, as well as able to offer something to others. These needs may be difficult for children with learning differences to fulfill. Such children may not understand why their best efforts go unrewarded, nor may they know how to change. They may have difficulty beginning and maintaining relationships with peers and be left out of groups because their behavior appears immature or because they lack social skills. They don't know the rules of relationships and don't pick up on the nonverbal clues others send. They struggle with the pain and frustration of failure.

In her book *Esteem Builders,* Dr. Michele Borba describes five feelings as sequential building blocks of high self-esteem. Figure 1.5 gives parents and teachers tasks that will assist them while they support the child as he struggles to build a solid foundation of self-worth.

The first requisite of high self-esteem in our children is a secure and safe environment. Psychologist Dorothy Corkill Brigg states that we must support the child's explorations, curiosity, and moves toward self-reliance if we want him to be intellectually stimulated and to use his creativity. This motivates the child to learn and to capitalize on his strengths.

Journalist John Stossel made the following comment about the importance of self-esteem in the video *I'm Not Stupid: Learning Disabilities*: "While educating an L.D. child—or any child, for that matter—don't forget about the heart. How children feel about themselves, their self-concept, their self-esteem is at least as important as solving a math problem or learning to read."

Below are some guidelines for protecting the heart of the child who struggles.

## The ABCs of Success

Accept the reality of the child's difference and its impact on all aspects of the child's life.

Buffer the child from undue criticism.

Capitalize on strengths.

Demystify the differences.

Encourage effort, not bottom-line productivity.

Focus on fairness, not equality.

Guide the child to gradual growth.

Honor the child for his individuality and uniqueness.

Insist on compassion and understanding.

Join all significant adults in a collaborative effort to help the child.

Know all aspects of strength and disabilities.

Love unconditionally and listen actively.

Move toward self-acceptance.

Neutralize the power of criticism with the power of praise.

Open your mind to new ways of achieving.

Plan interventions and bypass strategies to fit the child, not the other way around.

Question preconceptions and misconceptions.

Recognize the direct relationship between frustration and behavior.

Set realistic goals.

Teach compensatory skills.

Utilize community support

Vary instructional methods to utilize all learning channels—visual, auditory, and tactile.

Watch for scapegoating.

X-claim the child's individuality.

Yearly, monthly, daily reassess the child's progress and appropriateness of interventions.

Zero in on a failure-free environment.

---

**Fig. 1.5. The Building Blocks of Self-Esteem**

The following building blocks, based on the five feelings found in students with high self-esteem, are the sequential esteem-building steps incorporated in the curriculum.

| Building Block (Acquired Feeling) | Steps for Esteem Builder (Adult Functions) |
|---|---|
| **Security** | |
| A feeling of strong assuredness. Involves feeling comfortable and safe; knowing what is expected; being able to depend on individuals and situations; and comprehending rules and limits. | 1. Build a trusting relationship. |
| | 2. Set reasonable limits and rules that are consistently enforced. |
| | 3. Create a positive and caring environment. |

| **Building Block (Acquired Feeling)** | **Steps for Esteem Builder (Adult Functions)** |
|---|---|

**Selfhood**

A feeling of individuality. Acquiring self-knowledge, which includes an accurate and realistic self-description in terms of roles, attributes and physical characteristics.

1. Reinforce more accurate self-descriptions.
2. Provide opportunities to discover major sources of influence on the self.
3. Build an awareness of unique qualities.
4. Enhance ability to identify and express emotions and attitudes.

**Affiliation**

A feeling of belonging, acceptance or relatedness, particularly in relationships that are considered important. Feeling approved of, appreciated, and respected by others.

1. Promote inclusion and acceptance within the group.
2. Provide opportunities to discover interests, capabilities and backgrounds of others.
3. Increase awareness of and skills in friendship making.
4. Encourage peer approval and support.

**Mission**

A feeling of purpose and motivation in life. Self-empowerment through setting realistic and achievable goals and being willing to take responsibility for the consequences of one's decisions.

1. Enhance ability to make decisions, seek alternatives and identify consequences.
2. Aid in charting present and past academic and behavioral performances.
3. Teach the steps to successful goal-setting.

**Competence**

A feeling of success and accomplishment in things regarded as important or valuable. Aware of strengths and able to accept weaknesses.

1. Provide opportunities to increase awareness of individual competencies and strengths.
2. Teach how to record and evaluate progress.
3. Provide feedback on how to accept weaknesses and profit from mistakes.
4. Teach the importance of self-praise for accomplishments.

Reprinted from *Esteem Builders* by Dr. Michele Borba, Jalmar Press, 1989. Used with permission from Jalmar Press.

The good news is that each of us has access to the key ingredients for the development of the child's self-esteem. Our job is to empower the child. This job is not without roadblocks and pitfalls. That's why the *J* in our self-esteem alphabet is so important. Advocate for the child and join with other significant adults in the child's life to build a self-esteem network. There is no greater motivation than success. Each success reinforces and strengthens the child's belief that he can be successful.

# Points to Ponder

1. Each child develops at a different pace. Is the difference you are seeing a true disability or just a variation in development?

2. Even within each culture there is a wide variation in expectations, beliefs, and values. Is the child being stereotyped because of culture, race, or ethnic background?

3. Social stresses can have a huge impact on the child's development. What stressors can be identified in the child's environment?

4. Every child has potential and needs to be supported. Have you identified strengths, supports, and untapped resources?

5. A child may struggle when demands are developmentally inappropriate. Have the child's developmental stage and achievements been identified? Are the tasks that are required of him appropriate?

# 2

# The Elements of Learning

## My Child's Not Perfect?

The hardest thing for parents to hear is that their child is not perfect. As parents, we all like to think that our child is the brightest, most talented, and beautiful creation in the universe. Learning that our son or daughter may learn differently can be very difficult to accept. The shock of receiving this news often results in denial, which can delay getting the supports needed by the child. Many families actually go through a period of grieving (see chapter 25).

Nancy first realized that her son, Christian, learned differently when he was seven years old. Christian was referred to a neurologist because he was impulsive and had difficulty judging where his body was in space. These traits resulted in frequent accidents. The physician diagnosed his condition as minimal brain dysfunction. Nancy and her husband, David, were so frightened and overwhelmed by this terminology that they fled the office, vowing never to return. How dare this stranger say that there was something wrong with Christian's brain! He had a perfectly good brain, and no part of it was dysfunctional! Seven years later, Christian was diagnosed with attention-deficit disorder, formerly called minimal brain dysfunction.

Each day, many parents are faced with the realization that something is interfering with their child's ability to learn. A barrage of unfamiliar terms easily overwhelms them. Terms such as *disability, syndrome, disorder,* and *impaired* immediately strike fear in the hearts of parents. They fear that their child will not have a successful future. They feel guilty that somehow this mishap is a result of poor parenting. Neither of these assumptions is true. Yet, seeing the parent's concern, a child can begin to view himself as dumb or stupid. This begins a negative, self-defeating cycle often perpetuated by the way learners are classified.

# Differences Versus Disabilities

In education, differences are not always appreciated. Yet all one has to do is look in the mirror to see that no one is physically the same as another. We differ from our hair and eye color, to the shape of our noses and ears, to our stature and weight. Even identical twins are not exactly alike. Our interests and talents also make us distinctive. Some of us excel in sports while others are more artistically or musically inclined. Academically, it is because of our mental differences that some of us are math whizzes and others are better with words.

It is these diversities that make us unique and the world an interesting place. We have chosen to view the distinctive qualities children bring to the learning environment as differences rather than disabilities.

By definition, the term *difference* has a much less negative connotation than *disability*. Meaning "unlike, not the same as," *different* is not as judgmental a term as *disabled*, which is defined as "not able, without ability." Everyone has the ability to learn, each in his own way.

Unfortunately, the educational system is designed on the premise that to succeed in school, a child must excel in everything. When this fails to occur, the learner is often thought to lack the ability. This theory places the focus on what the learner cannot do and presents obstacles to success.

If each child were viewed as learning differently from another, this might be a more accurate and productive approach to education. This perspective would alleviate the negative feelings associated with the term *disability*.

## A Broader Umbrella

By legal definition, the term *disability* is narrow in scope. The focus is usually on specific areas with eligibility for services determined by federal and state criteria (see chapter 4). For example, a child who has difficulty processing written or spoken information, and this interferes with his ability to read, write, spell, listen, talk, or do math may be diagnosed with a specific learning disability under the Individuals with Disabilities Education Act (IDEA). (In this writing, we will use *disability* when referring to these qualifying conditions.)

Many children with differences in learning never meet the predetermined standards and are denied the supports that would meet their educational needs. These students are often more at risk than those who qualify for services.

However, if we think of children as having *differences* in learning, we can become more accepting of the qualities that make each learner unique. This puts the approach to education under a much broader umbrella. Once we understand the factors interfering with learning, we can make the appropriate skill-building adaptations. For example, Jim needs hands-on experiences in the lab before he can understand science concepts. He would struggle in a science class that consisted of lectures and work sheets. It is not that Jim cannot learn the concepts. Rather, learning is more meaningful if he is actively involved.

## The Factors Influencing Differences in Learning

The criteria for being identified as learning disabled is primarily based upon standardized test scores. While these tools offer one facet of how the child learns, they should not be used as the sole criteria. Too often, tests scores do not reflect the experiences and developmental maturation rates of learners who are not on the same time line as the educational program.

When we think of the child as having differences in learning, we look at the whole child, rather than focusing on the part that appears dysfunctional. Factors such as the rate of development, life experiences, genetics, gender, and individual strengths make each learner unique. It is a combination of these elements that determines the level at which learning will occur. What a student brings with him or her to the learning experience must be taken into consideration so that objectives and curricula can be adapted accordingly.

On the surface, our stance on using the concept of differences in learning rather than learning disabilities may appear to be one of semantics. However, what we wish to point out is that perhaps we need to reconsider the way we view the learning process. Maybe what we traditionally consider a disability may actually be an incompatibility between the factors influencing how each child learns and the learning environment.

Given the right circumstances, all children can learn. An increasing amount of research is indicating how unique the learning process is for each person. This is information that must be considered beyond the standardized test scores. Parents and teachers need to be aware of the factors that influence learning and how they make each learner unique. Figure 2.1 compares the components that are considered in determining whether a child qualifies as having a disability in learning and the factors that are encompassed by the concept of "differences in learning."

**Fig. 2.1. Comparison Between Learning Disabilities and Differences in Learning**

| Learning Disabilities | Differences in Learning |
|---|---|
| Not able, without ability | Not the same as |
| Meets specific criteria | Examines wide range of issues |
| Compares to what is considered age-appropriate | Considers body's internal clock |
| Brain's wiring not always considered | Recognizes brain's uniqueness |
| Labels and classifies children | Looks past labels and builds on strengths |

# Developmental Variations and the Role of Life Experiences

Each child reaches developmental milestones at different times depending on his or her internal clock. Piaget's explanation of the seven stages of development is perhaps the most familiar description of each milestone (see chapter 1).

Within your own family, you can observe different rates of development. One child may take off walking at nine months, while another may not accomplish this feat until fifteen months. Or your adolescent may be distressed because she is developing faster than, or not as fast as, her peers.

You may find yourself comparing your child to your neighbor's child. This can be frustrating and cause you unnecessary distress. Observing other children within the same age-group as your own can give you an idea of what the norm might be. However, we caution you not to jump to conclusions if your five-year-old would rather play with Legos than pick up a book and read.

It is important to keep in mind that a child's chronological age does not always match his maturation age. A child may be seven years old yet have the maturity of a five-year-old. This important factor is not always considered, especially in younger children.

Once we understand how a child develops, we can make adaptations to accommodate the biological and neurological rates of maturation within the classroom. Educators who ignore these developmental factors and approach education in a uniform way may be doing learners a disservice.

Developmental differences need to be examined before a student is referred for an evaluation. The child's level of maturity is linked to the developmental milestones. Consideration of his internal timetable can provide valuable information about his readiness to learn certain concepts. For this reason, caution should be exercised in using test scores as the sole criteria to determine a student's learning status. The child's developmental differences also need to be evaluated in relationship to the scores. This allows us to recognize that not all children mature and become ready for certain tasks at the same time.

## Life Experiences and Learning

Early exposure to a variety of life experiences should be considered, as long as it harmonizes with the body's internal developmental schedule. Research indicates that the timing and nature of life experiences are a crucial part of learning. For example, a first grader having difficulty identifying sounds may appear to have a reading disability. But there could be many reasons why learning to read appears difficult, and each should be explored before assuming a disability is present.

Perhaps reading is not a priority for the child at this time. He may still need to develop his social skills because he has had limited exposure to other children during his preschool years. Wanting to play and interact socially may take priority over learning. Or if it is early in the school year, maybe he has not adjusted to being required to sit and listen for long periods of time. His need to physically move may interfere with his attention. If he has not had much exposure to books, he may not be neurologically ready to make the connection that letters are symbols and each has a sound. He may not understand that when you combine sounds with symbols, words are formed. The teacher may want to examine each of these possibilities and adjust the instruction to provide the reading-readiness experiences this child may have missed.

In contrast, another child in the same class who has had playmates since she was six months old, been read to since she was born, and had exposure to a reading-readiness program may be whizzing through fourth-grade reading materials. Her early life experiences have developmentally prepared her beyond the typical first-grade curriculum. Likewise, the teacher will need to provide the instruction that will challenge this student.

These two learners are at different stages of development and have been exposed to different life experiences. By adapting the teaching goals and expectations to the experiences and developmental readiness of each learner, the teacher can accommodate the difference in learning.

The impact that early life experiences has on learning is just becoming evident. Educators and parents would benefit from familiarizing themselves with some of the findings, because they are showing that early life experiences are critical to the learning process.

In his book *Inside the Brain*, Pulitzer-winner Ronald Kotulak relates information about the brain that he compiled from interviewing more than three hundred researchers around the world. He points out that current research indicates that a highly stimulating environment for young children could increase their IQ by as much as twenty points. Such an environment could also reduce mental retardation by 50 percent and lower the rate of other school failures significantly.

The research suggests that the brain is primed to receive information at different times during the developmental process. These peak learning times, or "critical periods," provide windows of opportunity when optimum learning can occur. The brain is most receptive to the introduction of life experiences during these times.

The research of neurobiologist Martha Pierson, of the Baylor College of Medicine in Houston, has substantiated this theory. She has stated, "It's just phenomenal how much experience determines how our brains get put together. If you fail to learn the proper fundamentals at an early age, then you could be in big trouble. You can't suddenly learn to learn when you haven't first laid down the basic wiring."

While learning continues throughout a lifetime, it is thought that during the first twelve years of life humans learn by interacting with their environment. Because children reach different milestones and acquire skills at different stages of development, the question of when information and experiences should be introduced is a critical one. Information presented too soon or too late may not achieve effective results.

Current research indicates that younger children may be more receptive to learning new concepts than older youths. The first three years of life appear to be the time children are most receptive. This is thought to be when the "windows" are open, the child is most malleable, and the child's brain is making the most connections. Research shows that an infant's brain forms 3 billion new connections a second. By eight months of age, the brain has about a thousand trillion connections. It is during this time that the foundation for thinking, language, vision, attitudes, aptitudes, and other characteristics significant to future learning is established.

Depending on the stimulation in the environment provided for the growing youngster, the number of connections can increase or decrease by as much as 25 percent. Researchers think that if experiences are not presented during the critical periods, it becomes more difficult for the brain to make the necessary connections. This could result in delayed learning.

Each experience becomes a part of the learning process, providing a "hook" that connects to learning. Figure 2.2 shows the periods when researchers think the windows of opportunity may be open to enhance learning in certain academic areas. Providing the experiences during these peak times *may* enhance learning in the specific area.

We do want to qualify that this information is not meant to imply that giving a child a violin at age three will produce a Beethoven or an Itzhak Perlman. Nor does it mean that children who have not been exposed to music at an early age are doomed never to enjoy it. It does mean that learning is easier at an early age. Think in terms of your own life. Maybe you want to learn to play the piano or to speak French. If determined enough, you can accomplish this task, but it will be considerably more difficult than learning these skills as a young child. Perhaps Bruce McEwen of Rockefeller University stated it best when he said,

**Fig. 2.2. Windows of Opportunities and Experiences**

It is important to note that these experiences can benefit any child. For optimum results, the earlier they are introduced, the better.

| Skill Developed | Learning Window | Suggested Experiences |
|---|---|---|
| Math and logic | Birth to 4 years | Play classical music<br>Music or singing lessons<br>Counting games<br>One-to-one tasks (one cookie for each playmate) |
| Language | Birth to 10 years | Talk, talk, talk to your child<br>Introduce a foreign language<br>Treat ear infections early<br>Read to your child daily |
| Music | 3 to 10 years | Songs and rhymes<br>Lessons for a musical instrument |

"The most important thing is to realize that the brain is growing and changing all the time. It feeds on stimulation, and it is never too late to feed it." The most miraculous quality of the brain is its constant ability to create new channels to help the individual learn and function.

A word of caution: This research is still in the preliminary stages. This information is to make you aware, not to instill feelings of guilt or inadequacy. The experiences children bring with them to school are just one of the factors influencing how they learn. However, scientific research is indicating that life experiences do provide for children a larger pool of resources and information from which they can pull to make learning more meaningful. Therefore, this factor should not be overlooked in the overall picture of educating children.

It would benefit parents and teachers to consider this research carefully. Children need opportunities to touch, feel, see, taste, and smell their world. As a parent, use this knowledge to expand your child's world by sharing time and opportunities that bring you and your child together. As an educator, use this information to help design a multisensory, multidisciplinary curriculum that makes learning more meaningful for all learners.

The experiences provided for children should be enjoyable as well as learning opportunities. Guide the child in the selection of a variety of life experiences (see Figure 2.3). Remember: Each hook that is created will somewhere surface to make learning and life more meaningful. Many of the suggestions mentioned below are free or available at a minimal cost.

---

**Fig. 2.3. Life Experiences You Can Provide for Your Child**

Introduce playmates and arrange playtimes for your child at an early age.

Read to your child—books, magazines, cereal boxes, street signs, billboard ads.

Talk constantly to your child.

Take trips to libraries, bookstores, museums, zoos, amusement parks, farms, cities.

Visit airports, bus terminals, train stations. Many offer free tours.

Visit mountains, seashores, deserts, plains, to compare geographic differences.

Sign up for swimming lessons, gymnastics, ballet, Tae Kwon Do.

Go to concerts; play records, CDs, or tapes.

Encourage interest in musical instruments, even if they are pots played with spoons.

Ride bikes, skate, jump rope, kick soccer balls, practice hitting, and catching baseballs.

Celebrate birthdays, holidays, and special events.

Frequently interact with extended family.

Other ideas you can add:

---

# The Brain's Wiring

The brain is a miraculous creation. Billions of neurons carry impulses and messages from one part of the body to another. It is our body's control center. It is also very unique, in that it defines who we are. How we learn, our strengths and weaknesses, our feelings and emotions, and how we interact with our world all result from how our brain is wired.

Genetics has a great influence on how our brains are structured. Many learning issues experienced by parents are also experienced by their offspring. A mother with dyslexia may produce a son with the same disorder. Likewise, a dad with ADD may have a daughter with similar characteristics. Even with many genetic similarities, the brain is still a unique organ in each of us.

The way we use our brain to learn has always been a mystery. Researchers are beginning to uncover evidence that parents and professionals can no longer ignore when trying to understand how a child processes information. Their research needs to be considered by professionals responsible for developing programs, curricula, and classroom instruction.

This exciting research is becoming available as a result of the data collected from PET (positron emission tomography) and MRI (magnetic resonance imagery) scans. The technology is allowing researchers to "see" how a person thinks, displays emotions, and controls actions. With the use of color, activity levels in specific areas of the brain can be monitored. For example, red areas indicate the sections of greatest activity.

Through the use of this technology, researchers are beginning to unlock some of the mysteries of the brain. For example, PET scans have located our happiness center in the thalamus and prefrontal cortex regions. Sadness lights up the amygdala region.

Several researchers have asked individuals to perform academic tasks while being scanned. The clinicians have been able to observe which part of the brain is active during each task. Brain activity while reading differed from the activity of solving math equations. Interestingly, researchers found that more than one part of the brain was functioning while accomplishing a task.

If computer imaging can determine where brain activity differs from individual to individual, educators may someday know where learning differences occur and adapt the curriculum and classrooms with much greater accuracy. Perhaps then the idea that all learners must excel in all areas will diminish. With scientific documentation that we are not all neurologically the same, the focus can be placed on the strengths each student brings to the learning situation. Perhaps by teaching to the learner's strengths we might readjust our thinking about what truly defines a disability.

## Left Brain/Right Brain

Research shows that an individual may tend to use one side of his brain more than the other. The brain has two sides, the right hemisphere and the left hemisphere. The left side usually controls what happens on the right side of the body and vice versa. Each half of the brain has four smaller lobes that perform a variety of functions.

Technology shows that the left side tends to be slightly larger than the right in individuals who are more verbal. In 90 percent of right-handed people, speech and language are processed by the left side. This is true of only 30 percent of those who are left-handed.

Which hemisphere is most dominant in an individual is usually based on the prominent characteristics displayed by the individual and which side of the brain is most responsible for those functions.

The left side is believed to produce more rational, logical, sequential, mathematical, and language-oriented functions. Left-brain learners usually process the parts before seeing the whole. The right hemisphere inclines toward musical, emotional, and spatial memory (knowing where things are located in space) producing a more whole-to-part learner. Musicians and artists tend to be "right-brain."

## Fig. 2.4. Specializations of the Hemispheres of the Brain

| Left Hemisphere | Right Hemisphere |
|---|---|
| Part to whole | Whole to part |
| Right-handedness | Left-handedness |
| Eighty-five to 90 percent of language productions | Abstract verbal tasks; proverb |
| | Major region of spatial relationships |
| Limited spatial orientation | Musical ability |
| Language comprehension | Verbal abstractions |
| Calculations, analytical processing | |

While this theory is interesting, it is not meant to imply that we use only one side of our brain. There is an overlap, and the extent to which each side is used depends on the task involved. However, most of us tend to demonstrate the qualities of one side over the other more often than not. These tendencies are determined by how our brains are genetically wired.

Some teachers attempt to determine the brain dominance of their students. By using this information in general terms, they can decide how specific tasks might be approached. This may help the teacher set realistic goals and objectives for her students and present a variety of learning opportunities.

## Gender Differences

New technology is also changing our understanding of how males and females learn by indicating that the two sexes have different ways of processing information. This research, while in its infancy, is providing some very thought-provoking data that educational systems should not ignore.

Through the use of PET scans, researchers have learned that females can use both sides of their brain to produce language, while males use primarily the left side. Female brains show more activity in areas that help recognize and remember subtle differences and details, and in the use of symbols or symbolic language. Male brains are more active in areas that control action and spatial activities. The data are too limited to make any conclusive judgments. It is important to know, however, that the information available clearly shows differences within the brains of males and females that may affect learning.

Other gender differences occur in developmental and maturation rates. It has long been documented that females mature faster than males, physically, emotionally, and psychologically. In early childhood, the span between chronological age and the rate of maturation tends to be wider for males than females. It begins to narrow through the elementary years until the onset of puberty. At this time, adolescent girls again take the lead. They usually grow taller and undergo body changes several years before their male counterparts. By late adolescence, the gap again narrows.

This information should make us cautious of the expectations of our children based on age. How many times have you found yourself telling a seven-year-old to stop acting like a baby? The reality may be that while the child has celebrated seven birthdays, he has the emotional maturity of a five-year-old.

Perhaps as more information becomes available, the gender gap on the identification of individuals with learning issues may begin to close. Males historically have seemed to dominate the populations of the learning-disabled and the attention-deficit-disordered. Identification has occurred primarily because males, often less mature, tend to draw attention to themselves more often than do females.

Females assume at an early age the gender expectations that society has placed on them. They smile sweetly, don't make waves, and quietly vanish into the woodwork. They tend to develop better verbal and compensating skills to mask their challenges. Appearing more mature, they seem to be in control of the situation. These are the skills they use to function within the system and are thus overlooked more often.

The female adolescent may be at even greater risk. A report entitled "Girls in the Middle, Working to Succeed in School," published by the American Association of University Women Education Foundation, reveals the pressures on female teens. It points out the challenges girls must face at a very difficult developmental time of life. Besides being self-conscious and not wanting to draw attention to themselves, they are often uncomfortable when called on in class. Also, they are usually asked to do more in school than their male counterparts. This attention often results in being teased and ridiculed by male classmates. This pressure can further mask any symptoms of a learning difference.

These factors may help explain why many females are not identified with learning issues until young adulthood. This is particularly true in the area AD/HD. In childhood six males are diagnosed with AD/HD for every female. In adulthood the ratio is one to one.

Females need to be monitored closely when inconsistencies occur or when they work harder than their peers to achieve the same results. Even though they appear in control of the situation, they may be masking a learning difference. (Because both genders are affected, we will use the male and female pronouns interchangeably.)

# Look to the Strengths

All of this information and research is of little value unless we know how to use it effectively. Frank Vellutino, a professor of educational psychology at the State University of New York at Albany, points out that Americans do more education research than anyone else in the world but also ignore more of it. As educators and parents, we are challenged to use this research by employing all the senses, attributes of the brain, and life experiences each child brings to the learning process. When we can accomplish this, we honor and celebrate the individuality of each child.

It is important to keep in mind that children are multifaceted and learning issues are just one facet. Often it is the qualities that make the child unique that hold the key to how she learns most effectively. As learners we are more different than alike. If the focus of the learning environment is on our weaknesses, we fail. If our strengths are recognized and honored, we succeed.

Parents and educators who recognize this truism are beginning to develop collaborative problem-solving approaches designed to teach to the strengths of the learner. Initially, labels are being used to help understand what is interfering with the child's ability to learn. From there, the focus turns toward identifying the strengths and learning styles of the child and away from the labels. This allows for more acceptance and appreciation of the differences in learning, and values the learner as a unique and capable individual.

Figure 2.5 lists many areas of strength. Which describe your child? What additional strengths can you and your child add to this list? As part of the collaborative process, share your child's gifts and talents with his teachers. Point out how your child will be most successful when these strengths are a part of the learning experience.

# Points to Ponder

1.  Discovering your child has a difference in learning can cause feelings of anxiety and guilt. This condition has *not* occurred as a result of poor parenting! Is there someone with whom you can

**Fig. 2.5. Possible Strengths Your Child May Have**
Add other strengths that apply to your child. Take this list with you to conferences and share it with the professionals working with your child.

| | |
|---|---|
| Enjoys reading | Is organized |
| Enjoys math | Has a sense of humor |
| Musically talented | A good problem solver |
| Artistically creative | Enjoys people |
| Strong writing skills | Makes friends easily |
| Strong verbal skills | Helps others |
| A computer whiz | Is sensitive to others' feelings |
| Is athletic | Is outgoing |
| Is energetic | Is reflective |

Other strengths your child possesses:

---

talk to alleviate these feelings—a friend, perhaps, or a member of the clergy or a medical or mental-health professional?

2. The terms used by educators can leave parents feeling confused and overwhelmed. Ask professionals to explain the situation in plain English. Ask for resources you can obtain to get more information on what is interfering with the child's learning.

3. The term *disability* implies that someone is "not able" to do something. Often specific criteria must be met to qualify for support. Is the child truly not able to function at school? Have her strengths been identified?

4. *Different* means "not the same as." It is a much broader term that encompasses developmental rates of maturation, life experiences, the brain's wiring, and gender differences. Is the child a late bloomer or right on target? How many experiences have been available to broaden the child's world?

5. Labels may be useful only when they are used to identify the problem. Thereafter the focus needs to go back to the strengths

of the child to find the solutions. What are the child's strengths? What talents and special qualities does he possess? Examine Figure 2.5, the abbreviated list of possible strengths. Circle the ones that apply to your child. Add to the list. Share it with professionals.

6. In light of the information presented in this chapter on what makes learners unique, is it fair to identify those who learn differently as disabled? Luckily, this is the question many parents and educators are beginning to ask.

# 3

# Pathways to Learning

When the education of children is approached by using the experiences and strengths they bring to the learning situation, success can be achieved. Learners who can make connections between the subject matter and their own experiences struggle less with paying attention, completing tasks, and taking tests. An academic struggle begins when students do not have the hooks with which to connect the information given with their own experiences and strengths. Research is presenting strong evidence that a uniform approach to education is ineffective. Computer imaging continues to unlock the mysteries of the learning process and strongly indicates that acquiring knowledge is a unique experience. A one-curriculum-fits-all approach assumes all learners are the same. This just is not true!

To accommodate this diversity in learning, curricula and classrooms need to be designed to approach learning in a multisensory, multidisciplinary way. This means learning occurs through a variety of approaches, incorporating many subject areas and using all the sensory pathways. Understanding is facilitated when opportunities to see, hear, smell, taste, and feel are made available. For example, learning about a cow may be more meaningful if the child has the opportunity to feel, see, smell, and touch the real thing, rather than just read about the animal in a book.

Learning occurs most easily when information is presented through the pathways of our strongest modalities, or learning channels. Those who learn best by seeing and manipulating may struggle in a classroom where only lecturing occurs. Some learners need to see demonstrations of what is being said, and their learning is further reinforced by actually being a part of the demonstration. For example, a student may hear an explanation about sound waves and see examples in the science book but not fully understand the concept until he touches a tuning fork to water and sees the ripples. Optimum learning will occur if the student then has the opportunity to teach the concept to someone else.

Thus, *how* information is presented is an important factor in the learning process. From the research, we have learned that students retain 10 percent of what they read, 26 percent of what they hear, 30 percent of what they see, 50 percent of what they hear and see, 70 percent of what they say, and 90 percent of what they say and do. An ancient Chinese proverb states, "I hear and I forget. I see and I remember. I do and I understand." These words have meaning for us today.

In planning lessons, teachers need to keep these words of wisdom in mind. Presenting a variety of experiences benefits all students and increases their likelihood of learning and retaining the information.

# Learning Styles

One of Nancy's responsibilities as a learning specialist is to help parents and teachers identify the students' learning styles. This is done partly through careful observation of the learner in the classroom. Nancy looks for clues from the student that may indicate his strongest sensory pathways. Does he appear confused by verbal explanations, then perk up when visuals are shown? Does the lesson seem to come alive when manipulatives are provided? Is the child staring off into space yet able to respond immediately when asked a question? These are some of the hints that give Nancy the information she needs to determine the student's learning styles. She finds that some children may favor one learning channel, but usually it is a combination of sensory pathways that are identified.

Knowing on which sensory passages the student relies is very important. Teachers can use this information to select the instructional techniques that will make learning most meaningful for the learner.

We do not mean to imply that teachers need to prepare twenty-five different lessons. A teacher presenting a multisensory lesson may orally deliver the information that will benefit the auditory learners. Then she may use concrete objects or examples that will help visual learners understand the explanation, and provide a hands-on experience for the tactile learner. The class may then be divided into small groups where the students can share information and learn from each other. When the information is presented in a number of different ways, the student can process it through his or her strongest learning channel.

Sometimes parents become confused by the jargon teachers use when discussing a student's learning style. The terms parents may most often hear are described below. Provided are the characteristics that typically identifies each style of learner. Remember: The child may favor one modality but use some combination of the other styles. Which description best suits your child?

1. Visual learner
   - Often responds with "Just show me!" after hearing an explanation or when presented with new or confusing concepts.
   - Often asks for things to be repeated. Overuses, "Huh?"
   - Will often look at what other children are doing rather than ask the teacher to repeat the instructions.
   - May appear distracted when overwhelmed by too much information.

- May have word-finding problems, so uses a lot of hand gestures and *whatchamacallit*s or *thingamabob*s. Also may make verbal errors, such as "He got expended from school."
- Often completes many difficult tasks (change a tire, knit a sweater, weave a basket) but cannot explain in words how it's done.
- Unless directions or assignments are in writing, may have difficulty remembering them.
- Easily recognizes visual images and can distinguish the familiar from the unfamiliar.
- Distinguishes between similar visual images such as *b, d, p,* and *q*.
- Frequently doodles or draws on edges of paper.
- May have difficulty hearing and distinguishing sounds.
- Is aware of spatial relationships such as spacing, margins, directionalities, and sequencing differences.
- Needs to create a mental picture of what is being said. Examples, pictures, maps, charts, diagrams, modeling, or demonstrations help create the mental images.

2. Tactile learner
   - Needs to feel, touch, and manipulate objects.
   - Twisting, turning, rotating, pouring, and measuring enhance learning.
   - Is a tinker and designer.
   - Benefits from hands-on experiences, such as math manipulatives (counters, coins matrix, geoboards) building materials, and laboratory experiments.

3. Auditory learner
   - Gains understanding from what is heard.
   - Usually very verbal but has illegible handwriting.
   - Enjoys using language.
   - Can discriminate between similar sounds.

- May appear distracted as language is being processed. Learning style may be confused with AD/HD.
- May omit or transpose words or letters.
- Spells out loud better than on paper. May test better orally.
- Better retains what he hears in class, as opposed to what he reads.
- Comprehends better when read to or reads aloud.
- Not a detail person. May miss sign changes in math problems or incorrectly read numbers, letters, or words.
- Work appears sloppy or messy. Dislikes ditto sheets or workbook pages.
- Uses bookmarks, line markers, or fingers to mark place.
- Can be the class hummer or whistler.
- May complain of eye problems, but eye tests do not indicate a problem.
- Benefits from a tape recorder to play back information.
- Benefits from books on tapes. (Note: Parents in Nancy's school volunteered to be readers. They made a complete set of tapes for every textbook and all of the required reading in grades 5 through 8. Students who wanted recordings provided the tapes and copies were made for them.)
- Usually benefits from a phonics approach to reading when combined with whole language.

4. Kinesthetic learner
   - Uses bodily control and movement to express himself.
   - Has exceptional fine and gross motor coordination.
   - Eye-hand coordination is also well developed.
   - Is energetic and physical. Has difficulty sitting for long periods of time.
   - Expresses self successfully through dance, sports, gymnastics, martial arts.

These are examples in very general terms of the different types of learning styles that can be found in any general education classroom. Many researchers view learning styles through other lenses. Howard Gardner, Ph.D., for example, theorizes that humans have eight personal intelligences. His theory of multiple intelligences provides some very interesting food for thought.

# Multiple Intelligences

Howard Gardner, Ph.D., co-director of Project Zero, a research institute at Harvard University, began his research with brain-damaged patients in a Boston hospital. More than a decade ago, in his book, *Frames of Mind*, he presented the theory that humans possess, in varying degrees, seven intelligences. (Recently, Gardner revealed an eighth intelligence.) He introduced the theory that how intelligence is currently defined and determined may not be accurate or appropriate. Based on his research with the patients, Gardner discovered that the brain has many distinct abilities. From this data, he established a set of criteria to determine what constitutes an intelligence.

Interestingly, Gardner's work was targeted at psychologists, not educators. However, his theory of personal intelligences supports a multisensory, multidisciplinary approach to education. By proposing that our concept of intelligence needs to expand beyond a number determined by an intelligence test, it is changing the way educators perceive students and their potentials. By studying Gardner's work, educators are finding academic applications.

His theory is also changing the way other sectors of society are thinking about and defining intelligence. His book *Leading Minds: An Anatomy of Leadership* is catching the attention of businesses and CEOs of major corporations.

The eight human intelligences proposed by Gardner are linguistic, logical, musical, spatial, kinesthetic, intrapersonal, interpersonal, and naturalist (see Figure 3.1). Critics claim that many of these categories are gifts or talents and hardly qualify as intelligences. Whether it is stated as intelligences, strengths, talents, or modalities is not the issue. What this theory of multiple intelligences does confirm is that each of us receives, processes, uses, and stores information in different ways. Some of us tend to be more visualizers than questioners. Others learn best from other people, while for many learning is an individual activity.

It is important to keep in mind that no one is purely one type or another. We are a blending of all types. What Gardner is attempting to point out in his theory is that humans have stronger inclinations toward some channels of learning than toward others. These would be the center of our strengths, and through these channels, we would probably learn and function most effectively. In looking at the eight personal intelligences, therefore, we can also define eight learning styles.

## Linguistic Learners

Linguistic learners are skilled manipulators of language. They enjoy playing with words and can communicate well. They like to read and write and may be talented storytellers. Memorizing names, dates, places, and pieces of trivia comes easily to them. Hearing, seeing, and repeating words and information are their most effective avenues of learning. Being allowed to tape lectures may reinforce learning. Career choices may include writer, poet, or statesperson.

Students with this ability to communicate often make great peer tutors and peer mediators. Be aware, though, that this type of learner may tend to monopolize conversations or classroom discussions.

## Logical/Mathematical Learners

Logical/mathematical learners tend to question the world around them. They are inquisitive and have a need to find answers. Logical learners enjoy exploring patterns and relationships and like to work with numbers. Math, reasoning, logic, and problem solving are areas where they excel. They ask many questions and like to research and experiment to find the answers. Albert Einstein, who asked so many questions in school he angered his teachers, was a logical/mathematical thinker. Careers in mathematics, technology, or research would utilize this learner's special talents.

Learning situations presenting opportunities to categorize, classify, and work with abstract patterns and relationships are most meaningful.

**Fig. 3.1. The Multiple Intelligences Table**

| Intelligence | What Is It? | Students Like To | Teachers Can |
|---|---|---|---|
| **Interpersonal** | • Sensitive to the feelings and moods of others. <br> • Understands and interacts effectively with others. | • Enjoy many friends. <br> • Lead, share, mediate. <br> • Build consensus and empathize with others. <br> • Work as an effective team member. | • Use cooperative learning. <br> • Assign group projects. <br> • Give students opportunities for peer teaching. <br> • Brainstorm solutions to problems. <br> • Create situations in which students are given feedback from others. |
| **Intrapersonal** | • Sensitive to one's own feelings and moods. <br> • Knows own strengths and weaknesses. <br> • Uses self-knowledge to guide decision-making and set goals. | • Control own feelings and moods. <br> • Pursue personal interests and set individual agendas. <br> • Learn through observing and listening. <br> • Use metacognitive skills. | • Allow students to work at own pace. <br> • Assign individual, self-directed projects. <br> • Help students set goals. <br> • Provide opportunities for students to get feedback from each other. <br> • Involve the students in journal writing and other forms of reflection. |

**Bodily-Kinesthetic**

- Uses one's body to communicate and solve problems.
- Is adept with objects and activities involving fine or gross motor skills.

- Play sports and be physically active.
- Use body language.
- Do crafts and mechanical projects.
- Dance, act, or mime.

- Provide tactile and movement activities.
- Offer role playing and acting opportunities.
- Involve the students in physical activity.
- Allow the students to move while working.
- Use sewing, model-making and other activities using fine motor skills.

**Linguistic**

- Thinks in words.
- Uses language and words in many different forms to express complex meanings.

- Tell jokes, riddles, or puns.
- Read, write, or tell stories.
- Use an expanded vocabulary.
- Play word games.
- Create poems and stories using sounds and imagery of words.

- Create reading and writing projects.
- Help the students prepare speeches.
- Interest the students in debates.
- Make word games, cross-word puzzles, and word searches.
- Encourage the use of puns, palindromes, and outrageous words.

*(continued on next page)*

**Fig. 3.1. The Multiple Intelligences Table,** *continued*

| Intelligence | What Is It? | Students Like To | Teachers Can |
|---|---|---|---|
| Logical-Mathematical | • Approaches problems logically.<br>• Understands number and abstract patterns.<br>• Recognizes and solves problems using reasoning skills. | • Work with numbers, figure things out and analyze situations.<br>• Know how things work.<br>• Ask questions.<br>• Exhibit precision in problem solving.<br>• Work in situations in which there are clear black and white solutions. | • Construct Venn diagrams.<br>• Use games of strategy.<br>• Have students demonstrate understanding using concrete objects.<br>• Record information on graphs.<br>• Establish time lines and draw maps. |
| Musical | • Sensitive to non-verbal sounds in the environment, including melody and tone.<br>• Aware of patterns in rhythm, pitch and timbre. | • Listen to and play music.<br>• Match feelings to music and rhythms.<br>• Sing, hum, and move to music.<br>• Remember and work with different musical forms.<br>• Create and replicate tunes. | • Re-write song lyrics to teach a concept.<br>• Encourage students to add music to plays.<br>• Create musical mnemonics.<br>• Teach history through music of the period.<br>• Have students learn music and folk dancing from other countries. |

| Naturalist | | |
|---|---|---|
| • Sensitive to the natural world.<br>• Sees connections and patterns within the plant and animal kingdoms. | • Spend time outdoors.<br>• Observe plants, collect rocks and try to catch animals.<br>• Listen to the sounds created in the natural world.<br>• Notice relationships in nature.<br>• Categorize and classify flora and fauna. | • Use the outdoors as a classroom.<br>• Have plants and animals in the classroom for which students are responsible.<br>• Conduct hands-on science experiments.<br>• Create a nature area on the playground. |
| **Spatial** | | |
| • Perceives the visual world accurately.<br>• Creates mental images.<br>• Thinks three-dimensionally.<br>• Aware of relationship between objects in space. | • Doodle, paint, draw or create three-dimensional representations.<br>• Look at maps.<br>• Work puzzles or complete mazes.<br>• Take things apart and put them back together. | • Draw maps and mazes.<br>• Lead visualization activities.<br>• Provide opportunities to show understanding through drawing or painting.<br>• Have students design clothing, buildings, play areas and scenery. |

Reprinted from *Succeeding with Multiple Intelligences: Teaching Through the Personal Intelligences*. Used with permission of New City School © 1996, St. Louis, Missouri.

Science curricula should be hands-on and provide regular laboratory time for experimentation. Brain teasers and math challenges need to be a part of this learner's daily assignments. Providing multiple resources and opportunities to investigate and find answers to their questions is important.

## Musical Learner

Musical learners love rhythm and enjoy anything related to music. They sing and hum, enjoy listening to music, usually play an instrument, and respond to music with their whole body. The musical learner picks up sounds, remembers melodies, keeps time to rhythms, and is sensitive to varying pitches and rhythms. Through the use of rhythm, pitch, and timbre, these learners can create and make meaning out of sounds. Expressing their talent is their greatest joy. These learners may make career choices as composers, musicians, vocalists, or music directors.

Outside of music class or band, these learners often have little opportunity to express their talent. Humming or singing in the classroom is discouraged. Few opportunities are available throughout the school day for musical learners to use their skills. Educators need to be sensitive to providing opportunities for these learners.

Music is usually the first area where funding is cut by school systems on a limited budget, yet numerous studies indicate the importance of music in the intellectual development of children. The introduction of music during the first ten years of life is linked to the development of strong math and logic skills. Many schools are finding that piping classical music throughout the school building results in calmer, less disruptive and less distracted learners. Times of transition, such as changing classes or subject areas, are smoother and less chaotic when music is used to alert students that change is coming.

## Spatial Learner

Spatial learners are visualizers. Learning takes place when a picture is created in the mind's eye and then re-created. They are proficient at recognizing objects whose positions have changed. This is how they often orient themselves and navigate from place to place.

Often referred to as daydreamers, they like to draw, build, design, and create things from memory. They enjoy looking at pictures and watching movies. They are tinkers whose playing and manipulation of objects can result in masterpieces. Mazes and puzzles, maps and charts present little challenge to spatial learners. A career as an artist, an architect, or a navigator would capture the spatial learner's talents.

Learning occurs when the opportunity to work in a small group or team with peers is permitted. Numerous examples, demonstrations, and modeling makes learning easier. Hands-on experiences help spatial learners make sense of their world. Being able to turn, twist, rotate, and move objects in space is part of the learning experience. Math manipulative and laboratory experiences are especially important for this learner.

## Bodily Kinesthetic Learners

Most people think that body management belongs in the physical education class. The "mover" is the kinesthetic learner. Through touching and maneuvering, such learners use their bodies to process information in a highly effective way.

Highly developed gross-motor muscles allow kinesthetic learners to excel in physical activities such as dancing, sports, acting, and crafts. Equally developed fine-motor muscles assist this learner in skillfully and precisely handling objects. Gracefully they can perform the most delicate tasks. They may become athletes, actors, mimes, or ballerinas.

Learners who need to move have high energy levels. They express themselves and solve problems through the control and movement of their bodies.

## Interpersonal Learners

Interpersonal learners are socializers. Being extroverted, they have many friends, belong to many groups, and talk easily to people. They seem to have an innate understanding of people and their feelings. They are leaders who can organize, motivate, mediate, and effectively communicate with others. Politics, the church, and education would be likely career choices.

Any opportunity to relate to others enhances learning. A cooperative learning experience in the classroom, where students work together in small groups, would benefit this type of learner. The interpersonal learner needs to interact and share feelings and ideas with others. This social interaction develops self-awareness.

## Intrapersonal Learner

The individual, or intrapersonal, learner is more introspective. This learner prefers to work alone and follow his own interests. With a good understanding of self, this learner pursues his own feelings, dreams, goals, and interests. Ideas tend to be very original. Preferring to work alone, at their own pace, on their own thing, in their own space, these individuals are very aware of their strengths and weaknesses. They find creative ways to compensate in the areas where they do not excel. Likewise, they find opportunities to use and enhance their strengths. These individuals would be great in a think-tank career or as inventors.

This type of learner does best when she can work at her own pace. Individualized assignments and projects are successful. While there are times to accept these qualities in students, teachers need to make an extra effort to present situations where intrapersonal learners can successfully interact with others, sharing their ideas and feelings.

## The Naturalist

The final type of learner is the naturalist. This type is very interactive with the natural environment. "The ability to recognize flora and fauna, to make other consequential distinctions in the natural world, and to use this ability productively [in hunting, farming, biological science]" is Gardner's definition of the naturalist learner. Ordering, categorizing, and classifying are exceptional skills these learners possess. A career in forestry, agriculture, botany, biology, zoology, or as a naturalist would be an excellent choice.

Outdoor education programs provide meaningful experiences for this learner. Relating math problems, reading assignments, and projects to their environmental interests makes learning meaningful. Their ability to identify and organize can be applied to any area of learning.

# Learning Styles in the Classroom

The point of all this information is that each classroom teacher is faced with a variety of learning styles. No classroom has only auditory learners who would benefit from a lecture format. At times, even an auditory learner can profit from a hands-on experience. The presentation and development of lessons must be designed to say the same thing a number of different ways using a variety of experiences before meaningful learning can occur for all students.

## Classroom Examples

To understand how a curriculum can be adapted to accommodate each of the learning styles described above, let us examine three sixth-grade classrooms. Each teacher has the same objective—to teach writing skills—but three different approaches are used. How many learning styles can you identify? Which one describes your child? Which classroom resembles your child's?

In Mrs. X's class, the morning writing assignment is positioned on the front board. During the scheduled writing time, students are required to open their journals and produce a writing sample about the topic the teacher selected. The objective of this exercise is to develop writing skills through daily entries.

Some of the learners eagerly open their notebooks and begin to write. Their thoughts appear to flow onto the paper. Two pages later, they complete their assignment.

Other students appear to be having more difficulty. Jason is staring off into space, seemingly awaiting a bolt from heaven to get his creative juices flowing. Mary begins over and over again, only to erase her efforts. Eric, in the back row, leaves his seat and goes to the restroom. Maybe the change of scenery will help.

By the end of the writing period, many of the students have little or nothing written in their journals. For many, this is the most excruciating time of the day. Some have difficulty relating to the topic because they have no hooks available. Others find it difficult to hold a thought and write at the same time. A lack of organizational skills interferes with another's progress.

Down the hall, in Mrs. Y's class, the same writing time is approached a little differently. Mrs. Y is teaching the writer's workshop approach to developing writing skills.

At the beginning of each month, Mrs. Y and her class have a brainstorming session that results in the generation of a list of topics on which they will write. From that list, the students make selections based on their interests, experiences, and strengths. They will be writing on their selected topic for several weeks. Right from the start, the learners are writing about what they know and have an opportunity to develop it thoroughly with guidance and input from others.

Once the topic has been selected, the students enter the prewriting stage. They organize what they want to say and begin a rough draft of their work. During this time, the teacher is supporting and monitoring each student.

As students complete their first draft, conferencing occurs. Students meet with each other and share their first efforts. Constructive criticism is given on where improvements can be made. The teacher monitors the conferences, noting the skills that need reinforcing, and prepares mini lessons around those needs.

Following the conferences, the students use the suggestions as they edit and rewrite their work. Again, conferences are held, and additional recommendations are made before the final rewrite is completed. After the final draft is approved by the teacher, the work is published and displayed for all to enjoy.

In Mrs. Z's room, another approach to the writing assignment can be observed. The students have read a book of their choice. Rather than assign a two-page book report, Mrs. Z allows her learners to use their creativity. Today they are being asked to prepare an imaginative way to share their books with their classmates. On a three-by-five-inch card, they are asked to write how their presentation relates to the book.

Sarah is designing a book jacket showing her favorite part of the book. Joe is rummaging through magazines, selecting pictures for a collage that will depict the major events occurring in his readings. Two students enter the room. They have been working with the music teacher. Jacob has chosen a musical work that describes his book and will play the piece on the piano, while Karen, having read the same book, will dance to the accompaniment. Amy is planning to dress up as her favorite character. Tom is writing a speech, and Jim, assuming the role of a reporter, is preparing an interview.

The students are fulfilling the assignment in their areas of strength. Working in whatever medium they feel most comfortable with, the sixth graders are completing the assignment. Mrs. Z has provided the opportunity for her students to succeed by using their special talents to share what they know.

Three teachers with the same objectives are using very different approaches to the same end. Two teachers allow children to succeed by utilizing the diversity of learning styles in their classrooms. An experiential approach allows each learner the chance to successfully complete the writing assignment. The third teacher approaches writing in a uniform, "everyone learns the same" way. In two classrooms, learners are excited, eager to share, and actively involved. In the third, students are struggling and being turned off to writing.

This is interesting information, but what does it mean in terms of how our children learn? Learning can no longer be approached as one-dimensional. In order to tap the full potential of each learner, teachers need to be flexible in how they prepare and present lessons. They must find a variety of ways to say the same thing. Then *all* students will benefit from the opportunity to hear the concept, to see how it fits into their world, and to feel and manipulate the information.

The current trend in education is toward this multimodal approach to learning. Legislation is changing to provide an environment conducive to learning for all students.

# Points to Ponder

1. Learning styles are pathways that incorporate our experiences and our senses to make understanding possible. What type of learning style best describes your learner?

2. Diverse learning styles require a variety of teaching techniques. Are various methods of teaching being used in your child's classroom? Are manipulative and laboratory experiences available? Are individual and small and large group instruction provided to meet each learner's needs?

3. Howard Gardner's theory of eight personal intelligences allows us to think about how many different strengths and talents can be tapped to make learning more meaningful. Are curricula in your school district diverse enough to include learners from each of Gardner's multiple intelligences? Is the full potential of each learner being developed and nurtured?

4. It is important to remember that humans are complex beings. No one is just one type of learner or of just one intelligence. The channel through which we learn best is determined by the blending of all our senses and modalities. By using our strongest pathways, we can learn successfully.

# 4

# Students' and Parents' Rights

Since 1975, the rights of students with disabilities to receive a free appropriate public education (FAPE) in the least restrictive environment (LRE) have been protected. Over the past twenty years, the commitment to the education of all children has been expanded and strengthened. No longer is it legal to exclude children with disabilities from public school buildings and educational programs. No longer are these students separated from other students or placed in institutions.

Parents, being their child's strongest advocates, should familiarize themselves with the legislation protecting their rights and those of their child. Abbreviated explanations of the three major pieces of legislation are presented below. They include Public Law 94-142 and related legislation, Section 504 of the Rehabilitation Act of 1973, and the Americans with Disabilities Act.

# Public Law 94-142 and Related Legislation

In 1975 the U. S. Congress enacted a law which entitled all children with disabilities to a free appropriate public education. This was the Education of All Handicapped Children Act, also known as PL [Public Law] 94-142. For the first time, children with disabilities were guaranteed under the law the right to attend school and get an education. No longer were they shunned and refused entry into public classrooms. They were given the same rights as other children to acquire an education. The following summarizes the guarantees that were established by this legislation:

1. A "free appropriate public education" (FAPE) within the "least restrictive environment" was guaranteed to all children and youths with disabilities. This provided programs for special education and related services to all children meeting the established criteria for eligibility.

2. The legislation guaranteed the right to an individualized education plan (IEP) for children and youth with qualifying disabilities.

3. The law provided for federal funds to assist the efforts of state and local governments in providing full educational opportunities to all children and youths with disabilities.

In 1983 Congress amended PL 94-142 to provide incentives for preschool special education programs, early intervention programs, and transition programs. These provisions were made under PL 98-199. At the same time, all the programs under PL 94-142 became the responsibility of the Office of Special Education Programs.

In 1986 PL 98-199 was further amended to change the age of eligibility for special education and related services. Public Law 99-457 included children between the ages of three and five for special education services. The Handicapped Infants and Toddlers Program, established under PL 99-457, provided early intervention services for children from birth to three years.

In 1990 the Education of All Handicapped Children Act (PL 94-

142) was reauthorized and renamed the Individuals with Disabilities Education Act (IDEA). IDEA (PL 101-476) further expanded PL 94-142 by providing other significant changes. Under IDEA the term *handicap* was changed to *disabled,* and autism and traumatic brain injury were made eligible for special education and related services.

At this writing, the major provisions under IDEA are the following:

1. All children with disabilities must be provided a free appropriate public education. Special education and related services must be provided to meet the specific needs of each child. Related services include transportation, counseling, physical and occupational therapy, speech and hearing therapy, school health services, and diagnostic health services.

2. All children with disabilities must be located, evaluated, and identified by the school districts. The evaluation process is conducted by a multidisciplinary team, the members of which are determined by the specific needs of the child. From the beginning of the process, parents should always be part of the team.

3. An individual evaluation must be provided for the student, in his or her native language, at no cost to the parents.

4. Specific criteria have been established to determine the child's eligibility for special education services.

5. A child qualifying for special education and related services must have an individual education plan (IEP) prepared and implemented. This plan is reviewed annually to ensure the program is appropriate. (See chapter 5 for information about eligibility and IEP requirements.)

6. Children receiving special education services are to be placed in the "least restrictive environment" whenever possible. Decisions about placements are to be agreed upon by the team.

7. A child receiving special education services must be reevaluated at least every three years. A more frequent evaluation may take place at the request of either the parents or teacher.

8. Parents have the right to review and inspect all of their child's educational records with respect to the identification, evaluation, placement, and provision of a free, appropriate public education. Within forty-five days after a *written* request is made, the records must be made available to the parents. Parents must have access to any records they've requested before any evaluations, team meetings, or hearings transpire.

9. If parents dispute the school's evaluation or recommendations, they are entitled to a free, independent evaluation paid for by the school district. This evaluation must cover the same areas evaluated by the school district. The child is to "stay put" (a legal term) in the current educational placement until the evaluation has been completed.

10. Parents have the right to appeal a decision made by the school through due process.

11. All information regarding the child is confidential and may not be released to anyone without the written consent of the parents.

12. States must provide in-service training for special- and general-education teachers.

# Protection Under Section 504 of the Rehabilitation Act of 1973 and ADA

IDEA pertains specifically to the education of children with disabilities. Many children with learning differences do not qualify under this regulation but nevertheless have a condition that "substantially interferes with their ability to learn." Therefore the civil rights of these children are protected under two other federal statutes. One is Section 504 of the Rehabilitation Act of 1973. This is part of the Civil Rights Act of 1964. The second law, the Americans with Disabilities Act (ADA), was enacted in 1990. Both of these regulations protect the rights of students from discrimination because of their disabilities. Unlike IDEA, which is designed only to meet the educational needs of the disabled during the school years, Section 504 and ADA protect the civil rights of individuals throughout their life span.

Under Section 504, revised in 1991, anyone having a physical or mental impairment that substantially interferes with "caring for oneself, performing manual tasks, walking, seeing, hearing, speaking, breathing, learning, or working" qualifies for services. A 504 Plan should be written for qualifying students. Reasonable accommodations, the placement of the child, and the services to be provided should be included in the 504 Plan.

It may be prudent to clarify a specific point about Section 504. While a student's diagnosis may qualify him within the realm of the criteria stated above, this does not necessarily assure him of receiving accommodations. It must be demonstrated that the dysfunction *substantially* interferes with the child's ability to learn. In Nancy's position as a learning specialist, she sees many children with a variety of diagnoses who are functioning very well in the classroom. She makes a note of each diagnosis but does not intervene if the child is learning successfully. At some future time, when the curriculum becomes more difficult, the child may begin to struggle. It is at this time that Nancy intercedes and works to get in place the interventions needed to support the learner. This is when Section 504 protects the learner.

The Americans with Disabilities Act (ADA) also protects the right of children with disabilities to an education without discrimination. This regulation entitles students to all the educational services for which they qualify and access to all the programs and activities offered by the school. ADA requires accessible public transportation, telecommunications, and other services for the individual with a disability.

# The Compliance of States with the Federal Mandates

All of the laws mentioned above apply to any school district that receives federal funds. All states must be in compliance with the federal laws, but how far beyond the minimum standards services extend varies from state to state. States not in compliance with the guidelines established by the federal legislation are refused federal funding. To be in compliance, the following criteria must be met by each state:

1. All children and youths with disabilities, regardless of the severity of their disability, will receive a free, appropriate public education.

2. The education of children and youths with disabilities up to age twenty-one will be based on a complete, individualized the evaluation of the specific needs of each child.

3. To the maximum extent appropriate, all children and youths with disabilities will be educated in the least restrictive environment, which is frequently the general education classroom.

4. Parents have the right to participate in every decision related to the identification, evaluation, and placement of their child or youth with a disability.

5. Parents must give consent for any initial evaluation, assessment, or placement. They also must be notified of any change in placement that may occur. They must be included, along with the teachers, in conferences and meetings held to develop individualized programs. Parents must approve these plans before they go into effect for the first time.

6. The right of parents to challenge and appeal any decision related to the identification, evaluation, and placement of their child is fully protected by clearly established due process.

7. Parents have the right to confidentiality. Only school personnel with legitimate educational interests may see a child's records without the parents' written permission.

8. Parents have the right to access and review their child's records. They must put this request in writing.

9. "Reasonable" accommodations must be made for the individual whose disability is "substantially interfering with a life function."

10. Public facilities, transportation, etc. must be accessible to those with a disability.

Before parents sign anything, knowing how their child's rights are protected under the law is imperative. All of the federal regulations discussed in this chapter can be obtained by writing your congressional representative, visiting your public library, or contacting your state board of education. A well-informed parent is the child's strongest and most effective advocate.

# Intervention Assistance Teams

In this chapter, we have presented the current federal guidelines. However, at this writing, the regulations are again undergoing change. Because the state and federal regulations are in constant flux, it is imperative that parents remain aware of the changes as they occur.

Most of the changes in legislation appear to be moving education in one direction—away from labeling children. Through the use of intervention assistance teams (IATs), the focus is turning toward identifying the strengths and needs of the child and adapting learning environments to meet those needs. In most states, a multifactored evaluation is not recommended until after an IAT has met and numerous interventions have been tried.

This approach makes it easier for *any* child having difficulty learning to be referred to an intervention assistance team. An IAT is a collaborative problem-solving process that uses the resources of parents, teachers, paraprofessionals, and support-services personnel to identify the problem most interfering with a child's ability to learn. Once the problem has been identified, team members brainstorm ideas to produce viable interventions for the learner. Then the suggestions are implemented in the home and school environments. If, after a reasonable time, these attempts to intervene do not improve the child's situation, a multifactored evaluation may be recommended.

# Points to Ponder

1.  The right to a free, appropriate public education for all students with disabilities is protected under PL 94-142, reauthorized and renamed IDEA. The U.S. Department of Education is responsible for the interpretation and enforcement of IDEA.

2.  Section 504 of the Rehabilitation Act of 1973 and the Americans with Disabilities Act of 1990 protect the civil rights of children, youths, and adults from discrimination based on their disabilities throughout their life span. The Office of Civil Rights interprets and enforces both regulations.

3.  The confidentiality of a child's educational records and the right of the parents to have access to all of their child's records are also protected under federal law.

4.  To receive federal funding, states must comply with the guidelines established within the federal statutes.

5.  An intervention assistance team is a collaborative problem-solving model that helps cut down on multifactored evaluations.

6.  The trend in education is to focus less on labels and more on the strengths and needs of the child. This could be a two-edged sword. On the one hand, it could help many previously underserved children get their needs met. On the other hand, unless parents and educators are able to give a specific name to the issues interfering with learning, how will they form an effective plan of action for the child?

For more information or a copy of any of the federal legislation regarding the educational rights of children with disabilities, contact the following agencies:

Office of Special Education and Rehabilitative Services, U.S. Department of Education, 330 C Street, S.W., Room 3132, Washington, DC 20202-2524.

Your public library can provide the Code of Federal Regulations and the Federal Register. Both contain the public laws.

Your congressional or state representatives can provide copies of federal or state legislation. Your state department of education is another resource.

# 5

# The Multifactored Evaluation

Andy is struggling in his second-grade classroom. He is falling behind in his written assignments, and his reading ability is not keeping pace with his classmates. At a conference, his teacher and parents express mutual concern about Andy's struggle with reading and writing and how this is affecting his attitude toward school. They agree to refer Andy to the school's intervention assistance team. However, after numerous attempts to resolve the problem using the team process, it becomes clear that a multifactored evaluation is needed to provide more information about how Andy learns.

Federal law is very specific as to how eligibility for special education services is determined, how placement is made, and how the child's right to a free, appropriate public education is protected. To meet all the standards of the law, a multidisciplinary team is formed. This team includes the parents of the child, teachers, school specialists, and sometimes the child. The team determines in what areas a multifactored evaluation (MFE) should be performed. The results of this evaluation can determine the presence of a specific learning disability and/or a communication disorder. Once this determination has been made and eligibility for services established, an IEP is written and placement in the least restrictive environment is determined.

# How a Specific Learning Disability Is Defined

A multifactored evaluation determined Andy had a specific learning disability (SLD) in the area of reading and a written-language disability. A specific learning disability is defined as a problem in understanding or in using spoken or written language. This manifests itself in the inability to listen, think, talk, read, write, spell, or do mathematical calculations. Conservatively, it is estimated that up to 20 percent of all schoolchildren are evaluated with an SLD. Many researchers suspect more children are affected but not identified.

The term *specific learning disability* does not include differences in learning that occur as a result of neurobiological disorders; autism; mental retardation; emotional/behavioral disorders; visual, hearing, or motor impairments; or environmental, cultural, or economic disadvantages. Specific learning disabilities occur most frequently in reading and math. A communication disorder, while not considered a specific learning disability, often compounds the learning issues.

Children with SLD often have average to above-average intelligence. They often exert much more effort than their peers with minimal results. For this reason, they are often referred to as "lazy" or "unmotivated." The child interprets this as "stupid" and "dumb."

This, of course, is not true! The difference between them and other learners is not a matter of intelligence but of the way in which they perceive the world. They learn easily in some areas and have difficulty in others. Information presented through the student's channels of learning can bring significant results. A multidisciplinary, multisensory approach to learning is most successful.

The spectrum of SLDs can range from mild to severe. A child with a mild disability may require little or no accommodations to learn successfully. Students with severe impairments may need extensive intervention before they can become successful learners.

Specific learning disabilities are usually disorders of the central nervous system that interfere with one or more of the basic learning functions. Any of the following learning areas may be affected.

1. **Ability to collect information.** The child has difficulty making sense of information being presented. He may do well in one sensory modality but poorly in others. For example, he may learn from what he sees but get confused by what he hears.

2. **Ability to sort information.** A child with a learning disability may miss small details and have difficulty classifying and categorizing objects. He may confuse size, shapes, letters, numbers, and colors.

3. **Ability to store information.** Learners with poor memory skills have difficulty recalling sequences in words or processes. This may be especially apparent in spelling and math.

4. **Ability to express information.** Difficulty in giving back information may interfere with the child's ability to function. He may know more than he is able to relate either orally or in writing.

# Causes of a Specific Learning Disability

No one is sure of the cause of SLD. However, there is strong evidence of a genetic predisposition to the disorder. Students with SLD usually have a parent or relative who has experienced the same issues. Parents who have struggled in school often become very successful adults if they recognize their strengths and use them in their career choices. Parents who recognize from experience the difficulties they see in their child can help teachers understand how the child learns best. Appropriate accommodations can then be made to support the learner.

SLD can also result from illness or injury, especially to the head. Hearing and vision should be assessed before a multifactored evaluation is performed. Problems in these areas can interfere with learning. While emotional issues can also affect learning, they do not cause SLD.

# Observable Traits of SLD

According to the Association for Children with Learning Disabilities (ACLD), the following are warning signs of a specific learning disability. Parents and teachers should be aware of them. Rarely, however, is a single characteristic sufficient to indicate an SLD. Learners usually display a combination of symptoms.

1. Reading below age or grade level.
2. Poor spelling.
3. Difficulty with ideas or concepts easily mastered by other children the same age.
4. Poor penmanship and/or drawing. Writing is difficult for the child. Copying can also pose a problem.
5. A short attention span.
6. Poor performance on standardized tests and classroom exams requiring reading.
7. Experiences reversals, inversions, and/or omissions in reading and writing.
8. Irregular achievement—high in some areas, low in others.
9. Slow language development.
10. Low frustration tolerance.
11. Poor long- and/or short-term memory.
12. Physical awkwardness—tendency to stumble, fall, drop things.
13. Poor judgment of distance and time.

14. Difficulty in reading and interpreting nonverbal and social cues.

15. Tendency to make comments such as "I don't like school" or "I'm stupid."

In the table developed by Melvin D. Levine, M.D., Director of Clinical Center for Study of Development and Learning at the University of North Carolina at Chapel Hill, some observable traits that may indicate a learning problem are outlined at each stage of development. Figure 5.1 is another tool to alert parents and teachers to the warning signs in each age group.

# When Should a Child Be Referred for a Multifactored Evaluation?

Parents and teachers are often in a quandary as to when a referral for an evaluation is indicated. They may understand that the key to optimum success in learning is early diagnosis and early intervention. Often they want to wait long enough to see if maturation and intervention strategies will improve the situation but not so long that the child ends up frustrated and hating school. As a rule of thumb, if the child's learning difficulties intensify rather than lessen, a learning problem may be present. If the child has a learning disability, the traits do not go away. They are always present and usually intensify as the child gets older and the academic demands increase.

If a developmental or maturation issue is delaying the acquisition of a skill, remediation or intervention will often enable the child to close the learning gap, and the issue will subside. Remediation can give the child the extra support needed until the skill is developed. For example, a child who has difficulty identifying the main idea in reading may qualify for assistance from the reading specialist or tutor. With the appropriate intervention, the child will demonstrate a marked improvement, and a multifactored evaluation will not be necessary.

**Fig. 5.1. Learning Disabilities. What to Look For:** *Some First Signs of Trouble Keeping Up with the Flow of Expectations*

| | Language | Memory | Attention | Fine Motor Skill | Other Functions |
|---|---|---|---|---|---|
| **Preschool** | Pronunciation problems<br>Slow vocabulary growth<br>Lack of interest in story telling | Trouble learning numbers, alphabet, days of week, etc.<br>Poor memory for routines | Trouble sitting still<br>Extreme restlessness<br>Impersistence at tasks | Trouble learning self-help skills (e.g. tying shoelaces)<br>Clumsiness<br>Reluctance to draw or trace | Trouble learning left from right (possible visual spatial confusion)<br>Trouble interacting (weak social skills) |
| **Lower Grades** | Delayed decoding abilities<br>Trouble following directions<br>Poor spelling | Slow recall of facts<br>Organizational problems<br>Slow acquisition of new skills<br>Poor spelling | Impulsivity, lack of planning<br>Careless errors<br>Insatiability<br>Distractibility | Unstable pencil grip<br>Trouble with letter formation | Trouble learning about time (temporal-sequential disorganization)<br>Poor grasp of math concepts |

| Middle Grades | | | | |
|---|---|---|---|---|
| Poor reading comprehension | Poor, illegible writing | Inconsistency | Fist-like or tightly gripped pencil | Poor learning strategies |
| Lack of verbal participation in class | Slow or poor recall of math facts | Poor self-monitoring | Illegible, slow, or inconsistent writing | Disorganization in time or space |
| Trouble with word problems | Failure of automatic recall | Great knowledge of trivia | Reluctance to write | Peer rejection |
| | | Distaste for fine detail | | |

| Upper Grades | | | | |
|---|---|---|---|---|
| Weak grasp of explanations | Trouble studying for tests | Memory problems due to weak attention | (Lessening relevance of fine motor skills) | Poor grasp of abstract concepts |
| Foreign language problems | Weak cumulative memory | Mental fatigue | | Failure to elaborate |
| Poor written expression | Slow work pace | | | Trouble taking tests, multiple choice (e.g. SAT's) |
| Trouble summarizing | | | | |

These lists are guideposts for parents. They should not be used in isolation but may lead the parent to seek further assessment. Many children will, from time to time, have difficulty with one or more of these items. They should always be reviewed in a broader content of understanding about a child.

Used with permission of Melvin D. Levine, M.D., F.A.A.P., *Their World '90* published by the National Center for Learning Disabilities

# The Steps in the Multifactored Evaluation Process

If the warning signs persist, however, an evaluation should be requested. Several steps should occur before a child is evaluated for SLD. First, the parents may want to consult with the child's pediatrician to check for any physical impediments to learning. A hearing and vision screening may also be appropriate. If these examinations show no medical reasons for the child's learning difficulties, a school evaluation should be requested.

Anyone working with the child may begin the process by requesting an evaluation. *The request must be in writing!* Within thirty days of the written request, the school district must initiate the evaluation process. The district then has ninety days to complete the evaluation and hold a meeting of the multidisciplinary team, of which the parents are a part. This team meeting determines the child's eligibility for services under IDEA, and an IEP is developed if the child qualifies.

The multifactored evaluation is conducted to determine whether a student meets the criteria established by state and federal guidelines to identify children with a learning disability. The term *multifactored* means that an assessment must occur in more than one area of the child's functioning. This evaluation is performed by a multidisciplinary team of qualified professionals. Figure 5.2 displays the academic areas in which an evaluation can be conducted and the appropriate professionals in each area who may be involved in evaluating the child.

---

**Fig. 5.2. Required Areas of Assessment for Specific Learning Disabilities**

| Evaluation Areas | Sources of Information* |
| --- | --- |
| *General intelligence:* a measure of cognitive functioning that is designed for individual administration | Parent<br>Psychologist/school psychologist<br>Regular classroom teacher |

**Fig. 5.2,** *continued*

| Evaluation Areas | Sources of Information* |
|---|---|
| *Basic reading skills:* word attack, sight vocabulary, structural analysis | Psychologist/school psychologist<br>Reading specialist<br>Regular or special education teacher<br>Special education supervisor |
| *Reading Comprehension:* Factual, Inferential, Application | Psychologist/school psychologist<br>Reading specialist<br>Regular or special education teacher<br>Special education supervisor |
| *Mathematics calculation:* computation, time, money, measurement | Psychologist/school psychologist<br>Regular or special education teacher<br>Special education supervisor |
| *Mathematics Reasoning:* Application | Psychologist/school psychologist<br>Reading specialist<br>Regular or special education teacher<br>Special education supervisor |
| *Oral expression:* articulation, fluency, vocal quality, vocabulary, sentence structure, grammar | Psychologist/school psychologist<br>Regular or special education teacher<br>Special education supervisor<br>Speech and language pathologist |
| *Listening comprehension:* attending skills; perception; receptive knowledge of vocabulary, basic concepts, structure, grammatical forms | Audiologist<br>Psychologist/school psychologist<br>Regular or special education teacher<br>Special education supervisor<br>Speech and language pathologist |
| *Written expression:* sentence structure, semantic accuracy, use of grammatic forms, spelling, composition skills, handwriting | Psychologist/school psychologist<br>Regular or special education teacher<br>Special education supervisor<br>Speech and language pathologist |
| *Vision abilities:* acuity, perception, eye coordination, physical ear condition | Physician or school nurse<br>Vision specialist |

*(continued on next page)*

---

**Fig. 5.2. Required Areas of Assessment for Specific Learning Disabilities,** *continued*

| Evaluation Areas | Sources of Information* |
|---|---|
| *Hearing abilities:* acuity, perception, physical ear condition | Audiologist or hearing specialist<br>Physician or school nurse<br>Speech and language pathologist |
| *Motor abilities:* fine and gross motor development and coordination | Adapted or regular physical education teacher<br>Occupational or physical therapist<br>Physician or school nurse<br>Psychologist/school psychologist<br>Regular classroom teacher |
| *Social and emotional status:* behavior, social interaction with peers and adults, general affect | Guidance counselor<br>Parent<br>Psychologist/school psychologist<br>Regular classroom teacher |
| *Observation* | Psychologist/school psychologist<br>Special education supervisor<br>Special education teacher |
| *Environmental, cultural, economic disadvantage* | Guidance counselor<br>Parent<br>Principal<br>Regular classroom teacher<br>School nurse |
| *Learning experiences appropriate for child's age and ability levels* | Guidance counselor<br>Parent<br>Principal<br>Regular classroom teacher |

*In each evaluation area there may be other persons equally qualified.

Reprinted from *Ohio Tour Book*. Used with permission of the Ohio Department of Education.

---

The following steps should be a part of the evaluation process. The process begins with the prereferral step and progresses through the request for an independent educational evaluation.

1. **Prereferral Step**

   Parents and teachers identify learning concerns.

   They conference and share ideas that are helpful.

   Intervention assistance teams generate additional classroom interventions.

   Teachers try interventions to alleviate concerns.

   If attempts are unsuccessful, a referral for a multifactored evaluation is made by either the teacher or the parents.

   The referral must be in writing.

2. **Referral**

   Within thirty days after the referral is received, the evaluation process must be initiated.

   A multidisciplinary team is formed that includes the parents.

   Parents give written consent for the school district to test their child.

   Parents receive a copy of their rights.

3. **Multifactored Evaluation**

   The parents are informed when and where the MFE will take place and who will be participating in it.

   The testing is performed.

   The multidisciplinary team examines the results and determines the child's eligibility under legal guidelines.

4. **Before the IEP Meeting**

   Parents are notified of time and place of IEP meeting.

   Parents receive a draft of suggested goals for the child's individualized education plan. The goals and objectives of the IEP should be based on the strengths and needs of the child.

   Parents may choose to access and review their child's records.

   Parents should bring support persons, concerns, and questions to the IEP meeting.

5. **During the IEP Meeting**

   The evaluation results are shared, and the finding of eligibility for special services is explained.

   The IEP goals and objectives that were developed are explained and discussed.

   Questions and concerns are addressed.

   Parents give permission for the child to receive services.

   If child does not qualify for services, the following must occur:

   a. Appropriate accommodations are determined.

   b. Eligibility for services under Section 504 should be examined.

   c. If parents disagree with the results of the evaluation, they are to be informed of their right to an independent educational evaluation at the expense of the school district.

6. **Annual Review**

   When an IEP is put in place, it must be reviewed each year.

   Current IEP goals and objectives are reassessed at that time.

   Child's current progress is also discussed.

   New goals and objectives are written where appropriate.

7. **Reevaluation**

   By law, a reevaluation must be performed every three years.

   A reevaluation of the student may be requested before three years, if there is a major change in the child's skills.

   This reevaluation determines if the child still qualifies for services or if progress in skill development would indicate a release from the special education program.

8. **Independent Educational Evaluation**

   Parents inform the school *in writing* of any disagreement with the evaluation performed by the school.

   Parents have the right to an evaluator *of their choice*. This would be at the *school district's expense*.

If either the school or parents cannot agree at this point on the child's status, either party may request a due-process hearing. This means a state-appointed mediator may be asked to decide the next step.

# How Is Eligibility for SLD Determined?

For a student to qualify as SLD, a severe discrepancy must occur between the child's intelligence level and his level of achievement. This discrepancy must occur in one or more of the achievement areas listed above in Figure 5.2.

Many parents, as well as educators, have little knowledge or understanding about the tests given in an MFE. They have even less understanding of what the score means and how a discrepancy score is determined. For your convenience, we have outlined some of the tests that may be used to evaluate your child. This information includes the ages for which the test is designed and the areas being evaluated.

## Measures Used to Determine Intellectual Ability

The child's intellectual ability is usually measured by the administering of an intelligence test. The test most frequently used is the Wechsler Intelligence Scale for Children, Revised (WISC-R). This is appropriate for ages six through seventeen. Preschool and adult versions of this measure are also available. Most school psychologists are trained to administer this test.

The WISC-R is divided into two scales, verbal and performance. Academic success is measured by the verbal scale. The verbal scale is divided into the following subtests:

1.  Information: measures the child's knowledge about the world in which he lives.

2.  Similarities: measures logical and abstract thinking.

3.  Arithmetic: evaluates attention, concentration, and abstract reasoning.

4. Vocabulary: tests the present functional understanding and use of words.

5. Comprehension: a test of common sense.

6. Digit span: measures immediate auditory memory, which requires attention, concentration, and emotional control.

The performance scale is non-verbal and measures the ability to think and solve problems in practical, concrete, and manipulative situations. It is made up of the following subtests:

1. Picture completion: measures visual alertness to detail and visual memory.

2. Picture arrangement: measures logical thinking ability and interpretation of social situations without the use of language.

3. Block design: involves the ability to analyze an abstract design and integrate its parts into a meaningful whole.

4. Object assembly: measures the ability to see spatial relationships by putting together a whole concrete form from separate parts.

5. Coding: measures the speed of learning and writing visual symbols.

Other tests frequently used to measure intelligence ability are listed below.

1. **Wechsler Preschool and Primary Scale of Intelligence (WPPSI)**

   For ages four to six.

   The version of the WISC designed to measure the intelligence of the young child.

2. **Stanford-Binet Intelligence Scale, Fourth Edition**

   Age two to adult.

   An excellent intelligence test that is frequently administered.

## Measures to Determine Achievement

Achievement is measured through the use of standardized tests, administered individually to evaluate the areas of basic reading skills, reading comprehension, mathematics calculation, and mathematics reasoning. Some examples of measures used to evaluate these areas include the following.

1. **Brigance Inventory of Basic Skills**

   For grades K through 6.

   Tests in the areas of reading, language arts, and mathematics.

2. **Kaufman Test of Educational Achievement**

   For ages six to eighteen.

   This screening measure of achievement has two forms.

   The Brief Form measures overall knowledge in reading, math, and spelling.

   The Comprehensive Form measures more specific skills in decoding, reading comprehension, math applications and computations, and spelling.

3. **Key Math Diagnostic Arithmetic Test**

   For grades K through 9.

   Measures three areas of arithmetic ability.

   The content area measures knowledge of basic math concepts such as numeration, fractions, and geometry.

   The operations area measures the ability to use those concepts to perform mathematical computation processes such as addition, subtraction, multiplication, and division.

   The application area assesses the ability to use the mathematical processes to solve problems found in everyday life such as making change.

4. **Test of Written Language (TOWL), 3d Edition**

   For ages seven to eighteen.

   Measures the written language skills.

   Evaluates skill levels in vocabulary, maturity of the theme, spelling, word usage, style, and handwriting.

   This measure is extremely time consuming and difficult to score.

5. **Woodcock Reading Mastery Tests**

   For grades K through 12.

   Measures letter identification, word identification, word-attack skills, analogies, and passage comprehension.

6. **Woodcock Johnson Psycho-Educational Battery**

   For ages three to adult.

   Part I measures specific cognitive ability. Part II measures academic achievement. Part III are tests of interest level.

## Questions Parents Should Ask Before Giving Consent to Test

This is just a sampling of the tools available to assess the achievement levels of a student. As a parent, you are responsible for knowing exactly what will occur before you allow your child to be tested. Consideration of the following questions may help you make an informed decision.

1. Who will be doing the evaluation? Depending on the areas of concern, your child may encounter more than one professional. Parents may request that evaluations be administered in areas other than the school's recommendations. For example, if the parent suspects a language-processing problem, a language evaluation may be requested.

2. What tests will be administered? What will they measure? How long will the testing take? For what age levels are the tests appropriate?

3. How should I broach the subject of testing with my child? How can he prepare for the testing situation?

4.  When will the testing begin? When can I expect the results?

## Formula Used to Determine Eligibility

Once the testing has been completed, the determination of eligibility is the next step. For a child to qualify, he must show a severe discrepancy between his intellectual ability and his achievement level. A specific formula is used to determine the discrepancy score. This formula is extremely complicated, and it takes a trained professional to use it easily and accurately.

## Writing an IEP

Once a child qualifies for services, an individualized educational plan must be written. The multidisciplinary team, of which the parents are a part, meets and writes the goals and objectives of the IEP. The following components should be included in the child's IEP.

1.  A profile of the child's strengths and weaknesses.
2.  Current performance levels in *all* areas where services will be provided.
3.  Annual goals and short-term instructional objectives based on the current level of performance.
4.  Criteria and evaluation procedures linked to short-term objectives.
5.  Statements of specific special education and related services that will be provided.
6.  The regular education classes in which the child will participate.
7.  The dates for the beginning and ending of services and how frequently the services will be offered (daily? twice a week?).

For those of you not familiar with an IEP, a sample is provided in the appendix. All of the components listed above are in the written plan. When everyone is in agreement, the IEP is signed by the parents and each team member and services begin.

The multifactored evaluation is conducted by school personnel to determine the learner's capabilities in various academic areas. Many children with biochemical and/or physical disorders may qualify for an MFE and special education services but may also require a medical diagnosis. This is particularly true of children with biochemical disorders. The medical and mental health professionals involved with the child and her family should be included in the multidisciplinary team. Their expertise is a critical component of the child's support system.

# Points to Ponder

1. A specific learning disability is defined as difficulty in more than one of the psychological processes involved in understanding or using language in a person of average to above-average intelligence.

2. A multifactored evaluation is performed to determine SLD. A severe discrepancy must be present before a child is eligible for special education services.

3. A multidisciplinary team meets to write an individualized education plan for the student.

4. Parents should be active participants in the evaluation process and the writing of their child's IEP.

5. If "teacher talk" and professional jargon cause confusion, ask for clarification.

6. Parents should not sign anything until they are comfortable with all the provisions offered. They should keep working with the team until all of their child's needs are met.

Contact the following agencies and organizations for additional resources and information about SLD.

National Center for Learning Disabilities, 99 Park Avenue, New York, NY 10016 (212) 687-7211.

Learning Disabilities Association of America, 4156 Library Road, Pittsburgh, PA 15234 (412) 341-1515 or (412) 341-8077.

# 6

# Clinical Evaluations

Besides evaluating to determine the presence of specific learning disabilities and/or communication disorders, school personnel may also screen for hearing and vision impairments and some orthopedic conditions, such as scoliosis. However, children with complex physical and/or biochemical disorders need to be evaluated by a medical or mental health professional. While the information provided by the school is a critical component of the evaluation, the final diagnosis needs to be made by the clinical professional, not the school.

Many medical disorders exhibit physical symptoms that can alert parents and professionals that clinical intervention is necessary. These might include hearing, visual, and orthopedic impairments. Other conditions, like some forms of mental retardation, can be detected before or soon after birth. The extent of a traumatic head injury often can be determined at the time the injury is incurred. Astute medical professionals and specialists have the tools available to diagnose these disabilities based on physical symptoms the individual is demonstrating.

Other conditions, such as the biochemical disorders, are less easily identified. These include AD/HD, Tourette syndrome, obsessive-compulsive disorder, oppositional defiant and conduct disorder, and autism. Mental health professionals are guided by the criteria found in the *Diagnostic and Statistical Manual of Mental Disorders, 4th ed. (DSM IV)* in the diagnosis of these disorders.

More often than not, teachers are the first to recognize the symptoms of one of these disorders and approach the parents with their suspicions that something is amiss. Often the teacher's information confirms what the parents have suspected for many years. Together, they need to work to get a complete evaluation, both educational and medical.

# The Role of the School

Educators are often unsure how to approach parents with the idea that the child has a learning disorder. In her work as a learning specialist, Nancy cautions teachers about using medical terminology with parents. When this occurs, they become educators using medical terms they are not qualified to use. Nancy recommends that teachers keep the following suggestions in mind.

1. **Approach with caution.** Parents of a child with any learning difference are probably overwhelmed and frustrated. They need to be approached in a caring, sensitive way. Teachers should try to keep their frustrations under control.

2. **Walk a mile in their moccasins.** By heeding this old Native American quote, educators can accomplish a cautious approach. When Nancy was in the classroom working with children with learning issues, she would stop and think about her son who has AD/HD. How would she want his teacher to handle the situation? What would she want to hear from his teacher? When the situation was put into a personal context, Nancy's whole perspec-

tive changed. Teachers need to think in terms of their own child, grandchild, niece, or nephew when talking to the parents of their students. If you as an educator would appreciate sensitivity, so would the child's parents!

3. **Establish confidentiality.** First, schedule a conference when you are not pressured for time. Five minutes before the morning bell is rarely sufficient. Next, find a place that is private, quiet, and out of the earshot of students, teachers, and other parents. At the beginning of the conference, state that everything shared will be held in strictest confidence, and *mean it!* The right to privacy must be respected.

4. **Stick to the specifics.** Describe all the characteristics that are interfering with the learning process in specific terms. Then prioritize the areas of concern. For example, "Anne is having difficulty staying focused. It is interfering with her ability to complete assignments. She also has a problem staying in her seat and often disturbs other children. Anne seems to know how to do the work, but she has a difficult time beginning and completing the task." The teacher may be describing AD/HD, but she is giving the parents specific information that they can use and share with a physician.

5. **Classroom accommodations.** Explain the classroom accommodations that have been tried to resolve the problem. "I have tried cover sheets to help Anne stay focused and not feel so overwhelmed. Sometimes this has been successful. I have also suggested to Anne that she may want to use the classroom 'office' for a quieter place to work. She likes this suggestion because she can stand and not disturb anyone. Standing seems to help her stay focused."

6. **Refer to the IAT.** Ask the parent's permission to refer the child to the school's intervention assistance team for more support. Together with this team, the parents and teachers can explore more resources to help support the learner.

7. **Referral for a multifactored evaluation.** If a learning disability is suspected, a multifactored evaluation may be appropriate. This recommendation may come from the teacher or the IAT if all attempts to resolve the issues fail.

8. **Referral to the child's physician.** At this point, the parents may be referred to their child's physician for further screening and evaluation.

All of these steps are within the realm of responsibility of school personnel. All areas approach the concern from an educational perspective. When all educational avenues have been exhausted, then a referral to medical or mental health professionals is appropriate. All of the data the school and parents have collected in this process will be valuable in the diagnostic process. Therefore, educators would benefit by considering this approach when encountering any of the disabilities discussed in this sourcebook. However, when a medical disorder is suspected, educators should be cautioned about using terminology they are not qualified to use.

# The Role of the Medical or Mental Health Professionals

Usually the pediatrician is the first professional consulted. Screening for physical causes can be completed by this professional. Vision and hearing screening and any other physical reasons for the child's symptoms should be assessed.

Depending on the results of this initial evaluation, the pediatrician may refer parents to a specialized professional for a more comprehensive evaluation. Based on the pediatrician's findings, the medical or mental health professional will perform the tests necessary to make a definitive diagnosis. The child's family, developmental, and medical histories should also be made available to this professional.

Many professionals will contact the child's school to gather valuable information about how he or she functions within that environment.

This contact is an especially important component in the evaluation of the neurobiological disorders (AD/HD, Tourette syndrome, obsessive-compulsive disorder, etc.). Through the use of checklists, questionnaires, and anecdotal notes, teachers can provide the diagnostician with crucial data about the child. A diagnosis of the child's condition should result from the analysis of all this information.

# Forming a Collaborative Team

Once a diagnosis has been made, the medical and mental health professionals should become part of the child's support team. The parents and the school's intervention assistance team need to work with the clinical professionals to develop a management plan. The objective of the management plan should be to identify the strengths of the child and suggest ways to build skills that will be used for a lifetime. Team members should assume responsibility in their areas of expertise and work together to accomplish this goal.

## A Word About Medication

For many of the disorders, especially the neurobiological dysfunctions, medication may be recommended to ease the symptoms and make management more successful. While teachers may be requested to fill out evaluations as a way of providing feedback regarding the efficacy of the medication, it is the responsibility of the physician to carefully monitor all prescribed medications.

The use of medication is a personal decision that parents should make with the guidance of their physician. Since children may not respond to medication, it should not be used as a diagnostic tool. *Never* should teachers or any school professional suggest that a child be medicated. *Never* should parents feel pressure from the school to place their child on medication. This would be inappropriate and unprofessional!

More information about the management of medications can be found in chapter 26. The specific procedures used to make a diagnosis for each disorder will be discussed as we examine each disability individually.

# The Legal Rights of Children with Physical and/or Biochemical Disorders

Once the child receives a medical diagnosis and it is shared with the school, the child may become eligible for support services and accommodations. Some children with medical disorders qualify under IDEA, but many do not. Many meet the criteria of Section 504 of the Rehabilitation Act of 1973 and/or the Americans with Disabilities Act and receive reasonable accommodations to support their learning. For most of the children, the "least restrictive environment" is the general education classroom. With most states adopting a policy of inclusion, the general education classroom is taking on a whole new appearance and tone in meeting the needs of all learners.

# Points to Ponder

1. A diagnosis made by medical or mental health professionals requires the collection of extensive data, most of which is provided by the school. Because of the complexity of each disorder, caution and thoroughness are required.

2. Schools should not diagnose for physical and/or biochemical disorders. They can gather information, make accommodations, and evaluate for SLD or communication disorders to alleviate the concerns. Specific descriptions of how the observable symptoms are interfering with the child's learning are also useful and appropriate.

3. Together, the educational and medical evaluations can provide a picture of the whole child.

4.  Following the diagnosis, parents, school personnel, and specialists, working as a team, can find ways to help the child manage his disability. Medication may be part of the management plan.

5.  The use of medication is a personal decision made by the parents with the guidance of the medical professional. The use of medications should be closely monitored by the physician.

6.  Therapy may be part of the management plan for many of these disorders.

7.  The rights of the children with a medical diagnosis are protected under federal laws, and for many, the least restrictive environment is the inclusive, general education classroom.

# 7

# Inclusion–Bringing Services to the Student

Upon entering Mrs. Paul's classroom in Any School, USA, you may be surprised by the diversity of students. You could observe Sarah, seated in front of a computer tapping out her daily journal entry. As Sarah's skills group is called, you notice her place her materials in a basket on the front of a walker. She uses this walker to maneuver herself to the group. Sarah has cerebral palsy.

The teacher is wearing a microphone that amplifies her speech for Michael, who is wearing an FM monitor. Michael is hearing-impaired.

The language pathologist is working with a small group of students on interpreting facial expressions as an instructional assistant moves about the classroom helping students needing additional support. The classroom is humming, and no one seems to be aware of these differences.

The learning differences you have observed are part of a new direction in education. Rather than providing special placements for students with disabilities, educators are moving toward providing an education for all students within the general education classroom. This model is called inclusion.

# The Influence of Legislation

Before the passage of Public Law 94-142 in 1975, schools were not responsible for educating children with learning differences. Often children with severe behavioral or emotional needs were placed in institutions. Other children with learning issues were turned away from schools. Before 1975, not all children were entitled to a "free, appropriate public education."

The programs offered for children with special needs were questionable at best. Often classrooms were isolated in separate buildings or in fenced-off areas. Other popular sites for the "special" students were behind boiler rooms or in storage closets. The personnel staffing these facilities were usually not trained or certified to teach the students. They were paid much less for their efforts and often felt as isolated as their learners.

With the passing of PL 94-142, now called IDEA, children with disabilities were provided with several guarantees (see chapter 4). Even with these guarantees, the separation of the child with disabilities and the "typical" learner still exists in the following ways:

1. "Pull out" programs take the child from the general education classroom throughout the school day.

2. Some children are assigned to resource rooms for the entire day.

3. Funding for programs under IDEA is separate from general education funds.

4. Teacher training is specialized, and special education and general education personnel rarely collaborate or support each other.

5. Children are still stigmatized and labeled as "different."

# Mainstreaming

The practice of moving children from the special education facility to the general education classroom throughout the day is known as mainstreaming. This is an attempt to educate students in the "least restrictive environment."

Research is suggesting that this may not be the most effective way to meet the needs of children who qualify under IDEA. The students feel like they are being bounced from place to place and have a hard time relating to any teacher. They still feel like "dummies," and the movement from one place to another interferes with the continuity of learning and socialization opportunities.

Many students who enter special education programs often remain there throughout their school careers. One study of school districts in twenty-six large cities found that fewer than 5 percent of the students who received special education services ever left the system completely.

Please do not misunderstand. IDEA has provided the supports necessary for many students to receive an education and maintain a productive life as an adult. But it is important to understand that this law has its drawbacks, and educators are now looking in another direction to equalize the delivery of instruction to all learners. When the reality is that only about 20 percent of the school-age population are getting their needs met, the system needs to change. Inclusion may bring about this change. It is moving in the direction of using the general education classroom as the "least restrictive environment" to meet the needs of *all* learners.

# Benefits of Inclusion

The inclusion model is being adopted by many states to bring about a greater sense of balance in educating our youth. Inclusion is being defined as a commitment made by school systems to educate all students, whatever their needs, in their neighborhood schools with peers of the same age and grade as themselves. This means that instead of taking the child to the services, the services are brought to the child.

Inclusion does not reduce the rights of students. All the provisions under IDEA are still intact. Children qualifying for services under IDEA are still provided with an IEP. The difference is that the goals defined in the IEP are met within the general education classroom rather than in a special placement.

Inclusion is designed to expand, rather than narrow, the scope of opportunities. Rather than making children with disabilities appear more different and isolated, inclusion allows everyone to become more accepting and tolerant (see Figure 7.1). If inclusion is working effectively, it is invisible. Differences are accepted rather than feared. Individuals are valued for *who* they are, not *what* they are. The opportunity to interact with peers in a safe, supportive environment can be provided.

To accomplish this task, general education teachers are supported by available instructional assistants, consultants, and special educators. School psychologists, speech and language pathologists, occupational

---

**Fig. 7.1. Comparison of Traditional Special Education Placements and Inclusive Placements**

| Traditional | Inclusion |
| --- | --- |
| Special placement in resource rooms | General education classroom |
| Student goes to services | Services come to students |
| Limited number of children served | All learners benefit |
| Isolated and segregated | Part of general education community |
| Labeled and stigmatized | Differences accepted and appreciated |
| Protected under IDEA | Protected under IDEA |
| Limited collaboration among professionals | Collaboration of support services |

and physical therapists, and social workers are some of the paraprofessionals who need to be available to support the classroom teacher. Because team teaching and collaboration are imperative to make inclusion successful, it becomes the responsibility of these professionals to meet with the teacher to plan and schedule their participation in the support services they offer.

Inclusion has resulted in major changes in the roles of everyone responsible for the education of the students once the model is adopted as the policy (see Figure 7.2). The educational system becomes more collaborative and team-oriented. Working as separate entities is no longer accepted practice.

Having professionals provide services within the classroom benefits

---

**Fig. 7.2. Changes in Roles**

| *Traditional Model* | *Inclusive Model* |
|---|---|
| **Regular Educators** | |
| Refer problem students to others for "diagnosis" | Seek assistance for problem students from special educators and support staff *within* the regular class |
| **Special Educators** | |
| Provide instruction to identified students in a resource room or special class | Provide instruction in regular class Collaborate with regular teacher |
| **Support Staff (Social workers, school psychologists, etc.)** | |
| Diagnose problems, assign labels, and determine eligibility | Work with teachers to define problems and design interventions |
| **Administrators** | |
| Responsible for attendance area population and "house" special education Primarily manage the "regular education" portion of a dual system | Responsible for the education of all students enrolled Manage a merged system |

Used with permission of Northern Suburban Special Education District.

all the students. Many children who could benefit from services are not eligible to receive them under state or federal guidelines. These children can easily fall through the cracks. The specialists in the classroom for one or two students can offer support to any learner who may be struggling. For example, in the classroom described at the beginning of this chapter, the speech pathologist was working with a group of students who were having difficulty reading social cues. Only one of those students may have actually qualified for language services, but with inclusion, other students with similar difficulties were able to join the therapist's lesson. Thus any learner in the class can benefit from the specialist's services.

When the specialists' and teachers' roles become more those of facilitator and coach, the classroom becomes more child-centered. Children work with other peers at their own paces and developmental skill levels. Techniques such as peer tutoring, cooperative learning, heterogeneous grouping, multiage classes, and small groups for remediation help meet the diverse range of learning styles. The emphasis is on improved instruction and how to make learning more meaningful for each student, rather than racing to "cover the curriculum." The learning differences of the student are accommodated and supported (see Figure 7.3).

Research shows that the school districts in which inclusion is working most effectively tend to have the following characteristics in common:

1. All students are placed in the general education classrooms on a full-time basis.

2. Special education specialists are working collaboratively with the general education teachers to meet the needs of all students in the general education classrooms.

3. Special education services are not being replicated within the general education classroom. The curriculum is being adapted and modified to meet the needs of the students.

4. Each classroom receives a limited number of students with special needs so as not to cluster them in one placement.

**Fig. 7.3. Benefits of Inclusion**

1. Students with disabilities have more confidence in their ability to handle academics
2. Social interaction improves
3. Classroom behavior improves
4. Students exceed their teachers' expectations in academics and work habits
5. Students with disabilities are more accepted by their peers
6. Classmates learn to accept and appreciate differences rather than fear them
7. Students are more willing to help each other
8. All students benefit from the additional support personnel in the classroom
9. Educators benefit from collaborating with other professionals
10. Educators can adapt the curriculum to meet the needs of all students
11. Educators have the flexibility to take risks and try new approaches to educating
12. A major step is taken toward eliminating the labeling of children

5. Well-trained instructional assistants support the teacher in the general education classroom.

Clearly, there are many benefits to changing the way education views the placement of students with special learning requirements.

# Barriers to Inclusion

Inclusion appears to be an ideal way to avoid labeling and become more accepting of students with learning differences. While an inclusive program can offer many advantages to all children, many educators are cautious and concerned that it works better on paper than in practice.

The practice of inclusion is in its infancy. To date there is no legislation that would mandate this method. So adopting an inclusive policy is still optional. While all states are moving toward inclusion, the goals and objectives vary dramatically.

Some states have mandated the entire elimination of labeling and segregating children, while others are more conservatively approaching inclusion with pilot programs in selected districts and schools. This inconsistency is causing a discrepancy in how school programs are funded. States eliminating special classifications for students are losing significant funding. This can seriously affect the resource personnel available to support the general education teacher. In contrast, states maintaining special education programs can keep their funding and maintain their special education professionals.

Even within school districts, inclusion is optional. Some schools are involved, and others are not. Any school system adopting an inclusion policy must design it to reflect the resources available for the training and support of the general education teacher.

Initial teacher preparation and continuous training are mandatory before inclusion can work effectively. This training needs to be designed to meet the specific needs of each school situation. Unfortunately, teachers often feel that the guidance offered is too sporadic and general to be beneficial. This leaves them feeling ill-prepared to meet the diverse needs of their students.

Scheduling times with other professionals is an additional barrier to a smoothly functioning program. Often support professionals entering the classroom are unfamiliar with the curriculum and unsure what their responsibilities should be. For example, an occupational therapist with no training in classroom management may feel very awkward in a class-room environment unless her role is well defined. Adequate time is there-fore required to establish the role of each service provider entering the classroom. This can be very time consuming for everyone.

Another consideration is whether total inclusion is in the best inter-est of all children. Inclusion is designed to give all learners the oppor-tunity to learn from each other and accept each other's differences. Yet many researchers are questioning whether the general education class-room is the best placement for children with extreme emotional, phys-ical, and academic impairments.

**Fig. 7.4. Barriers to Inclusion**

1. A lack of well-defined goals and expectations consistent for every state

2. A lack of well-defined roles for support professionals providing services in the general education classroom

3. Awkwardness in the division of responsibility among professionals

4. Specialists' unfamiliarity with the classroom curriculum

5. Ineffective collaboration and communication among team members

6. Scheduling problems

7. Finding adequate time for planning

8. A lack of experience and training among general educators in teaching students with disabilities

9. The need to continually modify the curriculum

10. Inadequate support from the school system, reflected in insufficient resources and personnel

11. Inadequate funding

Many studies are being conducted on the implementation of inclusion in the nation's classrooms. At this writing, the data are still inconclusive. Many questions are still unanswered, and numerous barriers need to be overcome. In theory, inclusion appears to be a promising way for children with learning differences to gain acceptance. In practice, many obstacles need to be addressed before a smooth transition from special placements to the general education classroom can occur.

In an article titled "Full Inclusion Is Possible," education advisor Marsha Forest wrote, "To me the key . . . is that a new generation is being born—a generation who tolerates difference and change far better than I do, who is less afraid, and who are more loving to people with differences." If this is what inclusion can accomplish, what a powerful tool we have at our disposal!

Realistically, educators have a long road ahead of them before all the flaws are ironed out and inclusion becomes accepted practice in schools nationwide. Inclusion is a process that will require continual change and adaptation if the needs of all students are to be met within the general education classroom. With change comes fear and resistance.

Perhaps, through education and understanding, fear and resistance can be alleviated. In the next section, we will present and discuss each disability that could be part of any inclusionary program. We will begin with those disabilities that can be determined by an educational evaluation and progress to the disorders requiring a medical or mental health diagnosis.

# Points to Ponder

1. Inclusion is designed to meet the needs of all students in the general education classroom. If your child has severe physical, emotional, or academic differences, will the general education classroom meet his or her needs?

2. Inclusion reduces the fear of differences and encourages acceptance. How would your child (with or without a disability) feel about being in the general education classroom where inclusion is practiced?

3. Inclusion still provides for the use of an IEP and related services for students who qualify. How will the child's IEP goals be met in the general education classroom?

4. Training and support of the general education teacher is essential for inclusion to be successful. What training has the general education teacher received? Is it ongoing?

5. Numerous resource personnel must be available to the general education teacher for support and collaboration. These paraprofessionals must be available throughout the school year. What resources are available to support the general education teachers in your school? Will they be available to offer their services for the entire year?

6. Flexibility and the ability to communicate are key components of a successful program to address the diversity of learning styles. How open is your child's teacher to new ideas and to working with other professionals?

7. The school district and administrators must be totally committed to providing resources and training to the general education teacher. What is your school district's level of commitment to its inclusion program?

8. How each state classifies special education will determine how much funding is available. Has your state eliminated the labeling of children? If so, how does this affect the funds available to support inclusion?

Contact your state's board of education for information about its policy on inclusion and school funding.

# 8

# Reading–The Basis of Learning

If yon are fihbihp tnis seuteuce bifficnlt to reab yonr are exqerieucinp oue of tne asqects of wnat it neams to nave a reabiuq bisadility. No this is not a misprint! Yes, it is just one sentence. Now, before you look at the translation provided below, go back and try to figure out what this sentence says. Were you successful? How long did it take you? The translation reads: If you are finding this sentence difficult to read, you are experiencing one of the aspects of what it means to have a reading disability.

For thousands of students attempting to read, this is how written words appear. How long did you struggle to make sense of the gibberish? Did you give up in frustration and peek at the translation? If you stuck it out, how did you feel when you finally understood the message? Tired? Overwhelmed? Exasperated? Triumphant?

Now try to imagine yourself in a high school history course. The typical nightly reading assignment is at least ten pages, every sentence of which is as difficult to read as the one above. How successful would you be at completing the reading assignment? How much information would you retain? Innumerable learners confront this overwhelming task. Is it any wonder that many of them give up in frustration?

Well, why don't they just get help? you may ask. Believe it or not, many do not realize that their experience is abnormal; they assume everyone sees the written word this way. It is like the child with visual problems who puts on glasses for the first time and is astonished to learn the world is not a blurry place. It may be only after an astute observation by someone else that the child with a reading difficulty gets assistance.

# How Is Reading Defined?

You may be thinking this is a strange question. You just pick up a book, look at the words as your eyes move from side to side, and you are reading. It may surprise you to realize that reading is a little more complicated than just moving from side to side down a page.

Reading involves understanding what those written symbols mean. Being able to identify a written word or symbol but not to comprehend its meaning is not reading. It is word calling. Many parents and teachers are amazed by students who can read words fluently without any understanding of what they are reading.

The skill of reading involves identifying *and* interpreting words into a meaningful message. The groundwork for accomplishing this task is begun early in life. Learning opportunities provided during the first four or five years are directly related to learning to read. Children with limited experiences tend to have a limited speaking vocabulary. Research indicates that the larger the child's speaking vocabulary, the more developed the reading vocabulary becomes. Early life experiences help develop a large vocabulary bank.

Reading also involves having a wide enough experience base to relate to what is written. Children with limited life experiences may find reading difficult because they cannot relate to the subject matter before them. We all have experienced this from time to time. How many of you could make sense of a computer handbook without ever having used a computer? The same is true of children reading about animals in Africa when they have never visited a zoo. The only animal to which they can relate is the cat or dog they see on the street.

Skillful reading also requires knowledge of the word order, grammar, and punctuation used in a sentence—knowing, for instance, that the words *who, why, what,* and *did* at the beginning of a sentence indicate a response is needed. The question mark at the end is another clue. Verb tenses help the reader understand when things occur. "Susan went downtown yesterday" is very different from "Susan is downtown." These subtleties add to the complexity of reading.

Reading also involves the brain. How the brain is wired may affect how written symbols are visualized. Reversals and mirror imaging are a result of neurological differences. The ability to hear and distinguish between the subtle differences in letter sounds stems from the brain. Correctly sequencing letters in words and words in sentences to under-stand the intended message is a mental function. The brain helps us determine left from right, which we must do if we are to track words across the page and back again. Genetics, therefore, plays a huge role in the reading process. Many parents with reading problems have children with the same issues.

If reading goes beyond picking up a book, newspaper, or magazine and scanning the written symbols, how can this term be defined? Reading is the meaningful interpretation of printed or written symbols. Special emphasis should be put on the words "meaningful interpreta-tion." To be classified as a reader, one must understand the message words convey. It is only when the reader gets meaning from the printed word that reading has occurred.

# Seven Steps in the Process of Reading

Tony Buzan, in his book *Use Both Sides of Your Brain*, defines seven steps in the process of learning to read. Each step is briefly discussed below.

1. **Recognition.** This is the reader's knowledge of the symbols of the alphabet. One of the first things young children learn is their ABCs. They begin by learning to say the rote sequence of the alphabet followed by individual letter recognition.

2. **Assimilation.** This is the process by which light is reflected from the word and is received by the eye, then transmitted via the optic nerve to the brain—in other words, the ability of the eye to send the letter image to the brain.

3. **Intraintegration.** Basic understanding occurs when all the parts of what is read are linked to all other appropriate parts within the passage.

4. **Extraintegration.** This occurs when the reader connects previous knowledge to what he is reading. Life experiences, for instance, may help the reader analyze, criticize, appreciate, select, and/or reject the new information.

5. **Retention.** This refers to the storage of information in the memory for recall at another time.

6. **Recall.** This is the ability to get back out of storage what is needed when it is needed.

7. **Communication.** This is the ability to think through the information and use it appropriately.

# The Three Levels of Reading Materials

To make sense out of what is being read, the reader goes through each of these steps. However, if the reading selection is beyond the reader's capabilities, a breakdown can occur somewhere along the line. When it does, the reader gets frustrated and shuts down.

Parents and teachers need to determine the child's reading level.

Reading selections should challenge the reader but allow him to feel confident and comfortable with his choice. Material beyond the child's capabilities will cause him to avoid reading.

Understanding the levels described below can help you select reading materials for a particular learner.

1. **Independent Reading Level.** Readers at this level can read with relative ease. They need little or no help to understand the message. They comprehend 90 percent of the information and recognize at least 97 percent of the words. At this level, students are reading library books or supplemental materials for pleasure or practice.

2. **Instructional Reading Level.** Readers at this level make progress with the guidance of an instructor. Reading instruction is most successful at this level. The teacher's assistance is still required, but the student should be able to manage independently after the instruction. At this level, the student should be recognizing words with 93 percent accuracy and comprehend better than 75 percent of what is read. Reading materials at this level should be selected with the intention of providing instruction.

3. **Frustration Reading Level.** This is the level at which reading material is beyond the student's capabilities and he becomes frustrated trying to make sense of it. He gets so bogged down in trying to read, he does not know what he is reading. Finger-pointing, tension, hesitancy in reading, embarrassment, and avoidance are signs that the student is at his frustration level.

There are several ways a child's reading level can be determined. A standardized test is one way. Grade-level scores are another. For example, in October, a fourth grader received a grade-level score in reading of 7.6 on her IOWA test. This means that this child may be capable of reading material at the seventh grade, sixth-month level. Another fourth grader scored 3.9 on the same test. This means she is reading at slightly below grade level. Obviously, two different levels of reading materials would need to be selected for these students.

Oral testing—listening to a student read aloud and monitoring the errors—is another method of determining a student's reading level. Select a passage of about twenty words and ask the child to read it aloud. Use the following rule of thumb to determine the reading level.

Independent level: less than one error in twenty words.

Instructional level: about one error in twenty words.

Frustration level: more than one error in twenty words.

Teachers can use this method in addition to test scores to help determine the appropriate level of reading difficulty for their students. Parents can also use this method when helping their children make book selections in the library or bookstore.

# Methods Used to Teach Reading

Determining the reading level of the child is one step in reading instruction. Matching the method of instruction to the child's learning style is another. This is where things become a little more complicated. As we have stated throughout this writing, curricula need to be multisensory and multimodal to accommodate a wide range of learners. This is especially critical in teaching reading. Without the ability to read, a student's academic success will be severely limited.

When it comes to reading instruction, usually one method is adopted by the school district, building, or grade level teachers, and only that method is used. Students who cannot learn through that modality struggle to learn to read. As an example, auditory learners, able to discriminate between sounds may learn very well in a phonics reading program but struggle trying to learn sight words. Visual learners who confuse sounds would have a difficult time learning to read through the phonics approach.

Expecting children to learn to read using one method is not realistic. This is assuming everyone learns the same way at the same time. The one-curriculum-fits-all theory is making learning to read difficult for a large population of students whose brains learn differently.

Priscilla Vail, in her book *Common Ground: Whole Language and Phonics Working Together*, discusses the multimodal approach to teaching reading. She refers to the "texture" of language. She states, "If phonics is the structure, 'texture' refers to the ornamentation which gives language its color, intensity, rhythm, and beauty." The most successful teaching programs will integrate instruction in both structure and texture.

A variety of methods are used to teach reading. Let us examine some of the more common approaches.

1. **Basal Reading.** A look-say model incorporates a sight vocabulary within a system of basal readers, teacher manuals, and supplementary materials. Through repetition and practice, the learner memorizes key words that are repeated throughout the reading text.

2. **Phonics.** The emphasis is on sound-symbol relationships and the blending of sounds. This is a part-to-whole approach that begins with the letter sounds and then blends them into words.

3. **Linguistic Approach.** A whole-word approach that builds vocabulary on the basis of spelling patterns. This structural approach teaches learners to look at the whole word and analyze its parts. Word families, root words, prefixes, suffixes, and sound-symbol associations are all considered in this whole-to-part approach.

4. **Whole Language.** This multidisciplinary approach to reading integrates the language-arts program to include skill development in reading, spelling, writing, vocabulary building, listening, and speaking. Many critics of this approach are concerned because decoding skills are not taught. They feel this omission leaves many students ill-equipped to figure out words in more advanced reading material.

5. **Multisensory Approach.** This uses all of the learner's senses, or modalities, in the learning process. The child sees, touches, hears, and says in order to learn.

With the variety of methods available to teach reading, we have included the table below as a reference to distinguish one from another. Figure 8.1 lists some of the various reading programs being used around the country. Each program is described, as well as the types of learners

**Fig. 8.1. Matching Developmental Profiles with Specific Reading Programs***

| Reading Approach | Description | Children for Whom These Programs Are Well-Suited | Children Whose Learning Styles Are Not Well-Matched to These Programs |
|---|---|---|---|
| Whole Language, Language Experience Approaches (e.g., Open Court**) | These total language arts programs incorporate the child's own language experience and vocabulary and teach listening, speaking, reading, and writing in an integrated manner. | Most suitable for children with global language difficulties or children whose spoken English differs significantly from that contained in the basal readers. | Inappropriate for children with major attention problems, who benefit from a highly structured, sequenced approach. |
| Multisensory Approaches (e.g., Fernald, V-A-K-T) | Emphasize the simultaneous presentation of auditory, visual, and tactile stimuli (e.g., letters are learned through tracing sandpaper letters, saying the sound, and seeing the symbol). | Most young children respond favorably to a multisensory approach, as long as this is structured and organized in a sequential fashion, as in Montessori. | Children who show major strengths in one sensory area and significant deficits in another may learn optimally through a program which capitalizes on their strengths in specific areas rather than emphasizing all sensory modalities. |

| | | | |
|---|---|---|---|
| Modifications of the Traditional Alphabet (e.g., Distar) | Incorporate an expanded alphabet which simplifies written language by matching each sound with a different alphabetic symbol. | Helpful for children whose language/learning problems cause difficulty with the rules and exceptions of English phonics. | Because children must shift to a regular alphabetic system in third grade, these programs are problematic for children whose cognitive style prohibits easy transitions from one learning approach to another. |
| Basal Readers (e.g., Scott-Foresman, Houghton Mifflin) | Sequenced readers with structured vocabularies which emphasize reading for meaning. | Children with good language and visual perception strategies benefit from this approach. | May be inappropriate for children with attention deficits and/or language and/or visual perceptual problems because of their inability to attend to all the word features simultaneously. |

(continued on next page)

* This table also appears in Zadig, J. And Meltzer, L. J. Special Education. In M. D. Levine, W. B. Carey, A. L. Crocker, and R. T. Gross (eds.), *Developmental-Behavioral Pediatrics.* W. B. Saunders Co., 1983, pp. 1100–1116.

** The early Open Court reading materials include phonic-controlled vocabulary.

**Fig. 8.1. Matching Developmental Profiles with Specific Reading Programs,** *continued*

| Reading Approach | Description | Children for Whom These Programs Are Well-Suited | Children Whose Learning Styles Are Not Well-Matched to These Programs |
|---|---|---|---|
| Phonics (e.g., Hay-Wingo, Orton-Gillingham) | Stress sound-symbol associations and sound blending. | Helpful for children with visual processing weaknesses and strengths in sequential memory. Appropriate for children who need a structured, multistep reading program and who learn best when tasks are broken down into their component parts. | Not appropriate for children with weaknesses in sequential processing and auditory memory, since these children have difficulty blending the sounds into whole words. |
| Linguistic Programs (e.g., Merrill Linguistic Readers, SRA) | Vocabulary selection emphasizes phonemically regular words or word families, so that children learn rhyming patterns and associate sounds with particular patterns of letters. | Appropriate for use with children who display sequential memory problems and good oral language skills. | Not well-suited for children with weaknesses in processing whole words or gestalts. |

Used with permission of Melvin D. Levine, M.D.

who benefit from it and those who do not. Knowing how the child learns best should determine which approach would be most effective in teaching the child to read.

# The Developmental Stages of Reading

We would all agree that learning to read is essential. However, developing this skill can be extremely complex. There are many areas were a breakdown can occur. In this chapter, we will discuss reading problems that arise in the areas of sound/symbol recognition and discrimination, decoding, sight word and vocabulary development, and reading comprehension. The reading specialist, school psychologist, education specialist, or clinical psychologist are the professionals who usually evaluate for a reading difficulty.

Before we delve into the individual areas of disability, it is important to be aware of how reading evolves developmentally. There are several schools of thought on when to teach children to read. Some research supports that it should be started by kindergarten, and other data urge educators to wait until ages six or seven. When a child is developmentally ready to read is still being debated.

For Nancy, the issue of developmental variations in young children became apparent when she was teaching kindergarten. One year she had a class of twenty-four students. Twelve of them turned five by the end of September. The other half of the class turned six by the end of March. Never had she experienced a class as developmentally diverse. A third of the class was ready to read on the first day of school. By the end of the school year, many of the younger students still were working on their reading readiness skills and were not yet prepared to tackle the concepts of sound/symbol relationships.

The focus, therefore, should not necessarily be on the chronological age at which reading is taught but on the developmental readiness of the student. Some will be developmentally ready in kindergarten and others not until well into first grade.

Again, we issue a caution to examine all the factors a child brings to the learning situation before assuming a learning disability is present. To help you sort out the developmental aspects of reading, we refer you to the five stages that Jeanne S. Cahill describes in her book, *Stages of Reading Development.* The age ranges given are approximate.

### Prereading stage. Birth through kindergarten.

1. The child becomes familiar with the printed word.
2. The child develops, uses, and manipulates language.
3. He understands words and develops speaking vocabularies.
4. The child develops visual, hearing, and listening skills.
5. The child learns the symbols of the alphabet.
6. The child may pretend to read by retelling stories from memory, using picture contexts, or by "reading" what he thinks the stories say.

### Beginning reading stage. Initial reading and decoding. First and second grades.

1. The child becomes aware of sound/symbol relationships.
2. The child begins decoding words. (Research shows that learners systematically taught how to decode produce better reading results in the long term.)
3. The child begins to blend sounds into words.
4. The child's reading is dysfluent and awkward. He reads word by word, as if glued to the print.
5. The child begins to develop a sight vocabulary.
6. The child does most reading orally.
7. The child begins to understand and relate what he reads.

### Basic reading stage. Confirmation, fluency, and ungluing from the print. Second and third grades.

1. The child's sight vocabulary increases.
2. She develops more advanced decoding skills.
3. He reads paragraphs and longer passages. Becomes more proficient at reading silently.

4. The child's reading speed and accuracy increase as more familiar reading content is used.

5. She begins to understand literal and inferred meanings.

6. He can evaluate what he has read.

7. Fluency improves as the child practices by reading more.

## Applied reading stage. Learning to use acquired skills to read for new information. Fourth through ninth grades.

1. The child can relate prior knowledge to new information read.

2. He continues to develop new vocabulary skills, such as meanings, root words, prefixes, and suffixes. A vocabulary broadens through reading.

3. He reads to acquire new knowledge, follows special interests, reads for pleasure as he applies acquired skills, uses textbooks as a source of knowledge.

4. Reading material is less familiar—contains more abstract words in longer and more complex sentences.

5. Begins to think and read at the same time as reading skills become more proficient.

6. The child does more silent than oral reading.

7. Rather than reading to master the print, the child reads to master ideas. Reading matter usually from one viewpoint. Reads for facts, concepts, or how to do things.

8. By the end of this stage, reading ability is at the general adult reading level.

## Multiple viewpoint stage. Reading for a variety of reasons. Ninth through twelfth grades.

1. Reads to solve problems.

2. Reads to find facts.

3. Reads to compare ideas.

4. Reads to gain different points of view or perspectives.

5. Reads more detailed and complex subject matter.

6. Learns through reading.

7. Broadens vocabulary beyond words used in daily conversations.

### Construction and reconstruction stage. College through adulthood.

1. Has the ability to analyze, synthesize, and make judgments about what is read.

2. Can modify reading pace to fit the circumstance. Skims or scans more familiar material and slows pace for unfamiliar texts.

3. Draws own conclusions about information read. Develops personal views and philosophies from the writings of others.

# Early Diagnosis, Early Intervention

Many learners progress through each stage of reading development with little or no difficulty. However, for an estimated 15 percent of the school-age population, reading poses a major challenge in learning. Studies led by the U.S. Department of Education reveal that more than half of the students with a reading disability drop out of school before the twelfth grade. Given this frightening statistic, parents and educators need to become more aware of the warning signs indicating a possible reading disability. The earlier the identification and intervention, the brighter the prognosis for the learners struggling to make sense of the printed word.

## Observable Traits That May Indicate a Reading Problem

1. Confuses words and letters.

2. Increasingly reverses letters and numbers beyond the second grade.

3. Cannot remember sight words or vocabulary words.

4. Loses place often, omits and/or repeats words when reading.

5. Avoids reading.

6. Does not understand what is read.

7. Does not understand what is read to him. Cannot answer basic questions about the story.

8. Does not appear to be making progress in reading.

9. Regularly complains that reading is too hard.

10. Reads more slowly than others the same age.

11. Feels inadequate because other children are significantly better readers.

## General Strategies to Promote Strong Reading Habits in Children

1. Eliminate or remediate for biological causes. Have vision and hearing checked.

2. Read, read, read to your child. Begin when the child is very young. Introduce different types of books on a variety of subjects. Begin with picture books. Discuss the cover and what is happening in the pictures. Allow the child to select books of interest to him or her.

3. Establish a time for reading. Select a comfortable spot to share a story. Read from five to fifteen minutes each day.

4. Set the example. Make reading an important part of your life. It is important for the child to see parents and teachers reading.

5. Listen to the child's questions and respond. Use books to find the answers to questions you may not know. This helps children understand that books provide answers to our questions.

6. Encourage the child to write. Ask the child to share the message with you. Writing is the first step to reading. It helps children understand that the printed page relates a story or message.

7. Relate the idea of directionality. Move your finger from left to right as you read to young children. This makes them aware of

the directional flow of the words and the need to sweep back again to the next line of passage.

8. Visit the library often. Get a library card for the child as soon as possible. Many libraries offer story hours and special programs for young children. Some even invite youngsters to come for bedtime story hours. The children come in their pajamas ready to hear the librarian read a bedtime story. Most libraries offer summer reading programs for young readers. Books on tape encourage the reader to follow along with the text.

# The Specific Areas in Reading Posing the Most Difficulties for Learners

In this section, we will examine the different aspects of reading where difficulty is most likely to occur. *Dyslexia* is the term most frequently associated with a reading problem. The reversals, inversions, and omissions common to dyslexia can seriously interfere with word and letter recognition.

Earlier in this text, reading was defined. We said it was the meaningful interpretation of printed or written symbols. If we think of reading in this context, two distinct areas emerge where a breakdown can occur. One is breaking through the symbolic code to identify and recognize the words. The other is understanding those words and receiving the intended message. Both factors must be present before the skill of reading can be mastered.

A breakdown can occur in either or both of these areas. Some learners may have difficulty identifying the words, and others may not be able to interpret their meaning.

Learning to read is complex, as are the problems that interfere with the development of this skill. Entire textbooks have been written on this subject. The purpose of this writing is to introduce the reader to some of the terms and concepts related to learning to read. To accomplish this goal, this section is divided into three areas. First, dyslexia will be discussed. The next section will be the skills needed to break the symbolic code. The last section discusses the components of meaningful interpretation of the message.

# Dyslexia

For reasons not completely understood, the brains of individuals with dyslexia confuse the way letters and words are visualized. Numerous reversals, inversions, and mirror images occur, as demonstrated in the sentence beginning this chapter. This often interferes with the ability to put things in the proper sequential order. In school, math, spelling, handwriting, and reading are all subject areas that require precise order. In oral language, reversals can also surface in the speech patterns where words are expressed in the wrong sequence.

It is important to clarify that dyslexia is not a result of a vision problem. However, it is prudent to have vision checked as a first step in the evaluation process for a reading problem. The vision of children with dyslexia is usually normal or can be corrected with prescriptive lenses. If dyslexia is present, the symptoms remain after the vision has been corrected.

The intelligence of people with dyslexia is not to be questioned. Students with dyslexia are often labeled as dumb, stupid, lazy, unmotivated. In reality, they are very intelligent and creative individuals. Measures used to evaluate for dyslexia reveal that it occurs in individuals of average to superior intelligence. They just perceive the world differently.

The symptoms of dyslexia are listed below. As you look at these characteristics, a word of caution must be heeded. Young children learning to read and write display reversals with great frequency. This is part of the developmental process and is to be expected. By the end of second grade, reversals and inversions should be minimal. If a child has dyslexia, the symptoms are still apparent and may have increased in frequency.

## Observable Traits That May Indicate Dyslexia

1. Reversals are common.
   • Letters in words are reversed.

- Most common reversals are *b/d, g/p, p/q, u/n, m/n, h/n.*
- Numbers are reversed. They are usually inverted or written backward.
- Words are reversed. *Saw/was, on/no, god/dog, felt/left.*

2. Letters and words may be placed out of sequence. *Light* may be *ilght.*

3. Words are omitted.

4. Handwriting is poor.
   - Pencil grip is awkward.
   - Mirror writing occurs.
   - Hand preference may never be clearly established.
   - Writing is small and cramped.
   - Lines and spaces are ignored.

5. Confusion with tracking.
   - Left is not easily distinguished from right.
   - Up and down are often confused, as are top and bottom.

6. Words wiggle, move, and tumble off the page, which makes tracking and keeping one's place difficult for a reader.

7. Memorization is difficult. The child knows something one minute and not the next.

8. Concepts of time, such as yesterday and tomorrow, are confused.

9. Gross and fine motor control are awkward and clumsy.

10. Finding the appropriate words is difficult. A word can be on the tip of the tongue and yet the child cannot recall it.

## Strategies to Support the Learner with Dyslexia

1. A multisensory approach to reading is recommended. The Orton-Gillingham method is one program designed specifically for the learner with dyslexia. To use this approach, special training is required.

2. The strategies offered on page 177 may alleviate some of the handwriting issues.

3. Cues may help the child learn to track words across the page from left to right.

4. Line markers or bookmarks may help the child focus and keep his place on the page.

5. Windows or cover sheets may help reduce omissions on work pages and textbooks.

6. Give patience and understanding. Recognize that this is a condition beyond the control of the child. Review the beginning of this chapter to remind yourself of the obstacles learners with dyslexia encounter every day.

7. An enormous amount of effort is exerted by the child to complete each task. Parents and teachers need to understand that the child can become easily fatigued.
   - Consider reducing assignments.
   - Consider alternative evaluation methods, such as oral testing or a word processor with a spelling checker.
   - Construct lessons and learning opportunities that offer a variety of ways to deliver the information. Make learning as multisensory as possible.

8. Parents, teachers, and other professionals need to collaborate to develop a workable management plan that supports the student.

One final word. Individuals with dyslexia do learn and are capable of great accomplishments. Albert Einstein, Thomas Edison, Woodrow Wilson, Tom Cruise, and Bruce Jenner all struggled with dyslexia. With the patience, guidance, and appropriate learning environment, success can be achieved.

# Skills Needed for Word Recognition

Before reading can occur, young children need to understand that words are made up of individual letters and each letter has sounds associated with it. When the letters are placed together in a specific order, a word is formed. Each word has a meaning. The sequencing of words into a sentence gives a message.

Many children seldom get the intended message because they cannot break through the code of letters and the related sounds. In this section, the evolution of skill development in word recognition is presented.

## Sound/Symbol Relationships

At an early age, children begin learning the symbols of their language through observation. They see that letters are all around them. As books, signs, cereal boxes, and comic strips are read to them, they begin to understand that the letters stand for something. They begin to realize that this is a form of communication. As they enter school, they learn that twenty-six characters, or symbols, form the English alphabet. Eventually they learn the names of these letters and begin to identify them on sight.

Many preschoolers begin to realize that the written word is another way of communicating. Beginning with scribbling, they attempt to communicate through writing. Eventually, scribbling turns into more recognizable shapes and symbols. Interest in writing the letters of the alphabet begins to emerge. The children begin to combine letters to form "words." Spelling is inventive, and word order is primitive in the child's early attempts at writing. This is not of concern to the learner, who is quite able to "read" what she has "written."

Young children soon learn that letters have sounds associated with them. It is the order of the letters and sounds that creates words. This sound/symbol relationship is the basis for learning to read. The symbol, or *grapheme*, must first be identified, then the appropriate sound association, or *phoneme,* must be made. In the English language, there may be more than one sound for each letter. For example, each vowel (a, e, i, o, u) has at least two sounds. A long vowel says its name, such as the *o* in *hope.* The *o* in *hop,* however, says *ah,* the short vowel sound. This can make learning to read very difficult. For some learners, recognizing and naming the letters can be difficult. Discriminating and producing the appropriate sound for the symbol can be equally taxing.

## Decoding

Decoding is one skill used to identify words. In order to decode a word, the sound/symbol relationship must be made. Students have to recognize each letter and know the related sound before they can produce those sounds for the letter combinations in the word. Many refer to this process as "word attack" or "sounding out" words. Decoding is a pulling apart of the letter sounds in a word. For example, *h-ah-p* represents each sound heard in the word *hop.*

Once the word has been decoded, the reader needs to blend the sounds together to say the word. Blending can be thought of as the merging of sounds into a recognizable word. The blending of the sounds *h-ah-p* will produce the familiar-sounding word *hop.*

Learners may be able to make the sound/symbol associations but unable to successfully blend those sounds into a word. These students are often unable to hear the word the combination of sounds is producing. They may sound out *hop,* for instance, without recognizing the word. For students experiencing this difficulty, other methods of identifying words may be necessary.

## Other Techniques Used to Recognize Words

The configuration approach to word identification works best for some learners. By tracing its letters in sequence, students learn the shape of the word. Other children use context clues, such as the pictures on the page or other words within the sentence, as clues to what the troublesome word might be. These two approaches may be successful for young readers, but as the reading material becomes more complex, these methods usually fail.

Once the basics of reading are established, learning the way words are structured may assist in word recognition. Finding the meaningful parts of words requires some knowledge about root words, compound words, prefixes, suffixes, inflectional endings, and contractions. Once these concepts are understood, the reader can learn to break words apart to find their meaning.

For your convenience, these structural concepts are defined below.

1. **Root words.** This part of a word can be identified by removing the prefixes or suffixes to reveal the base word. For example, the root word in *fearless* would be *fear.*

2. **Compound words.** These words are formed by combining two or more root words to form a single word. Examples of compound words are *classroom* and *blackboard.*

3. **Prefixes.** Coming at the beginning of a root word, prefixes change the meaning of the word. *Happy* becomes *unhappy* when the prefix *un* is added.

4. **Suffixes.** Placed at the end of the root word, suffixes can also change the meaning of the word. Add *less* to *motion* and the new word *motionless* results.

5. **Inflectional endings.** These are endings added to words to create plurals and to indicate verb tenses. Examples of such endings are *s, es, ed, ing.*

6. **Contractions.** These are the shortened versions of two combined words. An apostrophe replaces the missing letter(s). *Cannot* becomes *can't.*

Identifying word families is another way children figure out words. Looking for small word segments within the word may help the reader with recognition. For example, *bat, cat, fat, hat, mat, sat* are all members of the *at* family. Rhyming words comprise the word families. All the members have the same ending sounds but different beginning sounds. It is just like a family sharing the same last name with each member having a different first name.

## Sight Word Vocabularies

As children build their sight word vocabularies, fewer words need to be decoded. Sight vocabularies consist of words and letter patterns that are easily recognized and can be read without having to figure out each sound in each word. This makes reading more fluent, enjoyable, and productive.

Many words cannot be sounded out. They are the quirks of the

English language and simply must be memorized, because they cannot be decoded. Beginning readers may be asked to learn these words from a list compiled by Dolch, Thorndike, or another published source. Examples of sight words are *the, was, do, were, none.* These are words that must be learned.

## Observable Traits That May Indicate a Possible Word-Recognition Problem

1. Not seeing likenesses or differences in pictures or words.
2. Difficulty identifying letters by name.
3. Difficulty associating letter sounds with the printed letter.
4. Problems identifying similar letters (*b-d, m-n, p-q*).
5. Difficulty hearing sound differences in letters.
6. Problems isolating the sounds of letters in words.
7. Difficulty blending sounds together.
8. Problems learning short vowel sounds.
9. Finding it hard to discriminate the finer differences in similar words (*farm-form*).
10. Difficulty retaining sight words.
11. Often guessing at words or saying, "I don't know."
12. Reading word by word, struggling to decode each word.

## Strategies to Support the Learner Experiencing Word-Recognition Problems

1. Teach letter names.
   - Select a letter and ask the child to find words on a page that begin with that letter. Circle or highlight them.
   - Have the child trace letters made from sandpaper or felt, or have the child create letters with clay or pipe cleaners or Elmer's glue, or trace them in finger paint or shaving cream.

- Use flash cards with capital and lower-case letters on them. Allow the child to keep the cards he correctly identifies. Review the letters he is confused about.

- Have the child match the upper-case letter with the lower-case one.

- Lay out letter cards and have the child point to the letter you mention.

- To recognize vowels from consonants, lay out letter cards and ask the child to point out and name the vowels in the series. Repeat with consonant identification.

- Write a series of letters, repeating one specific letter several times. Say the letter. For example, A G H P G L E V G. Point to all the Gs. Ask the child to point to and say the letter each time it appears in the series. Go back and have the child identify all the other letters.

2. Teach letter sounds.

   - Using flash cards, hold up a letter card, say the letter, say the related sound, have the child repeat the letter and sound.

   - Riding in the car, sitting in a restaurant, or at the dinner table, select a letter-sound combination and have the child relate all the words he can think of that begin with that sound. For *l*, he might say *lion, little, lemon, lunchroom.*

   - In a variety of situations, have the child identify objects beginning with a letter-sound combination. Going down the road, how may things begin with the letter *s?* (Stop signs, streets, stores.)

   - Teach classification and categorizing skills. (These same ideas can be used to reinforce letter recognition.)

   - Name all the fruits beginning with the sound *m.*

   - Use riddles: "I am thinking of an animal that begins with the sound 'jee.' What is the animal?"

   "In this classroom, I see something that begins with the sound 'stuh.' What do I see?"

"I am thinking of a word that ends like 'bed.' It is a color word. What is it?" (Red.)

- Encourage the child to make a collage of all the things found in a magazine beginning with a certain sound.
- Make picture cards with the letter on one side and a picture of something beginning with that letter on the other side.

(All these strategies can be adapted to include middle and ending sounds, consonant blends, or other areas of difficulty the reader may encounter through the reading process.)

- Say a series of words beginning with the same sound. Add a word that does not fit. Have the child identify that word. (*Light, lake, shoe, love*) This can also be done using individual sounds. A variation of this is to have the child clap when he hears the word or sound that does not fit.
- Place letters on the outside of empty containers (soup, juice, or coffee cans). Ask the child to fill containers with pictures or objects beginning with that letter.
- Put a new twist on ticktacktoe. Each player selects a letter. Words beginning with that letter are written in the empty spaces until someone wins.
- Sound hopscotch is great for active children. Put a letter within the playing squares. Give a clue. "Jump to the first sound you hear in *room*." The child jumps to the square with the appropriate letter, *r*.

3. Teach blending skills.
    - Use flash cards, three-by-five-inch file cards, plastic letters, clay letters, or anything movable with individual letters on it. (The magnetic letters work great!) Begin blending with two letters and build.
    - Have the child select the *a* and *t* letters. The letters are pushed together as the individual sounds are made.

- Using word families on cards, follow the same process. Have the child move beginning sounds together with the family name. For example, have the child push *b* together with *at* to form *bat.*

4. Build a sight word vocabulary.

    - Have a word search. Write the word you want the child to find. Have her circle or highlight all instances of the word on a page in a newspaper or magazine. Count the number of words found. Read the passage containing the word.

    - Use labels. Put signs around the house and classroom on familiar objects—*bed* on the bed, for instance. As you pass a label, ask the child to read it.

    - Use colors to identify color words. In red ink, write the word *red*, and put the label on something red.

    - Put basic sight words on cards and have the child arrange them into sentences.

    - Make an experience chart with the child. Write down (or have the child write) the experience, such as a trip to the zoo. Have the child read back what he wrote.

    - Make a sentence strip. Cut the sentence apart into individual words. Ask the child to reorder and read the sentence.

    - Put vocabulary words on one side of a card and a corresponding picture on the other. The child can self-monitor as he practices the words.

    - Lotto, concentration, and bingo word games reinforce word recognition.

5. Evaluate the computer software that is available to reinforce word recognition skills. Make selections based on your child's skill level and the areas needing reinforcement.

# Skills That Bring Meaning to the Printed Word

Once the word is recognized, it has to have meaning for the reader. Recalling our working definition, reading is the *meaningful* interpretation of the printed word. Once the reader can name the word, meaning or definition must be attached before the message can be comprehended or understood. The development of the reader's vocabulary and comprehension skills are essential before reading can become meaningful.

## Vocabulary Skill Development

In the early years, a child's vocabulary increases and develops rapidly (see chapter 10). By the age of three, the speaking vocabulary is quite sophisticated and extensive. The larger the child's speaking vocabulary, the more easily he will learn to read. In the reading process, the child's spoken vocabulary becomes the reading vocabulary. The more words he uses and understands when speaking, the more easily he'll make an association with the printed form of that word. The larger the reading vocabulary becomes, the more words the reader can recognize on sight. As the sight vocabulary increases, less time is spent decoding, and reading becomes more fluent.

Building large vocabularies increases the student's storehouse of ideas and helps the reader link one idea to another. Vocabularies can be expanded in many ways. Being exposed often to a variety of reading materials increases the child's knowledge in many different areas. Providing numerous life experiences is another way to enhance the child's exposure to words. Listening to and being a part of discussions opens the child's world to new words.

Children are inquisitive and enjoy playing with and learning new words. Encourage learners to ask about the new words they encounter. Offer resources where they can find out the meaning on their own. Provide opportunities for them to use and understand the word within a written context. There are many researchers who question the benefits of teaching vocabulary skills from a list of twenty words each week. Words out of context rarely have meaning for the child. This approach to increasing a child's vocabulary is often a test in who can memorize best. The data shows that even the learner with the best memory seldom remembers the definition when encountering the word in a reading passage.

This approach to building vocabularies takes the excitement out of learning new words. When the learner is directly involved, the results last much longer. Ideally, word-building skills should be multisensory. The more involved the learner, the better. Through a variety of experiences, the student becomes more actively involved and finds ways to make the word have meaning for him. Field trips are one way to increase vocabularies. A visit to the big-cat area at the zoo can expand the child's vocabulary to include lions, tigers, panthers, cheetahs, and pumas when thinking about cats.

Using the media is another way to make learners more aware of new words. Using newspapers, magazines, advertisements, television, and radio, the child can be exposed to a variety of new terms and concepts. Projects, demonstrations, and experiments are other ways that the learner's vocabulary can be expanded beyond the word list for rote memorization. These experiences can bring words alive by giving them meaning.

## Observable Traits That May Indicate a Limited Vocabulary

1.  Difficulty, when given a choice of objects, in selecting the object that corresponds to the word spoken.

2.  Difficulty identifying an object or situation described in detail.

3.  Difficulty relating the function of common objects (not knowing, for instance, that a hammer is used to pound nails).

4.  Difficulty finding the words to describe feelings.

5.  Confusion regarding homonyms, synonyms, and antonyms.

6.  A limited speaking vocabulary. Using the same words over and over.

7.  Persistent stumbling over the same words.

## Strategies to Increase a Learner's Vocabulary Skills

1.  Use flash cards with the word on the front and a picture or the definition on the back.

2.  Make a rebus (picture illustration). Cut apart sentence strips with rebus pictures for vocabulary words. Reassemble the sentence. Read it aloud.

3.  Have a word search. Write a vocabulary word on a card. Ask the child to circle the word every time it appears on a page (use newspapers or magazines). Go back and have the child read the word within the context it was found. Discuss how the word was used.

4.  Use classification skills. Set several categories. Write words pertaining to those categories on cards. Mix up the cards and have the child reclassify them by categories.

5.  On walks or drives, point out words and discuss their meaning with the child.

6.  Play charades. Hold up words that the child can act out. For example, *jump, run, hop, smile, chef, carpenter, astronaut, dingo*.

7.  Show the child a word and have her imitate the related sound or function. For the word *skate,* she would move her legs in a skating motion.

8.  Select a word each day. Discuss the word and its meaning. Every time the word is seen, read the context in which it is used.
    Put words the child has learned into a "Words I Know" box. Encourage the child to add to this box.
    Have the child use the words to create sentences, or give antonyms or synonyms of the words.

9.  Develop dictionary skills.
    Have a young child begin a picture dictionary.
    Older learners can make a dictionary containing the words they use frequently.

10. Use multiple names for things. Wash hands because it's good *hygiene.* It kills *bacteria.*

11. Urge children to read a variety of books.

12. Use similes, metaphors, and idioms to add color to your speech. Discuss what they mean and how they affect meaning. (The *Amelia Bedelia* books are enjoyable and offer great opportunities for discussion.)

13. Consider computer software and games such as Scrabble to increase vocabularies.

14. Crossword puzzles are a great way to increase vocabulary skills.

15. Develop synonym and antonym skills.
    Play synonym bingo. Use a synonym dictionary to construct the game. For each word called, the player finds the synonym written on their card and makes the match. The first to cover a card wins. (Antonym bingo works the same way using antonyms.)

16. To develop skills in understanding figures of speech, ask the child to make a cartoon or picture illustrating the expression.

## Comprehension Skills

Comprehension is making meaning out of the recognized words. This occurs when the reader uses past experiences and prior knowledge to make sense of new information.

It is important to distinguish between comprehension and word calling. A child may be a fluent reader, able to read a passage without missing a beat. Proud teachers and parents declare this child a reader. There is just one problem. The child does not have a clue what she is reading. She is recognizing words and naming them, but the words have no meaning for her. She may have excellent word-identification skills but cannot gain a meaningful interpretation from the words. Having the skills to recognize words does not always ensure comprehension.

Other children have a difficult time understanding the message because word recognition is so time consuming. Their struggle to identify the word causes them to forget what they have read. Their focus on one word becomes so intense, they lose sight of the other words in the sentence. Learners with a limited sight vocabulary need to decode frequently. This interferes with their reading fluency. They often read every word and become glued to the page.

More proficient readers, when reading silently, can comprehend a passage without reading every word. They can usually gain understanding by reading the key words and using context clues. They can adjust their reading pace to adapt to the reading material and purpose. They may read faster, skimming the words, when reading for pleasure. More detailed and complex subject matter might require a slower, more precise reading pace.

## Observable Traits That May Indicate a Reading Comprehension Problem

1. Does not know if story is fact or fiction.
2. Has difficulty with cause-and-effect relationships in the story.
3. Has difficulty describing the feelings of the characters in the story.
4. Has difficulty adapting reading pace.
5. Cannot interpret figurative language.
6. Does not recognize the elements of humor.
7. Seldom knows the main idea of the story.
8. Cannot predict the outcomes of stories.
9. Has difficulty summarizing information in a short, sequential manner.
10. Rarely uses context clues.
11. Has a difficult time relating the details of the story.

## Strategies to Support the Learner with Comprehension Problems

1. Check the reading level of the selections to see if it matches the reader's ability.
2. Consider books on tape. The student can read at his own pace, stopping frequently to check for understanding.
3. Ask a question and have the child read to find the answer.
4. Read with the student.

- Ask questions after each sentence. Eventually, check for understanding after each paragraph.

- Ask detail questions. "Out of what was the first pig's house made?"

- Ask inferencing questions. "How was the first pig feeling when his house was blown down by the wolf? How do you know that?"

- Ask cause-and-effect questions. "If the pigs want to be safe, then what could they do to stop the wolf from blowing down their houses?"

- Determine fact from fantasy. "Can a wolf really blow down a house? Why not? Is this a true story or a fantasy?"

5. Take turns reading aloud to reduce frustration and fatigue. The child can read one sentence or page and the parent, tutor, older sister, or grandma can read the next.

6. Use the illustrations to help establish feelings. "Looking at the picture on this page, how do you think the second pig is feeling?"

7. Teachers can use advance organizers to give their students a preview of what will be included in the reading assignment. The reader can then look for specific details.

8. Before introducing a new lesson, review old information, then build the new information on that foundation.

9. Create story or character webs to help students relate important facts and details and display them for easy review. Students can create a web that resembles a spider's web by placing the topic in the center and extending the subtopics out on the threads of the web.

10. Help the child summarize large quantities of information as he advances in school by learning how to outline, list, compare and contrast information, write out events in a sequential order, or construct a web.

11. Have the child relate or teach the information to someone else.

12. Have the child make up sample questions about what was read and test himself.

13. Students with the option of purchasing their own textbooks can highlight important information and make notes in the margins. If this purchase is not possible, making copies of the chapters may be helpful. Taking notes while reading is very helpful.

14. Allow students to work together, sharing ideas and having discussions. This enables students with comprehension problems to hear in a variety of ways the same information in the words of their peers. In this type of cooperative learning situation, weak readers need the opportunity to contribute in their areas of strength.

15. Encourage children to write their own books. They might write a story about a trip to the grocery, or create a poem or a riddle. Allow room for illustrations. Ask the child to share his efforts.

16. Write secret codes. Get a book of codes from the library or make up your own. You and the child can write secret messages that must be decoded.

17. Provide many reading opportunities through book clubs (often offered in school), children's magazines, and letters or notes from friends or relatives. Once skills and confidence begin to build, encourage more difficult selections. Help the child make selections in his particular areas of interest.

18. Teach visualization techniques. Have the child close his eyes and try to get a mental picture of what he is reading. This technique is also effective in remembering vocabulary words. For example, visualizing a serene lake to associate with the word *lake*.

# Points to Ponder

1. Reading is a complex process that involves the meaningful interpretation of the printed word.

2. Early life experiences build a speaking vocabulary that is needed to later build a reading vocabulary.

3. Sight words make word identification easier and reading more fluent. Some sight words must be memorized. Others are recognized through repeated use.

4. Words are recognized by making an association between the sound and the symbol, decoding and blending, and developing a sight vocabulary.

5. A large speaking and reading vocabulary and the development of comprehension skills bring meaning to the identified word. A breakdown in either area can result in a reading disability.

6. No one teaching method is successful with all children. Research studies strongly recommend that phonics skills be taught to young children. This approach can be integrated with other methods. Which methods work best for your child?

# 9

# Mathematics–The Language of Numbers

Joey's throat went dry, his hands were clammy, and his stomach churned. What a way to end a perfectly good lunch hour—a timed test on multiplication facts! He could barely remember the facts *without* the pressure of time. Completing fifty problems in five minutes or less! Is this teacher for real?

Not only could Joey not remember the math facts, but the sight of fifty small problems scrunched together on one page was overwhelming. They seemed to dance about and play tricks on him. He often omitted answers or put them in the wrong place because he could not keep track of all the problems. This, of course, added to the pressure.

For many students, breaking the code of numbers is very difficult. In reading, the graphemes, or symbols, are letters. In math, the symbols are numerals. The grouping of the numbers relays a message. As in reading, understanding the sequencing of the graphemes is necessary to break the code and get to the meaning.

In reading, there is no right way to get to the end result. The same is true in math. While it is true that there is only one right answer, how one derives that answer is often as unique and diverse as the individual learner. A multisensory approach to learning math is most successful.

When math is taught only as a lecture course with little opportunity to go beyond pencil-and-paper calculations, learners become anxious, confused, frustrated, and turned off. Students having a difficult time comprehending the spatial relationships involved in learning math need numerous ways to feel, twist, and turn objects to make the concepts more concrete. The use of math manipulatives and concrete objects can accommodate many of these learners. These learning tools can be as simple as buttons, crayons, beads, or raisins used as counters. More sophisticated manipulatives, such as Unifix cubes, pattern blocks, geoboards, graphing mats, tanagrams, and base-ten blocks, can bring math to life for struggling students. Many of these math manipulatives are available for purchase, but teachers, parents, and students can make their own out of common household items.

Learning math concepts begins with the basics of arithmetic. As one skill builds on the next, more abstract and complex concepts are introduced. Since the study of math is a cumulative process, understanding one concept before moving on to the next is crucial. If bricks are missing from the foundation, the house begins to crumble. As an example, without an understanding of addition, subtraction, and multiplication, learning long division is difficult. To successfully complete a long-division problem, you must be able to perform each operation in the correct sequence.

# Math Phobias

As the learner's understanding decreases, so does his ability function in math. This increases the anxiety level often producing a math phobia. For many students, math class is the most anxiety-producing time of the school day. Math phobia begins with an aversion to numbers. Difficulty in grasping math concepts and breaking the code of numbers adds to the anxiety. Many students feel like they are lost in the foreign land of numbers.

Researchers have concluded that success in math depends on three factors. The first is spatial ability, or the ability to imagine objects or represented objects in different perspectives or planes—rotating on an axis in space, for example. Even if the object can no longer be seen, the learner is able to remember its place in space. One is born with this capability.

Commitment and confidence are the other two factors determining math success. These are factors influenced by the environment. Studies have confirmed that students planning to move on to higher levels of math or pursue careers in math or science are more committed to studying and working harder in math. Even students with a lower natural math aptitude got higher math grades because of their efforts and commitment to the subject. Feeling comfortable in a world of numbers is difficult for learners who view the subject of math as a foreign language. As students lose their confidence, anxieties mount. There are several ways to help the anxious math student feel more comfortable and confident.

1.  Point out how math and reading are similar. Have the learner point out key words in story problems. Talk about what clues to a solution these words offer.

2.  In everyday experiences, when you point out words to your child, point out numbers. When shopping, for instance, or eating in a restaurant, read the menu or price tags.

3. Monitor the child's frustration level in math. How long does he work before getting frustrated? Allow him to take a break before that time is reached. Stop him at eight minutes if frustration peaks at ten minutes.

4. Break work into small chunks to alleviate the feeling of being overwhelmed. Stop before the child becomes fatigued or frustrated. Practice math facts for five minutes at a time, rather than pushing the child until he becomes frustrated. To make learning more fun and interesting, try computer math games, flash-card games, or other games that use math skills, even if it's only to keep score.

5. Once the child recognizes that math is a useful part of daily life, parents and teachers hear fewer comments such as, "When will I ever use this stuff anyway?" Make math as much a part of a child's world as eating or getting dressed, which should begin in the early years of life.

In their book *Teach Your Child Math: Making Math Fun for the Both of You*, Arthur Benjamin and Michael Shermer suggest to parents that they think of math in terms of playing a game. They give ten rules for parents to follow to make math enjoyable for the child. These rules could easily be used in the classroom by teachers.

1. **Be upbeat and positive.** Many parents and teachers have unpleasant memories of their school experiences in math. This was not a pleasant subject for them. It is important that the child not sense personal biases. Think positive! This is going to be an enjoyable experience for you and the child.

2. **Approach math as you would any other game.** Be enthusiastic. The more your child enjoys the game, the longer he will play.

3. **Do not be afraid to say, "I don't know."** You are not expected to know everything. In fact, if math is approached as a learning experience for both of you, the process will be more rewarding.

4. **Use real-world examples in math problems.** Utilize the child's areas of interest in the introduction of math concepts. If your

child enjoys soccer, you might have him figure out how many points he could earn if he scored three points in each quarter.

5. **Use household objects.** Involve all the senses. The more interactive math becomes, the easier it is to learn. As raisins are being added to the cookies, allow the child to find out how many raisins it takes to fill half a cup. Allow him to taste a certain number of raisins. As he counts them out, he is learning about counting, measuring, and fractions. As he eats his raisins, he uses all his senses to complete an exercise in math. Teachers of young children can offer these same experiences. Older children benefit from the use of math manipulatives to bring understanding to the concepts being taught.

6. **Find similarities in objects.** This can be accomplished by sorting, comparing, ordering, measuring, and counting. At home, children can learn these skills by sorting laundry, putting away groceries (all the cereal together; cans of peas, beans, and corn in their places), putting away silverware (the salad forks are smaller than the dinner forks and go in separate compartments), or baking brownies (children love to cook, especially when they get to enjoy the results!).

7. **Find the differences in objects.** This teaches discrimination skills that are necessary in math. Being able to tell a *6* from a *9* is an important distinction. Use every opportunity to have the child develop this skill. How is a stop sign different from a railroad crossing sign? How is a cherry pie different from a pizza?

8. **Don't work any math problem for too long.** Limit the time you involve the child in the math game. Math can be mentally fatiguing. Fifteen minutes may be a realistic amount of time. Stop while the child is still having fun and wanting more.

9. **Offer a moderate amount of assistance in solving a problem.** Offer hints or tips when your child reaches an obstacle. Teach the child to learn from you, not lean on you.

10. **Have fun.** The authors point out that these are just guidelines to help you make math more personal, practical, and enjoyable

for the learner. Some will work better than others. To these suggestions, you may add your own. Focus on the process, not the product. Emphasize the fun of doing math rather than getting the one correct answer. The time you spend with your child should be enjoyable for both of you.

The point of these rules is to help the parent or teacher think in terms of making math a part of the learner's everyday life, rather than that scary subject taught during fifth period. When the learner relates math to her own world, the concepts become more meaningful and less intimidating. The more comfortable the child feels with numerals and math concepts, the more confident she becomes.

# How Mathematics Is Defined

Up to this point, we have been looking at the subject of mathematics in terms of a numerical process that results in one correct solution. A formal definition goes beyond this realm. In her book *Solving School Problems: Kindergarten Through Middle School*, Elaine K. McEwan defines mathematics as the study of "a group of sciences dealing with quantities, arrangements, magnitudes, and forms, and their relationships and attributes." The four math sciences she identifies are arithmetic, geometry, algebra, and calculus. More simply, math might be defined as the science of quantity and space. In arithmetic, the symbol/quantity is fixed. The symbol 7 represents the quantity or amount of 7. In higher-order math, such as algebra, the symbols are more arbitrary, and the spatial positions become more important.

In math, a connection between the written symbol and what it means must be made before understanding can occur. There must be a link between the concrete and the abstract. The learner must be able to connect the idea that three apples in one basket and four apples in another equals seven apples (concrete) to three plus four equals seven (abstract), and then write it as $3 + 4 = 7$. This can be a very complex concept to grasp.

# Gender Differences in Learning Mathematics

The ability to create mental images of objects in space is a critical factor in learning math concepts. As discussed in chapter 2, the male brain has a greater capacity to comprehend spatial relationships than the female brain. Females tend to be more language-oriented. Males can often relate more easily to objects, while females prefer people. This may account for why males seem to have fewer problems in math than females.

Research does substantiate that males and females have some neurological differences. In their research at the University of Massachusetts, Patricia Davidson and her colleague Maria Marold found that children having difficulty learning math fell into two categories.

Students who demonstrated learning style 1 were more attentive to details and solved problems in a step-by-step manner according to memorized rules. They were better at addition and multiplication than subtraction or division. They had poor estimation skills and often did not recognize an incorrect answer. The researchers found that females often fell into this category.

Students who demonstrated learning style 2 were more holistic in their approach to problem solving. Seeing the whole problem, they more frequently noticed incorrect answers. They used language and rote memorization less often and disliked word problems. They were better at subtraction and division and good at counting backward. Learners in this group were able to mentally calculate the answers to problems and disliked having to go through the procedures step-by-step. Most of the students in this category were males.

What this tells us is that the differences between the male and female brain affect how math is learned. Females tend to do better in arithmetic, where concepts are concrete and memorization and sequential steps are required. They can depend on the use of their language skills. Males excel in the higher levels of math, which are more abstract. Calculus, analytical geometry, geometry, and algebra I are courses in which males tend to do better. These courses rely on the ability to see spatial relationships, visualize objects in motion, and remember their place in space. A word of clarification, however: This does not mean that all males are math whizzes and all females are inferior math students. It is only the most current explanation for why males appear to excel in math.

The common assumption that math and science are dominated by males results in many females with a high math aptitude feeling uncomfortable and pressured to suppress their capabilities. Appearing smarter than their male counterparts puts undue social pressure on them. Because they desire to fit in socially, girls will often discontinue their math studies prematurely. These social pressures are often coupled with the fact that females are not always encouraged and supported by teachers and parents to continue their studies in higher-level math courses as are male students. Sadly, many capable young females reject career choices in math and science.

This assumption about females and math is beginning to change. Research shows that under the right learning conditions, females can be as proficient as males in math and science. Studies conducted on females attending classes or schools without a male population are showing that the girls feel less inhibited about asking questions when there are no boys around. Second, they are more committed to learning math. Third, females in a learning environment without males show more confidence in their ability to learn. Most important, they score significantly higher in math, with the result that more females are pursuing careers in math and science. Hopefully, as we further research the learning process, this trend will continue, and the learner's strengths, rather than gender, will determine how he or she is educated.

We do not mean to oversimplify the ability to learn math. This is a very complex subject, and we will explore in detail the areas where a breakdown in learning can occur. First, let us examine several different theories about how math skills are developed.

# The Developmental Stages for Acquiring Mathematics Skills

When and how math skills are acquired is somewhat theoretical. As Diane McGuiness points out in her book *When Children Don't Learn,* mathematicians rarely teach math, and seldom are they involved in the psychology of learning math.

Most of the current research available supports Jean Piaget's theory that children develop math concepts in four stages: sensorimotor, preoperational, concrete operational, and formal operations.

All children pass from one stage to another in the same sequence. However, the age at which the child reaches each stage varies, depending on the individual's developmental rate.

1. **Sensorimotor Stage. Birth to 2 Years**
   Manipulates objects.
   Thinks through solutions mentally.
   Constructs world by interacting with it.
   Uses trial and error.

2. **Preoperational Stage. 2 to 4 Years**
   Uses reason but not logic.
   Begins to learn about conservation.

3. **Concrete Operational Stage. 7 to 11 Years**
   Can reverse a thought process.
   Can solve concrete problems.
   Develops classification skills.
   Learns to sort by various categories (shape, size, color, texture).
   Understands serial ordering (smallest to largest, shortest to tallest).

   Masters conservation problems in the following sequence:

   | | |
   |---|---|
   | Length | 6 to 7 years |
   | Number | 6 to 7 years |
   | Area | 7 to 8 years |
   | Mass | 7 to 8 years |
   | Liquid | 7 to 8 years |
   | Weight | 9 to 10 years |
   | Volume | 11 to 12 years |

4. **Formal Operation Stage. 11 to 15 Years and Beyond**
   Uses more abstract reasoning.
   Develops capacity to apply logical thought.

Can solve complex verbal problems.

Can solve hypothetical problems.

Can solve problems dealing with the future.

Develops capacity to think scientifically.

# Areas of Difficulty in Learning Mathematics

Math is more than just picking up a pencil and computing an answer. It is the understanding of math concepts and the ability to apply them. Visual, language, memory, sequencing, and problem-solving skills, as well as the ability to comprehend spatial relationships, are all needed to solve a math problem. A child who has trouble with math may be experiencing difficulty in any of these areas.

## Visual Skills

Math relies heavily on the use of visual skills, such as the recognition of numbers. Some children reverse and confuse numbers. Incorrect answers may occur because problems are copied wrong—for instance, 38 becomes 83 or 6 + 2 is read as 9 + 2. Or the learner may misread the letters used in higher-level mathematics.

Visual skills also affect the writing of problems. Many students have difficulty lining up columns of figures. Misalignment confuses place value. In the problem 45 + 76, it is necessary to place the 6 under the 5 to hold the ones place, and the 7 under the 4 in the tens place. Keeping columns aligned in problems requiring several steps, such as long division and double-digit multiplication, can be especially difficult. Even children who understand the concept of place value may have trouble aligning their work.

The changing of operational signs is another opportunity for errors to occur. By going back and checking their work, students may find errors caused by visual oversights.

## Language Skills

In many ways, math has a language of its own. Before one can recognize what is being asked in story problems, one must learn certain key, or signal, words. *Sum, total,* and *how many in all* signal the need to add. Subtraction is signaled by terms such as *difference, how much greater than, how much less than,* and *what's left.* Multiplication is indicated when either *product* or *times* is used. *Quotient* and *into* signal division.

The teaching of math concepts requires that a lot of information be conveyed in a short period of time, so the learner can easily become overwhelmed. Trying to understand unfamiliar terms imbedded in large amounts of information can cause the student to shut down in frustration.

Use of the blackboard, manipulatives, and class discussion is helpful, as is the constant review of old concepts as new ones are being introduced. Students who can visualize the concepts find that understanding the language is easier.

## Memory Skills

Because Math is a cumulative subject—that is, each new concept builds on previously acquired information. This demand on the student's powers of recall can become overwhelming.

Children with poor automatic memory get stressed when trying to learn and rapidly recall math facts, especially multiplication tables. As the math gets more complex, children may get bogged down in trying to remember the product of $7 \times 9$, for example, and never complete the problem. For some children, learning all the math facts may never be a reality. Therefore, it may be prudent for educators to ask at what point is this no longer a priority. If the recalling of math facts is interfering with a sixth grader's ability to complete math problems, perhaps it is time to allow the student to use a calculator or matrix.

In higher-level math, poor automatic memory may interfere with the recall of formulas. Students may know when and where to apply a formula but be unable to recall it. This can make testing situations very stressful. Educators who desire to evaluate the student's level of understanding, rather than his memory skills, may consider placing the formulas at the top of the test paper. A student who understands the concept will know which formula to use and how to solve the problem. In this way, memory issues do not get confused with understanding.

Multistep math functions require a particularly strong active working memory. Many students have difficulty in this area of memory. By the time they complete the first step required, they lose their train of thought and either forget what to do next or forget to finish the problem. Also, students who get so caught up in the recalling of math facts during the computation of one step often lose track of what they are doing.

## Sequencing Skills

Knowing how to do things in the correct order, or sequence, is an essential part of understanding mathematics. Whether counting from one to ten or solving complex problems in calculus, knowing the order to follow is necessary to obtain the correct results. One step out of sequence in solving an algebraic equation makes the answer inaccurate.

Remembering the sequence of steps required can pose a problem for learners with temporal-sequential organization problems. Ordering and sequencing of numbers and procedures can be overwhelming. In math there is only one correct answer. Arriving at that answer generally requires that some sequential process be followed. The inability to organize and follow a step-by-step plan can make learning math very difficult.

Students with temporal-sequential organization problems also have difficulty learning about time. Learning the days of the week and months of the year, how to tell time, and how to solve math problems involving the elements of time can be very confusing for learners with sequencing issues.

## Problem-Solving Skills

Problem solving requires planning and organization before execution. Using these so-called executive-function skills means that before an answer is given, the learner plans and organizes a plan of attack. The ability to develop this plan is a critical part of being a good problem solver. Students with weak executive-function skills jump right in without forethought and planning. They haphazardly and randomly attempt to solve problems.

Good problem solvers are like detectives. They stand back, look at the situation, collect all the clues, analyze the information, then come up with a plan to solve the mystery.

Solving a math problem requires the same strategy. A plan is needed. In solving a problem such as 3 + 4 + 6 = ?, the following procedure may be helpful.

1. **Identify the problem.** What is being asked? Do I add, subtract, or multiply?

2. **Analyze the problem.** What clues are given? What are the operational signs telling me? Are there signal words that give me a hint? What rules must I follow to solve this problem?

3. **Brainstorm ways to solve the problem.** Estimate what the answer might be. Decide what methods could be used to solve the problem.

4. **Implement a strategy.** Prioritize your choices. Select a method and try it out.

5. **Evaluate the results.** Does this plan feel right? Did it work? Am I comfortable with my answer? Does it look right?

6. **Implement other strategies.** If your first attempt did not work, what other choices from your brainstorming step can you try next? Implement and evaluate until you feel comfortable with the results.

This systematic approach to math can often ease the stress caused by impulsively rushing to get an answer. The planning and organizing steps that a good problem solver uses can be time-consuming, but the results are well worth the time invested.

## Spatial Relationships

The ability to visualize objects in space and remember their position even when they have been moved about involves spatial reasoning. As math becomes more abstract, this quality becomes more important. Being able to translate words into mental images helps in understanding math concepts. Beginning with the concrete before the abstract helps many learners make the spatial connections required in solving a problem.

The ability to track objects in motion appears to be connected to spatial ability. These are the same skills that are used in playing videogames. The abilities to translate two dimensions into three and track fine details in objects in motion are important in understanding mathematics.

## Not Knowing You Do Not Know

One last consideration needs to be addressed. It is not unusual for students to sit in math class and think they understand what the teacher has said. During the explanation, they are active participants. However, when they begin a homework assignment or take a test, they cannot work the problems. The problems may look different, and the students get confused and do not recognize what they need to do. These children have a difficult time generalizing information from one situation to the next. This can occur for several reasons. They may not understand the concepts involved. They may not have sufficient mastery of previously learned skills required to learn the new concepts. Or they visualize the concept only one way and cannot recognize when it is presented with a different twist.

# Observable Traits That May Indicate a Math Disability

1. Difficulty with classifying and categorizing things.
2. Difficulty ordering and sequencing things.
3. Difficulty with one-to-one correspondence.
4. Difficulty understanding conversion.
5. Difficulty identifying shapes and/or numbers.
6. Difficulty understanding operational signs and signal words.
7. Difficulty planning and organizing.
8. Difficulty aligning numbers on paper.
9. Difficulty remembering the steps in a multistep operation.

10. Difficulty estimating numbers.

11. Difficulty with the elements of time.

12. Difficulty reading and understanding word problems.

# Strategies to Support Learners with a Math Disability

1. Make math fun and functional by relating it to the child's everyday living experiences. The more familiar a child is with math, the more comfortable she will be. This reduces the anxiety associated with learning math. (See the beginning of this chapter for suggestions.)

2. Give the child opportunities to sort, classify, categorize, and order his world.

3. Use concrete examples to help the child visualize the concepts (e.g., sort all the socks).

4. Teach problem-solving skills early. For example, "I only have three cookies for four children. What should I do?" Brainstorm to come up with workable solutions.

5. Make the learner more visually aware.

   • Allow the child to highlight operational signs or signal words.

   • Use windows, line markers, or cover sheets to reduce the number of problems omitted because of visual confusion.

   • Try to give adequate space between problems without crunching them together. (This is especially important on test papers. One hundred math facts on one page is too many!)

   • To help the child properly align his work, either turn notebook paper on its side so the lines run from top to bottom, or use graph paper.

   • Folding the paper into fourths can provide adequate space for each problem. This can alleviate problems scrunched together or written at random all over the page.

- Copying errors can be avoided by either reproducing the page for the student or allowing someone else to copy the problems for her to solve.
- Encouraging self-monitoring skills may eliminate many computation errors. For students working too rapidly and making careless mistakes, extend the work time. For example, if Sally is finished in five minutes, tell her that you will not accept her math paper until she has worked at least ten minutes (or whatever time is reasonable).

6. Improve language skills.
   - Learning and understanding signal words is helpful.
   - Repetition and multisensory experiences can help make sense of complex math language.
   - The use of manipulatives may help create mental pictures.
   - Examples and models of correctly solved problems may serve as a template for the student to follow.

7. Improve sequencing and ordering skills.
   - Opportunities to work with calendars and clocks may help establish the concepts of time. Daily planners and large block calendars for entering important activities or assignments should be made available to the child.
   - Clearly list steps. Write them out as a visual reference. Put them on a card or a Post-It note to serve as a visual road map. Ask the child to relate what comes first, second, next, and last.
   - Give simple directions and ask the child to repeat them back in sequence. Then he should complete the task in sequence.
   - Learning the steps effective problem solvers follow will benefit the child with poor planning and organization skills. Teaching the child to slow down and go through each step can be beneficial in the long run. Making it a game where he is Sherlock Holmes or a detective solving a mystery may be an enjoyable way to introduce these skills. Games such as Clue can also be learning tools.

- Provide a variety of manipulatives for children to maneuver and move about to improve spatial ability. Involve the child in making his own manipulatives from household items.
- See chapter 23 for more suggestions.

8. Improve memory skills.
   - Play flash-card games with math facts to improve speed and accuracy.
   - Examine computer software.
   - Allow the use of calculators or a matrix. Remember: A calculator will only assist in computation. It will not help if the student does not understand the math concept or the process needed to solve the problem.
   - Use graphs and Venn diagrams to help the learner visualize math concepts and connect the relationships.

9. Allow the students to work together. Sometimes peers can simplify the most complex concepts.

10. Math can be very fatiguing for a student struggling to learn. Consider reducing the number of problems required. In testing situations, where anxiety mounts, requiring fewer problems will be appreciated. Circling the ones required, asking the student to complete a certain number of problems, and giving a different test are ways teachers can discreetly make this accommodation.

11. Avoid timed tests. The pressure of time adds to the anxiety. Giving an extended time period can reduce some of the anxiety.

12. A more interactive approach to math may be appropriate. Touch Math is one such approach that benefits many learners.

# Points to Ponder

1. Math is a cumulative subject. One fact and concept builds on another. Remembering what was learned in first grade is necessary throughout one's career in math. This can strain the

memory and cause anxiety if previously taught concepts are not understood and mastered.

2. Math is a very complex subject. Many facts and ideas are given in a very short period of time. This can overload the child who doesn't understand the vocabulary and is trying to process the foreign information.

3. Good problem solvers can organize a plan to help them find an answer.

4. Math is very detail oriented. Children who race through their work and do not self-monitor have frequent computation errors.

5. The ability to understand the spatial relationships of objects is crucial in math performance. Research indicates that, neurologically, males tend to be more spatially oriented than females. This may be why males tend to perform better in math than females.

6. Our lives are touched each day by mathematics. The more children can relate to math in their everyday lives, the less frightening and overwhelming the subject becomes. Many of the references in the bibliography share simple ways that parents and teachers can make math come alive for children.

# 10

# Communication Disorders

Communication is the transfer of information from the sender to the receiver. Before communication can occur, the message must be received. Many parents lament the lack of communication between their children and themselves. Requests to turn off the TV, begin homework, feed the dog, or run an errand often fall on deaf ears. Clearly, in most families, the messages sent from the parent to the child frequently are not received.

When this phenomenon occurs, many parents think they are not speaking the same language. The Ohio Language Task Force defines language as "An organized system of symbols shared among a group of people which represent objects, actions, feelings, processes, and relationships." Unique to each language are "the set of rules that govern the content, form, and use of that language." Teenagers often communicate with each other using symbols and a set of rules not always familiar to their parents. When this occurs, parents and child may truly be speaking a different language.

The selection of an effective modality through which communication can occur may be helpful. "Modality" refers to the vehicle or means used to exchange a message. Listening, speaking, reading, and writing are communication modalities. Sometimes parents find that they can communicate most effectively by using the modality of writing notes for their children to read.

The difficulty parents experience when attempting to communicate with their offspring is common and part of the developmental process. However, for many children, communicating can be a difficult and challenging ordeal. Children who struggle to understand what is said and/or to make themselves understood may be experiencing a communication disorder. This condition can occur in the areas of either speech or language.

# How Speech and Language Are Defined

When many parents and teachers are informed that the child has a language disorder, they immediately reply, "But there is nothing wrong with the way she speaks." They do not understand that there is a difference between a speech disorder and a language dysfunction. Therefore, a distinction needs to be made between the two.

Speech refers to the actual formation and pronunciation of sounds and words. The oral and nasal cavities and the ear are the areas most associated with the production of speech. Speech disorders can occur in three areas: articulation, tonal quality of the voice, and fluency. In articulation, the motor production of sounds and how those sounds are pronounced may be affected. A voice with poor tonal quality may produce sounds that are too soft or loud, hoarse, nasal, or monotonous. Fluency, or the flow of speech, may be affected by the repetition of sounds, stopping and starting of speech, the rate of speech, and stammering or stuttering.

Language, on the other hand, involves the brain's ability to interpret, organize, process, and communicate a message. It is through this channel that ideas, thoughts, and feelings are related. A language disorder may occur in receptive language (making sense of information received, in either oral or written form), expressive language (giving information back, either in oral or written form), and/or pragmatic language (social language).

# Components of Language

There are three integrated components of language. They are the content, form, and use of language (see Figure 10.1). Content gives our message meaning. It is the selection of words, phrases, and sentences and the way they are interpreted in context that determines our understanding of the message. Meaningful communication depends on the receiver's ability to understand the vocabulary and relate the information to his world. For example, a chemist's description of the molecular structure of a substance would have little meaning for anyone who had no knowledge of the technical vocabulary and no understanding of chemistry.

Form is how the message is structured. An understanding of how sounds are combined to form syllables and words and how words and sentences are constructed are all a part of the complexity of selecting the correct communication form. A message that doesn't follow the rules that govern form can be very confusing. For example, "The boy rided past a church going to a picnic." Not only is the verb choice incorrect, but is the boy or the church going to a picnic?

Pragmatic language is the way we use language in our everyday conversation. It involves the reason we communicate, such as to ask a question, comment or respond, and the appropriateness of the words we choose. For example, a child with a pragmatic language disorder may loudly announce to a classmate, "That's one ugly dress!" He doesn't understand that the consequences of his remark hurt his classmate's feelings.

To communicate effectively, these three components must work

**Fig. 10.1. Characteristics of Language and Communication Problems**

| Component | Problem | Characteristics | Potential Effect on Academics | Potential Effect on Socialization |
|-----------|---------|-----------------|-------------------------------|-----------------------------------|
| Semantics (Meanings) | Comprehension; gets little meaning from spoken/written language | Has trouble categorizing | Basic concept development | Stands out in the crowd |
| | | Lacks specificity | Talking around the topic | Can't understand jokes |
| | | Overuses verbal filers, e.g., "ah" | Inability to get point across (speech/writing) | Talks a lot but says nothing |
| | | Talks around and switches topic | Reading comprehension (can't identify main idea, distinguish fact from opinion, predict/infer, etc.) | Is irritating |
| | | Can't get point across (speech/writing) | Auditory comprehension of vocabulary (idioms, metaphors, etc.) | Appears spacey |
| | | Hesitates | | Relates poorly to peers |
| | | Has word-finding problems | | |
| | | Can't understand/ use multiple-meaning words and figurative language | | |
| | | Has difficulty with space, time, and quantity concepts | | |

Content

| | | | |
|---|---|---|---|
| Phonology (Sounds) | Decreased speech accuracy/intelligibility | Substitutes consonants<br>Omits sounds<br>Is difficult to understand | onics/word attack<br>Auditory discrimination<br>Listening skills<br>Verbal volunteering<br>Spelling | Is reluctant to participate<br>Interacts poorly with peers and teachers<br>Has low self-esteem |
| Morphology (Structure of Words) | Oral/written grammar atypical for age | Incorrectly uses plurals, possessives, comparatives, etc.<br>Has difficulty with subject/verb agreement<br>Has poor comprehension<br>Can't follow directions<br>Uses pronouns inaccurately | Auditory comprehension (e.g., generalization from root word to suffixes/prefixes)<br>Mathematics conceptualization (comparison/story problems)<br>Reading comprehension (doesn't pick up on tense markers)<br>Written expression<br>Spelling | Is reluctant to participate<br>May disrupt class activity<br>Has behavioral problems (e.g., withdrawal, acting out)<br>Has low self-esteem |

(continued on next page)

**Fig. 10.1. Characteristics of Language and Communication Problems,** *continued*

| Component | Problem | Characteristics | Potential Effect on Academics | Potential Effect on Socialization |
|---|---|---|---|---|
| Syntax (Sentence Structure) | Oral/written grammar atypical for age | Has improper sentence structure<br><br>Forms run-on sentences<br><br>Has difficulty understanding questions<br><br>Can't follow directions<br><br>Has poor comprehension<br><br>Is confused with time concepts | Reading comprehension (e.g., passive transformations, directions, sequencing)<br><br>Auditory comprehension (e.g., simple sentences, complex paragraphs)<br><br>Mathematics problems<br><br>Written expression<br><br>Response to questions (frequently answers incorrectly, such as "what," for "who") | Can't comprehend abstractions (e.g., riddles and jokes)<br><br>Has low self-esteem<br><br>Relates poorly to peers<br><br>Has behavioral problems<br><br>Is reluctant to participate |

**Morphology**

| Use | Pragmatics (Use and Purpose) | Inappropriate language/social behaviors | | | |
|---|---|---|---|---|---|
| | | Violates conversational rules | Is unable to do independent work | Interacts poorly with peers, teachers, and other adults |
| | | Violates personal space | Can't attend to discussion | Offends listeners |
| | | Interrupts frequently | Makes excessive or infrequent requests for assistance | Has behavioral problems |
| | | Makes odd, irrelevant comments | | Behaves immaturely |
| | | Confuses listeners | Has poor conversational skills (e.g., blurts out comments, is insensitive to others, lacks tact) | Has few friends |
| | | Has poor topic maintenance | | Can't alter behavior according to needs of a particular situation or setting |
| | | Can't interpret/use nonverbal cues | Has poor written expression skills (e.g., is not cohesive, does not provide sufficient information) | Behaves inappropriately |
| | | Doesn't ask clarification questions | Can't remain on the topic (speech/writing) | |
| | | | Can't engage in discussion | |
| | | | Has inadequate class preparation | |
| | | | Has poor study skills | |

Used with permission of the Ohio Department of Education.

together to maintain a delicate equilibrium. When one is out of balance, the child struggles to make sense of the world around him. Poor communication skills can interfere with every aspect of the child's life.

Learners with communication disorders quickly fall behind in school. Vocabularies dwindle, memories fail, and problem solving becomes difficult. Because social interactions rely on the ability to communicate effectively, children with communication disorders often appear awkward and inept in social situations. This results in alienation and isolation.

The literature is not clear as to how many children are affected with a communication disorder. The American Speech-Language-Hearing Association (ASHA) estimates that approximately 5 percent of the school-age population has some type of speech or language impairment. Because the available data is inconclusive, it is believed that this estimate is quite conservative and many children are not being identified.

# How a Communication Disorder Is Assessed

Early identification of a communication disorder is crucial if a child is to receive support before his life is seriously affected. An evaluation by a speech/language pathologist is often a component of the school's multifactored evaluation. An IEP is written for the child eligible for speech and/or language services, and therapy is provided by the pathologist. Students who qualify for services may have difficulties with speech; pragmatic, receptive, or expressive language; oral or written language; or any combination.

The measures more frequently used to evaluate for a speech/language disorder are described below. This information may help parents and professionals understand what each test is evaluating.

1. **Bracken Basic Concept Scale**

   Ages two to eight years.

   Measures basic readiness skills in the areas of color, letter identification, numbers/counting, comparison, shapes, direction/

position, social/emotional development, size, texture/material, quantity, and time/sequence.

2. **Clinical Evaluation of Language Functions (CLEF)**

   Ages four to eighteen.

   Screening and Diagnostic Battery has two levels: elementary (K through 5) and advanced (5 through 12). These are divided into Language Processing and Language Production sections.

   The Diagnostic Battery has thirteen subtests: six processing, five production, and two supplementary.

3. **Peabody Picture Vocabulary Test, Revised**

   Ages two to adult.

   Measures receptive vocabulary and verbal ability.

4. **Tests of Language Development (TOLD)**

   Ages four through twelve.

   There is a primary test (ages four to eight) that measures semantic and syntactic elements of receptive and expressive language. Subtests assess word articulation and word discrimination.

   The intermediate test (ages eight to twelve) also measures expressive and receptive language components. The subtests include sentence combining, characteristics, ordering, general comprehension, and grammar comprehension.

# Factors Interfering with Normal Speech and Language Development

Before a child is evaluated for a communication disorder, a hearing evaluation and examination of the oral and nasal cavities and the ear by a physician, speech/language pathologist, or audiologist is advised to rule out any physiological anomalies. Hearing impairments or malformations of these cavities due to illness or physiological conditions are factors to be considered. This advice is especially important if the child has suffered chronic ear infections, especially otitis media with effusion, at an early age. There appears to be a direct connection between young children who have had early bouts of otitis media and delayed language development and articulation. This is a result of not being able to hear and imitate language and speech sounds. When this condition occurs, speech and language therapy are part of the management plan.

Allergies can also interfere with speech and language development. Any allergy that produces fluid in the ear can result in a distortion of sounds. Allergies that affect the nasal cavities can change the tonal quality of the voice.

Ethnicity and cultural differences may also affect the pronunciation of sounds and sentence structure and may be reflected in the acquired vocabularies of children. These factors may be especially relevant in homes where no English is spoken or where English is spoken as a second language.

Another factor to consider is whether a child has an attention issue that may cause him to miss the subtleties of language. He may be busy attending to what is stimulating, interesting, and meaningful to him while the rest of what is being communicated is lost. It is important, therefore, to be aware of the child's focus of attention when communicating vital information.

Undetected, the presence of any of these factors can seriously interfere with or delay the child's speech and language development. A communication delay is when speech and language patterns are developing normally but at a rate behind what is expected for that age. A communication disorder is present when the observed speech and language behaviors are often delayed *and* deviate from the expected developmental patterns and forms. Figure 10.2 lists key questions that may be helpful in sorting out these factors.

# The Development of Speech Patterns

Below is a timetable for the development of speech sounds. The sounds are usually mastered around the age indicated. Please remember that not every child will produce these sounds at exactly the indicated norm. This is just an arbitrary measuring stick. Some children produce these sounds earlier than others and some later.

Most speech errors tend to self-correct as the child matures. Around the age of six, most speech distortions should begin to diminish. If they persist or increase in intensity, a speech pathologist should be consulted.

### Vocalization or prebabbling stage (lasts from birth to about 6 months).

1. Use of a wide range of sounds.
2. Random usage of sounds with no apparent pattern or control.
3. Use of sounds to get basic needs met (crying, laughing, cooing).
4. Discrimination between sounds.

    Between human voices and other sounds.

    Between angry and friendly verbal expressions.

    Between male and female voices.

    Between subtle sound patterns such as "pa" and "ba."

### Babbling stage (from about six months to one year of age).

1. Emergence of sound patterns and control as consonant sounds are repeated and strung with vowels.
2. Recognizable differences between types of crying (hunger, surprise, discomfort).
3. More melodic babbling, with rhythm, intonation, and stress.

### True speech stage (begins around first birthday).

1. Decreased babbling.
2. Attempts at meaningful words. These begin as distortions of adult speech and gradually refine pronunciations through imitation.
3. Articulation of basic sounds at the beginning of the words before the middle or ending sounds become present.

**Fig. 10.2. Guiding Questions for Consideration with Students Not Exhibiting Language Competence**

| | | **Listening**<br>Oral Reception | **Speaking**<br>Oral Expression | **Reading**<br>Written Reception | **Writing**<br>Written Expression |
|---|---|---|---|---|---|
| **Content** | **Semantics** | Does the student comprehend what is heard, i.e., the meaning of spoken words, the ideas heard in sentences, and the meaning of figurative spoken language? | Does the student express ideas that make sense? Can the student label common objects correctly and find the right words to convey the intended idea? | Does the student comprehend what is read, identify the main idea, and understand figurative language? | Does the student get the point across in writing? Does the student use age-appropriate vocabulary? Do ideas flow logically? |
| **Form** | **Phonology** | Does the student distinguish differences between similar-sounding words? | Does the student say sounds correctly? Is the student able to rhyme words? | Does the student make errors in word attack due to incorrect letter-sound association? Is the student able to decode words? | Does the student make spelling errors due to incorrect letter-sound associations? |

| | | | | |
|---|---|---|---|---|
| **Form** | **Morphology** | Does the student understand changes in past, present, and future word tenses? Can the student follow directions that differ only in number or comparatives? | Does the student use word endings properly when speaking to convey the intended idea? | Does the student miss the meaning of a sentence or story because of misunderstanding the intent of tenses, plurals, possessives, and comparatives? | Does the student use word endings correctly when conveying ideas in writing? |
| | **Syntax** | Can the student follow oral directions in the correct sequence? | Does the student tell stories or relate information in complete sentences using proper grammar? | Can the student follow written directions in the correct sequence? | Does the student's writing contain complete sentences, proper subject/verb agreement, word order, punctuation, and paragraphing? |
| **Use** | **Pragmatics** | Does the student understand when someone is teasing? Does the student comprehend nonverbal cues when communicating? | Does the student know how to begin, end, and maintain a conversation appropriately? | Does the student identify the intent of the writer? Does the student make appropriate inferences? | Does the student's writing correctly address the expectations of the reader, e.g., formal, business-like, and friendly? |

(continued on next page)

**Fig. 10.2. Guiding Questions for Consideration with Students Not Exhibiting Language Competence,** *continued*

| | **Listening**<br>Oral Reception | **Speaking**<br>Oral Expression | **Reading**<br>Written Reception | **Writing**<br>Written Expression |
|---|---|---|---|---|
| **Other**<br>**Graphics**<br>**(Visual**<br>**Features)** | | | Does the student perceive visual differences among shapes, letters, and words of similar configuration? | Does the student's handwriting have correct letter formation, size, spacing, slant, pencil pressure, and on-line writing? |

4. Acquisition of consonant blends (pr, kl, str) after the single consonants.

### Preschool years (from around age two to five).

1. By age four and a half, *m, n, ng, p, f, h, w, y, k, b, d*, and *g* sounds in constant use.
2. Signs of stuttering may emerge.
3. Nonfluency between the ages of three and five is not uncommon if there are no visual signs of tension (pursed lips, eye blinks, facial grimaces).

### Kindergarten.

1. Long vowel sounds (*a, e, i, o, u*) introduced.
2. Difficulty pronouncing the sounds *v, th, j, s/z, sh*, and *r*.
3. Presence of some mispronunciations (*clackers* for *crackers*) and word-form errors (*goed, comed*).

### First grade.

1. By six and a half, the sounds *sh, v, l, th* (as in *this*), *sz* (as in *treasure*), *ch, j* (as in *jump*) used correctly.
2. Short vowel sounds more distinguishable.

### Second grade.

1. By seven and a half, the sounds *r, s, th* (as in *thumb*), *z*, and *wh* mastered.
2. Phonetic identification of most sounds.

## Observable Traits of a Speech Disorder

1. Chronic ear infections or allergies early in life.
2. Stuttering or stammering that intensifies as the child reaches school age.
3. Sound distortions or problems with fluency or tonal quality that interfere with a school-age child's ability to make himself

understood, in which case a speech pathologist should be consulted and speech therapy considered.

## Strategies to Develop Appropriate Speech Sounds

To enhance a child's speech-sound development, the following suggestions may be helpful.

1. Avoid baby talk. Speak naturally to the child.

2. Accept speech errors during the learning process.

3. Remain patient, relaxed, and calm when listening to the child's efforts.

4. Model the correct pronunciation when the child mispronounces a word.

5. Have hearing checked and a speech evaluation performed if ear infections or allergies are chronic.

# The Development of Oral Language

Speech is the actual pronunciation of sounds that form words. Oral language is the stringing of those words into meaningful communication. The majority of oral language development occurs during the first three years of life. This is when extensive vocabularies develop that later are the basis for learning. Every opportunity should be made to provide experiences that allow the young child to hear, use, and experiment with language.

Below are the patterns that are considered the norm for oral language development (Figure 10.3). Again, some children reach these arbitrary milestones earlier than others depending on their developmental clock. A slight delay is not necessarily reason for concern.

### At birth.

1. Makes auditory discriminations between sounds.

2. Recognizes mother's voice within first few days of life.

3. Localizes sound by turning toward the source.

---

**Fig. 10.3. Developmental Milestones**

| Age | Language Behaviors |
| --- | --- |

**Age**        **Language Behaviors**

1 year

Recognizes his or her name
Understands simple instructions
Initiates familiar words, gestures, and sounds
Uses "mama," "dada," and other common nouns

1½ years

Uses ten to twenty words, including names
Recognizes pictures of familiar persons and objects
Combines two words, such as "all gone"
Uses words to make wants known, such as "more," "up"
Points and gestures to call attention to an event and to show
wants
Follows simple commands
Imitates simple actions
Hums, may sing simple tunes
Distinguishes print from nonprint

2 years

Understands simple questions and commands
Identifies body parts
Carries on conversation with self and dolls
Asks "what" and "where"
Has sentence length of two to three words
Refers to self by name
Names pictures
Uses two-word negative phrases, such as "no want"
Forms some plurals by adding *s*
Has about a 300-word vocabulary
Asks for food and drink
Stays with one activity for six to seven minutes
Knows how to interact with books (right side up, page
turning from left to right)

2½ years

Has about a 450-word vocabulary
Gives first name
Uses past tense and plurals; combines some nouns and verbs
Understands simple time concepts, such as "last night,"
"tomorrow"
Refers to self as "me" rather than name
Tries to get adult attention with "watch me"
Likes to hear same story repeated
Uses "no" or "not" in speech

*(continued on next page)*

**Fig. 10.3. Developmental Milestones,** *continued*

| Age | Language Behaviors |
|---|---|
| 2½ years *(continued)* | Answers "where" questions<br>Uses short sentences, such as "me do it"<br>Holds up fingers to tell age<br>Talks to other children and adults<br>Plays with sounds of language |
| 3 years | Matches primary colors; names one color<br>Knows night and day<br>Begins to understand prepositional phrases, such as "put the block under the chair"<br>Practices by talking to self<br>Knows last name, sex, street name, and several nursery rhymes<br>Tells a story or relays an idea<br>Has sentence length of three to four words<br>Has vocabulary of nearly 1,000 words<br>Consistently uses *m, n, ng, p, f, h,* and *w*<br>Draws circle and vertical line<br>Sings songs<br>Stays with one activity for eight to nine minutes<br>Asks "what" questions |
| 4 years | Points to red, blue, yellow, and green<br>Identifies crosses, triangles, circles, and squares<br>Knows "next month," "next year," and "noon"<br>Has sentence length of four to five words<br>Asks "who" and "why"<br>Begins to use complex sentences<br>Correctly uses *m, n, ng, p, f, h,* and *w, y, k, b, d,* and *g*<br>Stays with one activity for eleven to twelve minutes<br>Plays with language, e.g., word substitutions |
| 5 years | Defines objects by their use and tells what they are made of<br>Knows address<br>Identifies penny, nickel, and dime<br>Has sentence length of five to six words<br>Has vocabulary of about 2,000 words<br>Uses speech sounds correctly, with the possible exceptions being *v, th, j, s/z, zh,* and *r*<br>Knows common opposites |

| Age | Language Behaviors |
|---|---|
| 5 years *(continued)* | Understands "same" and "different"<br>Counts ten objects<br>Uses future, present, and past tenses<br>Stays with one activity for twelve to thirteen minutes<br>Questions for information<br>Identifies left and right hand on self<br>Uses all types of sentences<br>Shows interest and appreciation for print |
| 6 to 7 years | Identifies most sounds phonetically<br>Forms most sound-letter associations<br>Segments sounds into smallest grammatical units<br>Begins to use semantic and syntactic cues in writing and reading<br>Begins to write simple sentences with vocabulary and spelling appropriate for age; uses these sentences in brief reports and creative short stories<br>Understands time and space concepts, such as before/after, second/third<br>Comprehends mathematical concepts, such as "few," "many," "all," and "except"<br>By second grade, accurately follows oral directions for action and thereby acquires new knowledge |
| 8, 9, 10, 11 years | Substitutes words in oral reading, sentence recall, and repetition; copying and writing dictation are minimal<br>Comprehends reading materials required for various subjects, including story problems and simple sentences<br>By fourth grade, easily classifies words and identifies relationships, such as "cause and effect"<br>Defines words (sentence context)<br>Introduces self appropriately<br>Asks for assistance<br>Exchanges small talk with friends<br>Initiates telephone calls and takes messages<br>Gives directions for games; summarizes a television show or conversation<br>Begins to write effectively for a variety of purposes<br>Understands verbal humor |

*(continued on next page)*

**Fig. 10.3. Developmental Milestones,** *continued*

| Age | Language Behaviors |
|---|---|
| 11, 12, 13, 14 years | Displays social and interpersonal communication appropriate for age<br>Forms appropriate peer relationships<br>Begins to define words at an adult level and talks about complex processes from an abstract point of view; uses figurative language<br>Organizes materials<br>Demonstrates good study skills<br>Follows lectures and outlines content through note taking<br>Paraphrases and asks questions appropriate to content |
| Adolescence and young adulthood | Interprets emotions, attitudes, and intentions communicated by others' facial expressions and body language<br>Takes role of other person effectively<br>Is aware of social space zones<br>Displays appropriate reactions to expressions of love, affection, and approval<br>Compares, contrasts, interprets, and analyzes new and abstract information<br>Communicates effectively and develops competency in oral and written modalities |

Developed by the Ohio Statewide Language Task Force, 1990. Used with permission of the Ohio Department of Education.

## By age of one year.

1. Learns turn-taking first by smiling, then cooing, babbling, and then uses words.

2. Makes eye contact with the speaker.

3. Responds to his or her name.

4. Repeats speech and points to what he wants.

5. Has real names for things, such as *mama, dada,* and *cat.*

## By eighteen months.

1. Increases vocabulary to anywhere from twelve to fifty words.

2. Points to things he is asked to identify (ears, nose, mouth).

3. Follows simple commands.

## By two years.

1. Combines two words into meaningful phrases.
2. Understands simple directions and commands.
3. Understands most of what is said to him.
4. Invents words for words he does not yet know.

## By three years.

1. Has a vocabulary of around 1,000 words.
2. Speaks in sentences of five to ten words.
3. Carries on conversations.
4. Enjoys playing with words and language in using rhyming and nonsense words.

## By kindergarten.

1. Has a vocabulary of around 2,000 words.
2. Language styles and usage representative of experiences from home, community, ethnicity, and cultural background.
3. Uses complex sentence structures and a variety of sentences (questions, statements).
4. Uses pronouns, articles, plurals, and comparative endings.

## School years.

1. Develops a more sophisticated use of language by refining how words are used (semantics), sentence structure, and grammar usage (syntax).
2. Learns how to use language more effectively and efficiently to serve a variety of communication functions.
3. Fine-tunes metalinguistic skills—that is, becomes more aware of the correct and incorrect forms of speech and language that makes sense from nonsense (puns, jokes, etc.).

## Observable Signs of an Oral Language Disorder

1.  By eighteen months the child is not saying some meaningful words (e.g., *mama, dog, dada*).

2.  By twenty-four months, the child is not using some words in meaningful phrases (e.g., "Me go!)"

3.  By age three, speech is not understandable, or the child does not communicate comfortably with others.

4.  By age three, he continues to point and grunt to get what he wants, instead of using words. (Younger children will do this because of limited vocabulary. By three, they should have the words for everyday items and requests.)

5.  The child does not seem to understand what is being said and appears confused by simple directions or requests.

6.  The child has difficulty sequencing steps and events.

## Strategies to Develop Oral Language Skills

Language development can be promoted by providing the following experiences for the child.

1.  Read, read, read, beginning in infancy. Select many different topics.

2.  Talk, talk, talk to your baby and young child, even if it is "I'm opening a can of soup now and pouring it into a pan."

3.  Provide opportunities to identify likenesses and differences in shape, size, color.

4.  Provide opportunities to name things by category.
    - Sort laundry, silverware, toys (a good way to teach a skill and responsibility at the same time).
    - Categorize foods (fruit, meats, vegetables).
    - Categorize animals (farm animals, pets, jungle animals).

5.  Provide opportunities to sequence.
    - Count things whenever possible.

- Follow a recipe. Discuss the order in which the ingredients are added.
- Use terms indicating sequential order, such as *first, second, next, last.*

6. Provide a variety of experiences, such as trips to the grocery, the firehouse, a farm to pick apples or pumpkins, the zoo, and museums. Sequence the events.

   - Discuss what is happening, about to happen, or did happen during the experience.
   - Capture the experience with photos. Recall the experience when film is developed and encourage the child to share the pictures and experience with others.
   - Write about the experience. Have the child recall his experiences as you record his words on paper. Allow him to draw a picture to go with his story. Urge him to share his story with someone.

7. Urge children to ask questions about their world (be sure to listen and respond carefully).

8. Make up stories about pictures (e.g., an advertisement in a magazine or a comic strip).

9. Provide a variety of tasting experiences. Discuss the food's taste and texture.

10. Use travel time in the car to find license plates that are the same or different, identify street signs and buildings, count specific objects (e.g., red cars, trucks, cows).

11. Provide opportunities to work with construction paper, paste, glue, scissors, paints, markers, crayons.

# The Development of Written Language Skills

Written language is the presentation of thoughts and ideas in visual, rather than auditory, form. Often the first attempt at written language is the decorating of walls with markers or crayons. The horrified mother may see only a confused array of strokes, but to the child, they are an attempt to communicate.

The way written language develops in the individual is outlined by Melvin Levine, M.D., in his book *Developmental Variations and Learning Disorders*. As with the speech and oral language developmental timetable, the age guidelines for each stage are approximate.

### The scribbling or prewriting stage: before the age of three.

1. Large and diverse configurations with little pattern, shape, or control.
2. Inability to copy or trace figures or patterns.
3. Very little fine muscle control.
4. No concept of line and space.
5. Use of different writing implements on a variety of surfaces.

### The imitation stage: preschool to first grade.

1. Scribbling, drawing pictures, and talking about his creations are the child's first attempts at communicating through the written form.
2. Early writing mimics true writing. Child will draw lines across paper to represent words in sentences and "read" back what he "wrote."
3. Fine motor muscles are still weak but allow more implement control as child matures.
4. Child develops a sense of line and space, but fine motor control is still too weak for precise placement within these boundaries.
5. Child begins letter and number formations later in this stage.
6. Child enjoys writing and is willing to share efforts.
7. Inventive spelling occurs.
8. Child learns to write own name.

### The graphic presentation stage: first and second grade.

1. Child masters numbers and uppercase and lowercase letters. Reversals are common.

2. Spacing and line orientation become more refined. Child is aware of margins, left-to-right direction, and placement of letters on lines and in spaces on the paper.

3. Fine motor control becomes more precise.

4. By the end of second grade, hand preference is usually established.

5. Spelling ability increases.

### The progressive incorporation stage: late second to fourth grades.

1. Child develops awareness and use of grammar, punctuation, and capitalization in the writing process.

2. Simple sentences are still used with little thought to organizing ideas.

3. Child begins to learn rewriting techniques.

4. Cursive writing is begun by the end of second grade.

### The automatization stage: fourth through seventh grades.

1. Writing becomes a communication tool as child writes with more ease and fluency.

2. Child produces a larger volume of writing that is more sophisticated and complex.

3. Child can write about as quickly as he can speak.

4. Writing is more organized and planned, often entailing outlines and refining drafts before the final version is completed.

### The elaboration stage: seventh through ninth grades.

1. Writing is used to express a viewpoint, solve a problem, and summarize.

2. Child can do research using information from numerous resources.

3. Cohesive ties such as *for example, finally,* and *therefore* are used.

### The personalization-diversification stage: ninth grade into adulthood.

1. Individual writing styles emerge.

2. Different styles are used for different purposes.

3. Writing becomes more simple and speechlike.

4. Student enjoys experimenting with writing and writing styles.

## Observable Traits of a Written Language Disorder

1. Unwillingness to use pencils, pens, markers, crayons in early stages.

2. Poor or awkward pencil grip. A tripod position is most effective and desirable.

3. Difficulty with spatial orientation (line and space, spacing between words, margins).

4. Difficulty with directionality (left-to-right progression, top to bottom, form letters from bottom to top)

5. Difficulty with tracing or following patterns.

6. Difficulty copying from board or other printed materials.

7. Avoidance of writing assignments.

8. Testing poorly on long-answer or essay tests.

9. Poor note-taking skills.

10. Fatigue.

11. Switching hands.

12. Excessive erasures.

13. Writing too fast or in a slow and labored manner.

14. Combining capital and lowercase letters or manuscript and cursive in same word.

15. Difficulty with learning and applying spelling, grammar, and punctuation rules.

16. Frequent spelling, grammar, vocabulary, and syntax errors. Failure to spot errors when proofreading work.

17. Limited vocabulary for age level.

18. Difficulty coming to and making a point.

19. Abbreviated writing samples often with disorganized thoughts.

20. Poor sequencing skills.

## Strategies to Develop Written Language Skills

1. Develop fine muscles in the hand by providing opportunities to pummel cookie dough, work with modeling clay, use a hole puncher, and cut with scissors.
   - String beads, use lacing cards, trace pictures, shapes, letters, or numbers.
   - "Write" in sand, flour, sugar, or shaving cream. (This also cleans the writing surface.) Introduce a variety of mediums and textures.
   - Begin the writing experience on large areas. Paint with a bucket of water and a paintbrush on the driveway, use chalk on the sidewalk or blackboard, put large sheets of paper on the floor or wall.
   - Begin with fat writing implements: pencils, crayons, markers.

2. Delay the teaching of letters and numbers until the child is comfortable drawing or scribbling and relating his experiences.

3. Do not expect perfection at the start. Encourage and accept the child's first efforts. Demands to color within the lines or perfectly reproduce letters early in the writing process will frustrate and discourage the child.

4. Be realistic. Allow your child to take the lead and go where she is developmentally ready to venture. If she is still scribbling in coloring books, she may not have the precision and control needed to form the letters in her name.

5. Display with pride your child's finished creations.

6. Have the child talk about what he has written. Have him explain the *what, who,* and *why* of his writing.

7. Use words such as *first, next,* and *finally* to help your child develop sequencing skills.

8. Give your child space at the end of letters to relatives or friends to add a message.

# Exploring Speech Disorders

In relating an episode involving his brother, five-year-old Joey explained, "My wittle brudder, um, um, wunned into the, um, tweet and almost got, um, wunned ober. My mudder, um, was, um, was um, weally, um mad. Um, um she 'reamed, and um, and um, she, um lelled at 'im."

This is typical of a young child with a combination of speech disorders. In this section, we will discuss three disorders—articulation, fluency, and voice problems—that speech pathologists can evaluate and remediate with therapy.

## Articulation

Articulation problems are the most common of the speech disorders found in childhood. It is not uncommon to hear children mispronouncing words and using incorrect verb forms. This concern can be found in Joey's account given above.

Other articulation problems may be the result of abnormalities in the dental formation, the shape or structure of the hard or soft palate, or poor muscle control of the tongue or lips. A hearing loss can also affect articulation. Children with immature speech patterns, like baby talk, also may exhibit articulation problems. Articulation can be affected by cultural dialects, especially in homes where English is spoken as the second language. Articulation errors range from very minor to speech that is barely understood.

### Observable traits of an articulation disorder.

1. **Distortions.** These are inappropriate sounds that replace the correct ones. For example, "shing" for "sing," "lollow" for "yellow."

2. **Omissions.** This term refers to sounds that are not stated at all, e.g., "hep" for "help," and "fiend" for "friend." Word endings are also dropped.

3. **Substitutions.** These occur when one sound is substituted for another, as "wead" for "read" or "wittle" for "little."

## Fluency Disorders

Fluency refers to the rate and flow of the spoken word. Some children speak very rapidly, and all their words seems to mush together in one continuous flow. With other children, you can wait forever for one complete thought to be uttered. The use of sentence fillers, such as "er," "um," and "uh" is common.

Children with fluency problems may have word-finding problems and often express themselves by demonstrating an action. For example, a child cannot think of the word *hammer* but can describe a hammer and show you how it's used. He may use facial expressions, gestures, or generic words, such as *stuff, junk,* or *whatchamacallit,* to communicate.

For young children with limited vocabularies and motor control, these characteristics are common and a part of the developmental process. When these symptoms persist after around the age of five and a half, an evaluation may be warranted.

### Observable traits of a fluency disorder.

1. Repetition of syllables, words, or phrases.
2. Stopping and starting of speech, filled with pauses and fillers (um, er, uh).
3. Speech that is too fast or too slow.
4. Stuttering or stammering.
5. Visual signs of tension, such as pursed lips, eye blinking, or facial grimaces.

## Voice Disorders

Voice disorders have to do with the resonance, tonal quality, pitch, and volume of vocalizations. These disorders may occur as a result of hearing loss or structural abnormalities of the nasal or oral cavities. Also abusive vocal behaviors that result in vocal nodules may cause a change in the production of speech sounds.

### Observable traits of a voice disorder.

1. Voice is too weak and soft to be heard or too loud and boisterous.

2. Voice is nasal, husky, guttural, breathy, or hoarse.

3. Voice tends to be monotonous, without inflection or variety.

### Strategies to support the child with speech disorders.

1. Arrange for a speech and hearing evaluation for students with suspected speech disorders.

2. Speech therapy provides structured support.

3. Model appropriate speech.

4. Be cautious about correcting speech.

5. Limit the demands on oral speech.

   - Allow the student to read prepared work rather than speak from memory.
   - Allow written reports if oral reporting is too stressful.
   - Oral reporting should allow for the use of written notes.
   - Provide a "wait time" for the child to find his words.
   - Ask questions that require a yes or no answer, a demonstration, or a visual response, such as pointing to a map or a picture.
   - Avoid asking the child with severe voice problems or stuttering to read aloud in class.

# Exploring Language Disorders

It is not clearly understood what occurs within the brain to cause a malfunction in language production. Interference can occur in the individual's ability to understand or express information, oral or written. For example, Susan gets confused and overwhelmed in class discussions. The information comes too quickly for her brain to process it. Seeing the information in visual form is a much more effective way for her to learn. She can take the time required to break it down into manageable chunks. Susan has a receptive language disorder.

Brian has problems writing out information. It is a slow and painful process whenever he is asked to respond in writing. Copying from the board is difficult, and the results are often inaccurate. His writing assignments, short with jumbled ideas that never come to the point, are returned with numerous spelling and grammar errors indicated. Expressing himself verbally is the easier and more comfortable communication channel. Brian struggles with a written expressive language disorder.

Kevin has a hard time making sense of the information he receives, either orally or in writing. Because he takes so long to understand the message, his response is usually inappropriate. He becomes embarrassed when his peers laugh at his errors. With combined receptive and expressive language disorders, Kevin needs a variety of experiences to make learning successful.

We will discuss four language disorders that can interfere with the learning process. They occur in the areas of pragmatic, receptive, expressive, and written language.

## Pragmatic Language

Pragmatic language is our use of language in everyday conversation. Sometimes referred to as our social language, it combines nonverbal language (dialects, humor, slang words) to convey a message. It is a system of rules that relate to the use and purpose of language. This rule system determines appropriate and effective communication in various contexts. Effective communication requires the complex ability to integrate many variables to determine when communication should occur, where, why, and with whom, and of what is should consist. We use pragmatic language skills when we take turns in our conversations, maintain topics, use eye contact, respond appropriately to the nonverbal cues our partner is sending, respect personal space, and modify our conversations to match the social position of our communication partner.

A child with weak pragmatic language skills often has poor social skills. Knowing how to say the right thing at the right time is an essential social skill needed to communicate effectively with others. Children with pragmatic language skills have a knack for making inappropriate comments, such as telling a joke when a classmate is talking about her grandmother's illness.

Children with pragmatic language issues often miss the subtleties of conversation. When they overlook facial expressions, gestures, posture, tones of voice, and other nonverbal cues, they do not formulate an accurate response. Telling a joke when someone is upset about a grandparent's illness may appear cruel and heartless. But the child with pragmatic language difficulties may be unaware of the tone of sadness in her classmate's voice and the expression of pain or worry on his face. Overlooking these nonverbal cues results in an inappropriate response, which causes the child to be misunderstood and ostracized.

The social register is another area often affected by children with pragmatic language disorders. The term *social register* refers to the adjustment of speech to fit the situation. For example, calling the school principal "dude" is not appropriate. Students who make errors of this kind appear to have a lack of respect for authority and get into trouble. Usually these are not disrespectful children but students who have difficulty reading the situation and adjusting their responses accordingly. They are often at a loss as to why they upset or infuriate people.

A child with a pragmatic language disorder may violate the personal space of others. This aspect of pragmatic language involves maintaining a comfort zone that serves as a buffer between you and another person. If your space gets violated, someone is too close to you, and your instinct is to back away. Children with pragmatic language issues frequently violate this personal space by getting into the face of other children. This creates a very uncomfortable situation and presents another reason to exclude the child who is trying to fit in.

Students with pragmatic language difficulties may lack an awareness of classroom routines. Because they are not aware that there are certain rituals the teacher follows each day, they do not know the rules and routine and therefore do not respond appropriately. For example, many teachers make it a point to be in a certain place when they're relating important information. This is called the "teacher place." Most students quickly pick up the subtle cue that when the teacher is in this place, they are to pay attention and listen. Children with pragmatic language issues never pick up on this visual cue. They also have a difficult time understanding classroom rules and following a daily routine.

Observable traits of a pragmatic language disorder. Children with pragmatic language issues tend to demonstrate certain characteristics. An evaluation by a language pathologist can confirm your suspicions if you have a child with these traits.

1. Interrupts conversations.

2. Confuses listeners by switching topics, often to unrelated subjects.

3. Begins conversations at awkward moments. For example, in the middle of a teacher's explanation, Bobby may ask Christy what she brought for lunch and carry on a conversation about his lunch.

4. Either misses or cannot interpret the nonverbal cues that set the tone of the conversation and determine the appropriate response.

5. Talks excessively.

6. Makes odd or irrelevant comments that seem to come from nowhere.

7. Violates personal space.

8. Lacks a social register.

9. Sends the wrong message through personal nonverbal cues (e.g., appears to be angry but really not).

10. Makes insensitive comments without meaning to hurt anyone's feelings.

11. Has few friends and is often used as a scapegoat by peers.

12. Is oblivious to classroom rules and routines.

13. Demonstrates poor body language.

14. Lacks eye contact.

15. Has difficulty initiating, maintaining, and/or terminating a conversation, as well as entering an ongoing conversation.

**Strategies to support a learner with a pragmatic language disorder.**

1. Arrange for therapy with a qualified language pathologist.

2. Use scripts to set a structured format for the child to practice and follow. For example, a script to teach telephone manners might outline the following scenario: *The telephone rings.*
   BETTY: *(calmly)* Hello.
   CALLER: Is your Dad there?
   BETTY: I'm sorry—he's here but can't come to the phone right now. *(A safe response when adults are away from home.)* Would you like to leave your name and number and I'll have him call you back? *(Paper and pencil should be attached to the phone for this purpose.)*
   CALLER: No, thanks. I'll call back later. Good-bye.
   BETTY: Good-bye.

   Scripts can be structured to fit any social situation. For a script to be effective, the child must help design it to read in a way that is comfortable for him. Then it should be practiced and rehearsed until the routine feels natural to the child.

3. Role-playing and modeling help the child learn what responses are acceptable in various situations. The child who missed the seriousness of the conversation about the illness of a classmate's grandmother may benefit from role-playing.

   • Have the child put himself in another child's shoes. For example, how would he feel if *his* grandmother were ill? What words might he choose to relate his feelings? What facial expressions would express his concern?

   • Then discuss how someone telling a joke at this time would make him feel.

   • Next brainstorm what might be appropriate responses to someone feeling sad or worried.

   • Model acceptable responses for the child. ("Oh, I'm so sorry. You must be so sad.") Point out the tone of voice, facial expressions, and gestures that would match this response.

- Have your child practice the suggestions most comfortable for him.

4. Build the child's awareness of the social register.

   Discuss how to adjust conversations to the other participant. Have child practice talking to authority figures (police, teachers, principals), strangers (store clerks, waitresses), acquaintances (barber, minister), relatives (grandparents, aunts), and peers.

5. Build an awareness of personal space.

   - Draw a line on the floor. Identify who is at one end of the line (teacher, sister, neighbor, cashier). Have the child practice moving along the line to the appropriate place to stop, depending on the communication partner. Farther away from authority figures and strangers than from more familiar people. Family members and close friends would be closer to the individual.
   - Demonstrate the looks and reactions of a person whose personal space has been violated.
   - Help the child understand that when a person begins to back up or look uncomfortable or threatened, the child needs to check his distance from that person and adjust accordingly.
   - Use a Hula Hoop around a child to demonstrate the buffer zone required between other people and himself.

6. Build responsiveness to nonverbal cues.

   - Use charts or pictures with faces showing different feelings. Have the child study the different expressions. Cover up the labels and have the child identify the feeling.
   - Ask the child to demonstrate in a mirror different facial expressions related to feelings.
   - Using pictures from magazines or books, ask the child to describe how the person is feeling and what may be happening in the picture to cause this reaction. Discuss how he might respond if he were talking to this person.
   - Videotape TV programs. Stop the tape and have the child identify the feelings shown and predict what is occurring and why the actor is showing those emotions.

- Demonstrate different postures that relay feelings (e.g., clenched fists for anger or aggression, stooped shoulders for sadness, crossed arms for defiance, open arms for acceptance).
- Demonstrate different tones of voice and the feelings associated with each.

7. Develop the child's awareness of classroom rules and routines.

- The teacher needs to cue the child when it is time to listen. Establish a "teacher place" and explain that when you're in that place, it is time to listen. This can be done with a silent signal. (This would need to be decided upon privately with the child.)
- Post classroom rules in a prominent place early in the school year and review often. Maybe even put rules on a post-it note and place on student's desk.
- Demonstrate the rules through role-play.
- Write the daily schedule on the blackboard. Erase or cross off each activity as it is completed.
- Have a copy of daily routines that can be placed on the student's desk as a reminder.

## Receptive Language

Receptive language refers to the information, either oral or written, received by our brains. Once it has been received, the brain needs to make sense of it. A decision must be made as to what will be used immediately, what will be stored in our memory, and what will be discarded.

Receptive language skills allow us to receive the thoughts and ideas that others share. We take in the information through our eyes and ears and then it goes to the brain. The brain then tries to make sense of it by sending the data through the appropriate channels.

Children with a receptive language disorder have a glitch in the way information is received. It goes in, but making sense of it quickly enough to organize and formulate a response is difficult. This may cause the child to appear disinterested or aloof.

There are several factors that may interfere with understanding the language we receive.

1. **Auditory overload.** Information that comes too quickly becomes overwhelming. Listeners wear themselves out trying to keep up with the rapid pace of conversation until they finally shut down in frustration. Long, complex sentences, complicated explanations, and multistep directions can add to the confusion. When this is coupled with huge quantities of information presented in a short period of time, the student's receptive skills shut down. These children tune out and appear very distracted and are often thought to be AD/HD. In reality, they may be both AD/HD and language impaired.

2. **Abstract terms and concepts.** Inferences, figurative language, higher-level concepts, and ambiguities become an issue as the student advances through school and learning becomes more abstract.

3. **Student's own lack of awareness that a problem exists.** Often students are unaware of their own lack of comprehension. For example, the child may think she understands how to regroup in a subtraction problem. It is not until she works on her own that she discovers she does not understand. Often children do not have a clear enough understanding of a concept to be able to formulate questions for clarification.

## Observable traits of a receptive language disorder.

1. Difficulty understanding and following oral directions.
2. Difficulty following conversation, especially when rapid and complex.
3. Difficulties with words related to space (*over, under, between, less*).
4. Difficulty recognizing meanings of homonyms (*blue, blew*).
5. Difficulty interpreting cause-effect relationships.
6. Frequent requests to have information repeated.
7. Looks of confusion or blankness during a conversation or explanation.

8. Missing the humor in a joke or a pun. May laugh before the punch line, or because everyone else is laughing, but does not get the joke.

9. Not knowing how to phrase a question to get the desired information.

### Strategies to support the learner with a receptive language disorder.

1. As a more visual learner, he will benefit from a multisensory approach to learning. Lectures or classes relying heavily on oral presentations of information are difficult for this learner.

2. Supplement oral information with written materials or directions.

3. Allow students to use a tape recorder for extensive lectures or detailed instructions.

4. Provide a note buddy to supplement the student's notes.

5. Make a classroom notebook for daily notes available to those who need supplementation or students who have been absent. Carbon copies of notes can be placed in a binder for classroom use.

6. Monitor the speed with which you present information. Slow down or go back and check for understanding.

7. Ask other students to restate the information in their own words. Classmates often use simpler, clearer, more familiar language.

8. Use materials and manipulatives whenever possible to make abstract learning more concrete.

9. Give the gift of time. Allow the child at least ten to fifteen seconds to process what is being said.

10. Give simple directions. Be sure you have the child's eye contact. After stating the directions, ask the child to restate them in her own words.

11. To assure understanding, write out complex directions.

12. Students testing poorly may not understand what is being asked of them. Out-of-class testing with someone available to restate the questions for the student may improve test results.

# Oral Expressive Language Disorder

"It is a luxury to be understood." This quote by Ralph Waldo Emerson may have captured the essence of an expressive language disability.

Once the message is received and interpreted, the brain needs to formulate a response. This ability to express one's thoughts is called expressive language. Many students can easily understand what is being said to them, but when they try to formulate and express an answer, they have trouble.

A response can be in either written or oral form. However, before ideas can be expressed, the appropriate words must be selected. Then the words must be organized into sentences and the sentences placed in the proper sequence. This often needs to be done with split-second accuracy.

Normal everyday conversation moves at a very rapid pace. Responses usually need to be made immediately to keep the dialogue alive. Children with an expressive language disorder find it extremely difficult to formulate an immediate reply. This may result in social problems because the child appears shy, unresponsive, or antisocial because he appears to be ignoring the communication partner. Peers think this child is zoned out when he gives a delayed response to a topic discussed five minutes ago or stands there looking blank. This can be devastating for the child.

Children with an expressive language disorder seldom have the luxury of being understood as they struggle to get out a response. This becomes very upsetting and frustrating for them. They try with little success to find the right words to tell a story or give an answer. Their thoughts come out jumbled and chaotic. When expressing their feelings becomes difficult, they often resort to acting them out using negative behaviors.

### Observable traits of an oral expressive language disorder.

1. Often appears shy and withdrawn. Has a difficult time interacting socially and making friends.

2. Gives delayed responses to questions. Usually is two or three topics behind in conversations.

3. Has a difficult time finding the correct words. Uses many fillers (e.g., *er, um, uh*) to buy time while thinking of a response.

- Uses a lot of pronouns and vague references (*stuff, thingamajig*).
- Uses many gestures or sounds.

4.  Uses single words or short phrases.

5.  Thoughts are disorganized and disjointed and frustrate the listener trying to make sense of the jumble.

6.  Has difficulty coming to the point or staying on the topic.

7.  Appears to understand the information but struggles to respond.

8.  Has difficulty finding the main idea. Everything seems to be of equal importance.

9.  May have inappropriate behaviors as a result of the frustration of not being able to make ideas and feelings known.

10. Often uses the incorrect verb tense and has vocabulary and other grammatical errors.

11. May omit integral parts of the sentence or information needed for understanding.

### Strategies to support the learner with an oral expressive language disorder.

1.  Give the gift of time to help the child organize his thoughts and formulate a response.

2.  Provide wait time. Teachers can ask a question, then erase the board as the students prepare answers.

3.  Provide a silent signal that lets the child know when you will call on him.

4.  Accept one-word or yes/no answers, as well as demonstrations, and pointing to pictures or objects in response to questions.

5.  Avoid having the student read aloud in class. Oral tests or reports can be stressful and embarrassing.

6.  Provide the correct model when the child responds with incorrect syntax. When Sam replies, "I goed to the store," respond in a neutral tone, "Oh, you went to the store?"

7. Provide choices, give the option of naming several items included in a list, or provide the initial sound for children with word-finding problems.

## Written Expressive Language Disorders

The organization and sequencing skills needed in oral expressive language are also necessary in written expressive language. A child may be challenged by the mechanics, the content, and/or the correct form of the written word. A learner having difficulty with content struggles with jumbled thoughts as he tries to make a point. His sentences may be incomplete, often omitting essential words and phrases. Jumping from one idea to another and back again is common. The vocabulary the child uses is often less sophisticated than expected for his age. Difficulty with form can be detected by numerous errors in spelling, word endings, subject-verb agreement, grammar, word order, punctuation, and paragraphing.

Many people think it is simply a matter of picking up a writing implement and putting down thoughts. This belief is an oversimplification of a very intricate process. Just reproducing the written symbols is difficult for many children.

In order to write a single word, a very detailed procedure must occur. First the brain must make a mental image of the word. Then the word must be held in the memory long enough to get the correct sequence of the letters and remember how to create them. In order to reproduce that symbol on paper, the positioning becomes critical. The margins and left-to-right direction must be remembered. The letters must of on the line, and there must be enough spacing between them so they do not all run together. This does not even address the use of capital and lowercase letters. All of this for just one word!

Writing a sentence becomes even more complex. Word order, grammar, punctuation, capitalization, vocabulary, the correct sequencing of the thoughts, and the ability to physically record everything must all be executed with precision. The writer must perform all of these functions simultaneously while trying to hold the ideas in his head. For some of us, this process is so automatic, we hardly give it a thought. For others, it becomes an excruciating exercise in futility!

Individuals who do not clearly understand this mental process often think a writing disorder is a result of poor fine motor control. This may be true of young children. The task of writing may be difficult because of the undeveloped muscles in the hand and fingers. Opportunities to strengthen these muscles should be a major focus during the preschool and kindergarten years.

Older children having difficulty with the mechanics of writing find printing much easier than cursive writing. Others find the continuous flow of cursive writing more manageable. Some children combine the two in the same word, sentence, or paragraph. Children with a written language disorder need to learn keyboarding skills early. As writing demands increase in the later grades, word processing will be their link to survival.

### Observable traits of a written expressive language disorder.

1. A strong resistance to drawing, coloring, copying, or writing.

2. Short, simplistic writing samples with unorganized, disjointed thoughts with little or no elaboration.

3. Errors in applying the rules that govern the form of communication.

4. Vocabulary below age and grade levels.

5. Poor self-monitoring, resulting in spelling, grammar, punctuation, capitalization, and word-order errors.

6. Difficulty reproducing written symbols (dysgraphia).
   - May show a preference for printing over cursive writing or vice versa. May use both styles in the same piece.
   - Illegible writing and a messy finished product.
   - Awkward pencil grip. A tripod position (pencil rests on middle finger supported by the thumb, the second finger is on top) is the preferred and most effective grip. Many students assume awkward grips that make the writing process more difficult and very fatiguing.

Strategies to support learners with a written expressive language disorder.

1. To help with dysgraphia:
   - Encourage the young child to cut, paste, draw, knead, trace, lace, draw, and paint to develop fine motor muscles in the hands and fingers.
   - Color-code lines on the paper to help children with the concept of lines and spaces. Use a traffic signal, star, or other cues to indicate the left side of the paper, where writing should begin.
   - Use dotted lines to write out words and have children trace them with solid strokes.

2. Teach keyboarding skills early. Begin younger children on a typewriter to strengthen fine motor muscles. Graduate to word processing once the keyboard is mastered.

3. Modify testing situations. (Few educators have a problem making these modifications when their object is to find out the student's knowledge and understanding of a subject rather than his test-taking skills.)
   - Allow the student to use a word processor to take essay or long-answer tests.
   - Allow the student to take essay and long-answer tests with his classmates, then orally test in private any missed questions to get an accurate assessment of his knowledge and understanding. (Use this strategy if the student's verbal skills are adequate.)
   - Allow for untimed, out-of-class testing.
   - Extend the testing time. Have the student test with classmates, then complete the test at a predetermined time.
   - Reduce the number of questions. Either allow the student to select a given number, or select them for him.
   - Enlarge the print so the text is clearer.

4. Never exempt students from learning to take notes. Their efforts do need to be monitored and supplemented, however

5. Give students enough time to respond. Last-minute assignments for the assignment book before the bell rings will either not be entered or entered incorrectly. Copying from the blackboard or overhead projector also requires extra time.

6. On writing assignments or tests where time is an issue and where spelling and grammar count, consider giving two grades—one for content and one for writing mechanics (grammar, spelling, etc.). Allow the student to make corrections to improve his grade.

7. When time is not a factor, writing assignments should have proper spelling, grammar, and punctuation.

8. Parents and teachers can help the student develop a system to complete writing assignments. Using the following steps, the child can learn to break down the assignment into manageable chunks spread out over time.

   • Have the learner begin by expressing all her ideas about the topic.
   • Get her thoughts in writing. Provide a tape recorder to store those thoughts or find a "secretary" to write them down.
   • Have the child edit out the ideas that are not pertinent to the assignment.
   • Help the child organize the ideas sequentially. An outline may make this job easier.
   • The child begins to write a rough draft.
   • Then she edits the draft, organizing and rewriting as necessary.
   • Next she edits for mechanical errors, approaching only one aspect at a time—for example, find all the spelling errors, then the capitalization errors, then the grammar errors.
   • Now she is ready to complete the final draft.

9. Reading the text aloud or reading it backward can be effective ways to edit. The child is able to hear the errors.

10. Provide opportunities where writing occurs every day as an enjoyable experience.

- Ask your child to write a grocery list as you dictate items needed.
- Send postcards or note cards the child selects.
- Arrange for a pen pal from another city, state, or country.
- Purchase a notebook, journal, or diary and urge your child to make daily entries.
- Send notes to your child that require a response. This is especially effective with adolescents, who tend to tune out adults.

# Points to Ponder

1. A speech and language pathologist is the professional who evaluates for a communication disorder. The testing may be a part of the multifactored evaluation performed by your local school district or a private agency.

2. Speech disorders involve the way words are pronounced (articulation), rate of speech (fluency), and vocal quality.

3. Language disorders involve the way the brain organizes and uses information. Pragmatic, receptive, expressive, and written expressive language are all areas where a disorder can occur.

4. Therapy offered by the pathologist provides support and delivers favorable results.

For more information about language disabilities, contact the American Speech-Language Hearing Association, 10801 Rockville Pike, Rockville, MD 20852 (301) 897-5700.

# 11

# AD/HD–The Invisible Disorder

In the middle of math class, the fish swimming in the classroom aquarium caught John's eye. Without a moment's hesitation, he was up out of his seat hovering over the fish tank. "Bleep, bleep!" "Bleep, bleep!" were the sounds John made as his hand made a circular motion over the fish. Oblivious to the eyes of his classmates and his teacher, who were now focused on him, he continued his actions.

When the teacher was finally able to break John's fixation on the aquarium, she asked for an explanation. "Why, Miss T.," John replied, surprised that she needed to ask, "I'm the frog helicopter patrol directing fish traffic!"

This is an example of attention-deficit/hyperactivity disorder, known as AD/HD. Individuals with this disorder are unable to maintain attention because they attend to *everything*. Poor impulse control and a high activity level are other hallmark characteristics of AD/HD.

# What Is Attention-Deficit/Hyperactivity Disorder?

Attention-deficit/hyperactivity disorder is a neurological syndrome. This means that the wiring in the brain is somehow affected. Researchers still do not know exactly what occurs. They do know, however, that the synapses within the brain release inconsistent quantities of neurotransmitters. This interferes with the message reaching its destination.

In simpler terms, the brain is the body's control central. Messages from all over the body come into the brain. Acting as a switchboard, the brain sends the incoming messages to the appropriate section. From there, assistance is sent back to the place of origin. It is like a fire station. When the alarm is sounded, the communication center finds out where the fire is located and notifies the closest firehouse. The fire station receives the information and knows exactly where its assistance is needed.

In the brain, the communications are sent via nerve endings. At the end of each nerve is a small gap called a synapse. The purpose of the synapse is to produce the neurotransmitters, or chemicals, necessary to keep the message moving along within the brain. It is thought that within the brain of an individual with AD/HD the neurotransmitters are not consistently released. This fluctuation results in some messages getting lost. This may explain why people with AD/HD appear consistently inconsistent.

To complicate matters, researchers are now indicating that rarely, if ever, is AD/HD found in isolation. It is usually accompanied by at least one other disorder. The severity of the AD/HD depends on the number of other issues involved.

Specific learning disabilities are one comorbidity, or related disorder, of AD/HD. The current statistics indicate that between 50 and 90 percent of students with AD/HD also have a learning disability. Paying attention to detail, as one needs to do when solving math problems, is not easy for the impulsive child who rushes through the task. The vast bombardment of words on a page only adds to the confusion of a child who is already struggling to stay focused and attentive (see chapters 8 and 9).

Communication disorders also affect a large population of students with AD/HD. Their poor ability to process and express information often intensifies the symptoms of AD/HD. Poor pragmatic language skills further complicate the lives of those overactive and impulsive children, who cannot pay attention long enough to pick up the subtle nonverbal cues being sent by other children (see chapter 10).

Other neurobiological disorders related to AD/HD are Tourette syndrome, sensory integrative dysfunction, obsessive-compulsive disorder, oppositional defiant disorder, and conduct disorder. Depression, mood, and anxiety disorders, fetal alcohol syndrome, and prenatal exposure to crack are other comorbidities that can mimic the symptoms of AD/HD.

AD/HD is frequently referred to as the invisible disorder, because there are no visible signs of a disability. This can pose a major concern when educators and parents do not understand, or remember, the neurological involvement and erroneously believe the child "could do it if he only tried." The amount of effort these children exert to stay focused and control their impulsivity and high energy level is extreme. They do not want to constantly be in trouble or hear their name called every five minutes. They wear themselves out trying to fit in. This is why it is important that parents and teachers understand how the child manifests the disorder, so that they can distinguish between what the child can control and what he can't. (See the symptoms checklist on pages 206–207.)

The real tragedy of AD/HD is a loss of self-esteem and confidence. When the focus is only on what the person cannot do, it becomes a self-fulfilling prophecy. By remembering that AD/HD is an invisible disorder caused by the brain's different wiring, we can begin to focus on all the positive traits of the child and appreciate his uniqueness.

Individuals with AD/HD have average to above-average intelligence. They are creative, humorous, talented people with boundless energy. Their perspective on the world is unique. When we can appreciate their differences in a positive way, the benefits can be endless. Too often, test scores and grades become the primary measure of how successful a person will be in life. If they were truly reliable, we might still be reading by candlelight, because Thomas Edison was a school dropout. It was his mother's encouragement of his doodling and creative curiosity that kept him inventing and seeking answers to life's questions. We, too, must find ways to keep the curiosity and creativity of children with AD/HD directed toward positive outlets.

# The Causes of AD/HD

Research has substantiated that AD/HD is a neurobiological disorder. The frontal lobe appears to be the area most affected, but other areas may also be involved. The disorder seems to occur because of difficulty in the brain's regulation of the neurotransmitters dopamine, serotonin and norepinephrine.

Research shows that at least 30 percent of children with AD/HD have a parent with AD/HD. Often one or more siblings also demonstrate the characteristics of AD/HD. This would substantiate the theory that in the majority of cases, AD/HD is inherited.

In Nancy's family, this was the case. When she suspected that her son, Christian, might have AD/HD, she took him to a psychiatrist for an evaluation. The physician was more interested in evaluating Nancy's husband, David. Both father and son were diagnosed with AD/HD.

This interest in David's background was not unusual; a family history is a crucial part of the evaluation for AD/HD. More often than not, the disorder can be traced back through several generations. Johnny may be just like Dad and Uncle Mike, who are just like Grandpa.

An impressive amount of AD/HD research is being conducted with adults. This is strengthening the genetic theory. Adults are providing valuable insight into understanding the effects of AD/HD, because they are often better able to articulate their youth and school experiences.

Two amazing findings are surfacing from this research. First, just like Nancy's husband, more adults are being diagnosed with AD/HD as they bring in their children to be evaluated. With continued research, the conservative estimate that 30 percent of children with AD/HD have a parent with the disorder is expected to increase.

Second, an increasing percentage of adult females are being diagnosed with the disorder, resulting in a reexamination of the idea that AD/HD is a male-dominated disorder. Young females are being observed for the more subtle signs of AD/HD.

A conservative 6 to 10 percent of the school-age population has been identified with AD/HD. Of this population, the ratio of males to females is 6 to 1. In the adult population the ratio changes drastically to one male for every female diagnosed.

There are also environmental factors that may cause the symptoms of AD/HD to appear. Lead poisoning from air pollution or from peeling paint ingested by small children can cause neurological changes that result in the characteristics of AD/HD.

During World War I, many soldiers who sustained head injuries began to display characteristics of impulsiveness and inattention. Also during this time, an encephalitis epidemic occurred, and many survivors of this outbreak experienced similar problems, leading researchers to conclude that they had sustained "minimal brain damage." It was later discovered that these changes caused by external factors resulted not in brain damage but in "minimal brain dysfunction." Today, this is known as AD/HD. Head trauma, a brain-related illness such as encephalitis or spinal meningitis, a brain tumor, AIDS, or prenatal exposure to crack or alcohol can all result in the characteristics of attention deficit/hyperactivity disorder.

There is little research to substantiate the theory that factors such as food additives, sugar, poor diet, or ineffective parenting will cause AD/HD. In fact, the research is finding just the opposite to be true. Mark L. Wolraich, M.D., in his research at Vanderbilt University, published his findings stating that diets high in sugar do not appear to affect the learning or behavior patterns of children.

As Nancy found out firsthand, food additives do not cause AD/HD but can intensify the symptoms. She dreaded the beginning of every school year because Christian would literally "bounce off the walls." Nancy assumed he was having trouble adjusting to a new teacher and learning environment. The real cause was not discovered until Christian was in the fourth grade. The red dye used in the antihistamine that was prescribed for his late-summer allergies was causing his bizarre behavior. A change in medication alleviated the problem, but the AD/HD remained.

Many children with AD/HD have a wide range of allergies. Some are more sensitive to certain foods and additives. Reactions to these irritants may mimic some of the characteristics of AD/HD. When the source of the irritation is eliminated, the child's behavior may improve.

Living with a child who has AD/HD can be a challenge. This is especially true if the parents also have the disorder. Households can become chaotic free-for-alls. Even under the best of circumstances, parenting children with AD/HD can be exhausting and frustrating. Many parents feel guilty and responsible for their child's struggles.

It must be clearly stated that AD/HD *is never a result of poor parenting*. It is more a matter of not knowing how to manage the child. Parents need information and support! Education of the parents, siblings, extended family, teachers, and especially the child is very important. Once demystification has occurred, understanding can begin. With understanding comes patience and tolerance. In a positive atmosphere such as this, skill building can help the child learn to manage the AD/HD.

As a parent, you can find support and become better informed in several ways. Join local parent support groups. Work with the school. Become familiar with the laws that protect your child's rights. While working to help your child, do not forget to take the time to rejuvenate and refresh yourself.

# The Developmental Differences of the Child with AD/HD

Parents and teachers agree that one of the most frustrating aspects of AD/HD is that it constantly changes. Just when they think they have the disorder under control, things shift. The manifestations of AD/HD can change as the individual matures.

It is suspected that the central nervous system of the individual with AD/HD develops at a slower rate than those of other children the same age. The maturation level of young children with AD/HD can be two to three years behind that of their peers. Not until late adolescence is the central nervous system completely developed and the gap closed.

AD/HD is not outgrown, but because the presenting symptoms are replaced by other characteristics, it often appears that the disorder is no longer present. If AD/HD is not identified and addressed by about the seventh grade, the manifestations of the disorder often take on a new appearance. This transition in symptoms is outlined below.

1. **Infancy and early childhood.**

   More prenatal activity.

   Irritability, frequent crying.

   Many allergies to formula and food.

   Frequent tantrums.

   Overactivity.

   Attraction to climbing and dangerous situations.

   Frequent injuries.

   Short, irregular sleeping patterns.

   Delayed speech because of inattention.

2. **Childhood.**

   Inattention, hyperactivity, impulsivity (the three hallmark characteristics).

   Manageability in the early grades gives way to lessening academic struggles in the higher grades.

   High energy and activity levels.

3. **Adolescence.**

   If not addressed, the three hallmark characteristics are still present, but they begin to manifest themselves differently.

   Diminished hyperactivity but increased impulsivity.

   Lack of basic skills, which causes the student to fall behind in school.

Frequent frustration.

Experiences failure often.

Dropping out of school common.

Involvement in drugs and/or alcohol abuse.

Involvement with the judicial system.

Need for intervention and therapy to deal with feelings and issues.

Need for a place to excel and feel good about himself.

4. **Adulthood.**

Undiagnosed adults still have the underlying hallmark characteristics present in childhood.

High energy levels (e.g., may run, not walk, behind the lawn mower).

Frustration over difficulty of holding down a job.

Poor relationships with peers, spouses, and children.

Anger because they cannot get ahead in life.

Severe mood swings.

Low tolerance for stress.

Difficulty completing tasks.

Tendency to pile or stack things as a form of organization.

# How AD/HD Is Diagnosed

Thomas Brown, Ph.D., of Yale University refers to AD/HD as the "wide umbrella" disorder because it can encompass so many issues. Since no one demonstrates the disorder in the same way, a careful, expert diagnosis is strongly recommended to understand completely everything that is affecting the individual. Once the diagnosis has been completed, prioritization of the most interfering symptoms is required. Then a management plan can be developed and carried out by all the appropriate professionals needed to support the individual with AD/HD.

A medical evaluation for AD/HD should be conducted by a psychiatrist, clinical psychologist, neuropsychologist, or pediatrician specializing in the disorder. These are the professionals qualified to make the diagnosis. Blood tests, X rays, and other medical tests are not yet available to diagnose for AD/HD. The diagnosis is made on the basis of more subjective data.

Schools provide the evaluator with information needed in the diagnostic process. Teachers are often the first to suspect a child may have the disorder, but they are not qualified to make this diagnosis. They are often asked to complete checklists and write anecdotal reports on their observations of the child in the school setting.

Parents and often the child also complete checklists based on their observations in the home and school environments. These checklists, along with parent and child interviews, a family history, and prenatal and developmental data, supply the professional with valuable information. Assessing for other comorbidities is an important aspect of the evaluation. Once all the information is collected and assessed, the diagnosis is made. The criteria used to make the diagnosis are found in the *Diagnostic and Statistical Manual of Mental Disorders IV,* or *DSM IV.*

This criteria has undergone many changes in the past two decades. Before 1980, AD/HD was referred to as minimal brain dysfunction, or MBD. It was renamed attention deficit disorder and appeared as such for the first time in the *DSM III* in 1980. At that time, it was identified under three major symptoms: inattention, hyperactivity, and impulsivity. Any combination of these three symptoms could have resulted in the diagnosis.

In 1987, the *DSM IIIR* reclassified and renamed AD/HD. It became known as attention deficit/hyperactivity disorder, or AD/HD. The three categories no long existed. All of the symptoms were lumped into a list of fourteen characteristics. Confusion arose from the new title. Many teachers, parents, and professionals assumed that the child had to be hyperactive before she could be diagnosed AD/HD. This of course is not true. Hyperactivity is just one symptom of the disorder. The confusion was eased when the *DSM IV* was released in 1994. It has two separate classifications for the disorder. If the child is just inattentive, the diagnosis would be attention deficit/hyperactivity disorder, predominantly inattentive type. If hyperactivity and/or impulsivity is the diagnosis, then the diagnosis would be attention-deficit/hyperactivity disorder, predominantly hyperactive/impulsive type. If a child demonstrates all three characteristics, the diagnosis would be attention-deficit/hyperactivity disorder, combined type.

# Observable Traits of AD/HD

Some of the signs that AD/HD may be present are categorized under the three hallmark characteristics.

1. **Inattention.**

    Lack of attention to detail.

    Careless mistakes.

    Difficulty sustaining attention in play or in tasks.

    Difficulty listening when spoken to.

    Failure to complete tasks.

    Difficulty organizing tasks and activities.

    Avoidance of dull, repetitive tasks or tasks requiring sustained mental effort, such as homework.

    Tendency to lose things.

    Distracted by external stimuli or own thoughts.

    Forgetfulness.

    Inattention; thoughts that flit about like a butterfly; flights of imagination.

2. **Hyperactivity.**

    Fidgety hands and feet.

    Squirming in seat.

    Tendency to leave seat often.

    Preference for standing over sitting.

    Running about or climbing excessively and at inappropriate times.

Playing or engaging in leisure activities difficult.

Always on the go as if driven by a motor.

Excessive talking.

Boundless energy.

3. **Impulsivity.**

Blurting out answers before questions are completed.

Beginning a task before it has been fully explained.

Difficulty waiting one's turn.

Interrupting.

Leaping before looking.

Frequent apologies and expressions of remorse.

Failure to learn from mistakes.

# The Three Hallmark Characteristics of AD/HD

## Inattention—The Butterflies

Many people assume that a child with AD/HD has a problem paying attention. This assumption makes little sense when the child is sitting in front of a video game so engrossed that he is not aware of anything else going on around him. Another contradiction is the child who cannot pull away from a project that she is thoroughly enjoying. The issue is not that the child cannot pay attention. It is that the child cannot *selectively* attend. The child gives equal importance to everything. Constantly in search of the new and exciting, the child flits from one thing to another like a butterfly going from flower to flower. She pays attention to everything!

There are two types of inattentive children. One is the student who is distracted by everything going on around him. He is unable to select the teacher as his object of focus and filter out all the other stimuli.

The second type is the child who is distracted by her own thoughts. She gets lost in the wonderful mind journeys within her head. This free-flighting of ideas is usually sparked by something that is said, and one idea links to another and another until minutes have passed without the child's realizing it. For example, Holly's math class is discussing money and making change. They are going to set up a classroom grocery store. This triggers Holly's thoughts about her trip to the grocery with her mom. They saw Mrs. Jones. Mrs. Jones has a pretty cat. Once there was a lost cat on the playground. The playground! With whom will she play at recess? Recess! Boy am I hungry! When is lunch? While these thoughts have been commanding Holly's attention, the class has moved from math to a science lesson. Once again, Holly is lost in space and drawing negative attention to herself as she flounders to catch up with the class.

Children with AD/HD, predominantly inattentive type, may experience either way, or both, of distracting themselves. More often than not, females tend to be distracted by their thoughts. This is one reason why their diagnosis may be delayed. They quietly sit, lost in their own thoughts, not disturbing anyone or drawing attention to themselves.

A malfunctioning in the reticular activating system in the brain is thought to cause this inability to maintain selective attention. This is the brain's filtering center. It is responsible for deciding where the focus is directed and what is not important. It acts as a camera lens, in that it focuses on what the subject of the picture will be and crops out the surroundings. If you attend a concert, your focus is on the performers. Someone sitting near you may sneeze or drop his program. While you are aware of this, you would not necessarily divert your attention to that person. This is an example of your reticular activating system at work.

This type of inattention often angers adults, who think the child is ignoring them. This is not usually the case. The child just gets distracted and either forgets what she is doing or gets lost in the process. On the way to emptying the trash, she sees a basketball in the driveway and stops to shoot hoops. Unfortunately, the garbage bag is still sitting in the driveway the next morning.

The same issue can cause social problems for the child, whose flitting from one thing to another may confuse and frustrate peers. This results in the child with AD/HD being socially isolated by peers who think he is a "space cadet."

Students with AD/HD may also appear to have a language processing problem. In fact, both disorders may be present. A complete evaluation by professionals is the only way to reach an accurate diagnosis.

**Management strategies for inattention.** There are ways that teachers and parents can help the child having difficulty with maintaining attention develop skills to compensate. Discreetly helping the child become aware of the times his attention is drifting is important. Once he is aware, having the tools he needs to help him maintain his focus is then necessary.

Study the suggestions listed below and select those that are most comfortable for the child. Introduce only one at a time so as not to overwhelm. Be consistent and patient in its implementation. It may take days, months, or even years to develop the skill. Add skills as old ones become internalized.

1. Get the child's eye contact.
   - Use other people as a model: e.g., "I see Mary's eyes."
   - Use whole-group directives: "Eyes up here." "I don't see everyone's eyes."
2. Use secret signals. Ask the child what secret signal the two of you could share.
   - A tap on the shoulder.
   - Standing next to the child.
   - Pointing to your nose or a tug on your ear.
   - A nonsense or silly word. One family came up with the word, "Pickles!" They found a bonus in that the word often broke the tension with humor.
3. Make lists to help the child remain focused. If you need to say it, write it! This gives the child a point of reference.
   - List chores to be completed.
   - List schedules for meals, extracurricular activities, homework.
   - List steps in a routine. For example, what needs to be done each morning before school?
   - Teachers can write the daily schedule on the blackboard or a personal schedule for the child's desk.

4. Eliminate distractions.
   - High noise levels can be distracting. Some children need complete silence. Others get distracted by the silence and need some background noise. Help your child find the best learning environment.
   - Keep the workplace clear. In school, on the desktop should be only what the child needs for the lesson. At home, only the materials needed to complete a task should be visible.
   - Cover sheets, bookmarks, three fingers scanning the page, folding back the book so that only one page is seen at a time, folding up the bottom of the page to expose only one line at a time, and "windows" cut from construction paper are ways to hold one's place and reduce the bombardment of information.

5. Get the child organized (see chapter 25).
   - Color-code books, notebooks, folders.
   - Use a daily planner to keep track of activities and events.
   - Use a plan book for assignments.
   - Long-term assignments can be broken down into smaller assignments and written in the blocks of a large desk calendar.
   - Provide drawers, shelves, or hooks for storing belongings.
   - Locker organizers separate materials for morning subjects from those for afternoon subjects.

6. Provide a working environment with limited distractions.
   - Bedrooms are not ideal places to do homework, presenting too many opportunities for distraction. A place out of the mainstream that can be monitored is a better choice.
   - Study carrels or an "office" in the classroom or at home may be helpful.
   - In the workplace, use baskets, tubs, or other containers to hold all the supplies the child may need to complete his assignments. This reduces the need to get up and wander around.
   - Earplugs may be helpful.

7. Timers may help the child focus on a task. When you set the timer, give instructions such as "You have ten minutes to get dressed and down for breakfast. I'm setting the timer."

8. Break tasks into manageable parts. Getting easily overwhelmed and not knowing where to begin are characteristics of children with AD/HD. Help them see the smaller parts of the whole. This will make the task seem possible. Seeing only one or two problems instead of twenty is much less intimidating.

## Hyperactivity—Even Without Batteries, They Keep Going!

Children with hyperactivity have a difficult time sitting still, require little sleep, are curious and forever seeking adventure, and must be monitored constantly for their own protection. These children often seem out of control. Many distraught parents are told that a swat on the behind will cure the child's ills. This of course does not help.

This constant need to move is beyond the control of the child. Hyperactivity is the body's inability to regulate the need to move. These high-energy children appear to be stuck in high gear all the time. They cannot sit in a chair, walk down the hall, wait quietly in line, or keep their hands to themselves. *Run*, *skip*, *hop*, and *climb* are terms they are more likely to understand. They are rockers, chewers, and nonstop talkers.

Movement is the way they process information. Children with hyperactivity *must* be allowed to move in order to learn. Chewing on a pencil may be a strategy the child uses to keep her body in the chair while thinking of what to write in her journal.

The active child who is sitting quietly in his chair may be pleasing his teacher, but he is not learning. The child is probably trying so hard to keep still, so the teacher will not get upset, that he hears nothing being said. For example, Brian had promised his mother before leaving for school that he would not get into trouble. To Brian, this means no fidgeting in his desk. At school, Brian begins to reach inside his desk for something. Immediately, he remembers his promise to his mom. He thinks, "I will not roll pencils in my desk. This makes Mrs. K. angry, and I get into trouble. I will sit on my hands to keep them still. I need to move. I know, I'll go to the bathroom." Brian gets up, leaves the room, and misses more of the explanation Mrs. K. is giving.

As the child reaches adolescence and his central nervous system matures, he is likely to become less hyperactive but developmentally more impulsive. Studies indicate that adults who were probably hyperactive as children retain high levels of activity. When they are able to direct this energy, what they can accomplish is remarkable.

**Management strategies for hyperactivity.** Children with hyperactivity often end up in a position of control within the family. How this happens is unclear. One possible explanation is that the parents, who are overwhelmed and stressed, find it easier to give in than to battle with the child. This can create a dangerous situation for everyone involved.

For the child in control, it can be very frightening. Children expect adults to make the decisions and set limits. When they don't, the child may feel burdened with the responsibility of doing the parent's job. This is too much to ask of any child at any age. Rules and boundaries must be established and consequences must be put in place and exercised. Sometimes the natural consequences are sufficient, and sometimes the results of certain actions must be spelled out. Avoid making threats you do not intend to carry out, because the child will test the limits.

For younger children, "time out" chairs where self-control can be restored may be one consequence. Older children may benefit from contracts outlining expectations and consequences. Having family meetings and a few house rules with which the whole family complies are other ways to keep peace and harmony while providing an open forum for opinions and feelings.

Suggestions to help the child harness and direct some of his energy are given below. Building skills early will help your child feel more comfortable as he enters school and the social environment.

1. Establish a compromise.
   - Recognize the child's need to move.
   - Set the parameters in which the child can appropriately expel the energy, e.g., "Running in the house is dangerous. If you need to run, you may go out in the backyard."

2. Use a secret signal to cue the child that she is losing control.

3. Provide a safe place for the child to regain control.
   - A quiet corner with a rocking chair or pillows.
   - Under a table or desk. (Young children feel safe in these places.)
   - A time-out chair—a designated chair where the child may sit to calm down and regain control.
   - A "safe place"—a private place that is supervised away from the eyes of others. At school, the health room or counselor's office may be an ideal location.

4. Allow the child to discreetly manipulate an object to channel the energy.

5. Allow frequent breaks so that the child can get up and move around.
   - During homework time, allow a few minutes between tasks to get a snack or go outside.
   - At a fast-food restaurant, ask the child to get a napkin or straw or throw away the containers.
   - Between subjects, allow the child to turn in papers, run an errand, get a book.

6. Give the child a job to do.
   - Order the meal at a restaurant or pay the check.
   - Get the can of coffee in the grocery while you get the bread.
   - Erase the blackboard while the teacher prepares for the next lesson.

7. Provide a space in which the child can move. Children with hyperactivity tend to spread out into the territory of others without realizing it.
   - Tape off a space on the floor so that the child can see the boundary.
   - Sit the child on the end of the row.
   - Sit the child next to an empty desk.

- Most children with AD/HD should not sit in the back of the classroom. However, for some, the last row is an ideal place to spread out without disturbing anyone. The teacher should closely monitor the child, however.

8. Allow the child to stand or kneel to eat or do work if this is a more comfortable position.

9. Involve the child in sports and activities that allow her to use her energy in positive and beneficial ways. Individual sports, such as swimming, gymnastics, ballet, biking, or Tae Kwon Do may be more successful than team sports, where waiting a turn can be frustrating.

10. Retain control.

    - Give choices to eliminate power struggles. Adults never win, so they need to avoid power struggles. Tell the child he may either do one thing or another, for instance, "Your curfew is eleven o'clock. You may either go out with your friends until eleven o'clock or stay home. You choose."

    - Choices also narrow the selections. Children with too many options get overwhelmed. They can choose between two items but not six. "You may wear either your blue shirt or your red" may be easier to deal with than "Go put on a clean shirt."

    - Select and post house rules. Just a few will maintain family harmony.

    - Clearly state the consequences of undesirable actions. Do not threaten. Say what you mean. The child's job is to test and challenge you to see if you mean what you say. Your job is to remain consistent and firm. Remember: Children want *you* to be in charge! They want boundaries and limits.

    - Contracting with older children is very effective. Clearly state the expectations and the contingencies. Everyone, including the child, signs the contract.

## Impulsivity—"Did I Do That?"

The world of children with AD/HD, predominantly hyperactive/impulsive type, moves so quickly that they are usually unaware of their actions. Like Steve Erkel on the television sitcom *Family Matters*, they are always asking, "Did I do that?"

These are not children with a defect in their moral character. They do know the difference between right and wrong. They just do not stop long enough to think through the consequences of their actions, i.e., "If I do that, then this will occur. Are these the results I want?"

Because they do not stop to consider the consequences, they often offend and hurt the feelings of those around them. They are not mean, vindictive children. They just speak or respond before they think. Impulsive children find themselves constantly apologizing and are truly sorry for the pain they have caused. Unfortunately, they do not learn quickly from their mistakes. They will turn around and do the same thing again. This does not endear them to family, peers, or teachers.

**Management strategies for impulsivity.** Impulsive children need to learn to stop and think before they act. They need to develop skills to slow down their world so they can think things through and make good choices. Developing a sense of awareness that they are out of control helps reduce some of the impulsivity.

1. Give secret signals or use visual reminders to help the child stop and think before he acts. The STAR technique is effective. The initials can stand for "stop, think, act responsibly" or "stop, think, and respond." The child can learn to stop and think about his behavior whenever he is signaled with a star symbol.

2. Help the child develop skills by asking if-then questions: "If I do this, then what will result? Is this the result I want?"

3. Analyze situations that produce negative results. Ask questions to help the child find solutions.

"What do you think happened?"

"How do you think that made the other person feel?"

"If someone said that to you, how would you feel?"

"What could you have done? What would have been a better choice?"

4. Role-play with the child. Suggest alternative ways of handling a situation.

5. Use a timer to slow down the child. If he races through his math in ten minutes, making careless errors, set the timer to twenty minutes. Urge him to use the extra time to check his work for errors.

6. Maintain a consistent schedule as much as possible. Transitions and change can be difficult. Whenever possible, prepare the child for change.

7. Urge the child to mark key words in written directions. Have him highlight, circle, or underline the words that give clues to what is being asked. For multistep directions, have him number each step or highlight it with a different color. This helps the child to remember to do all the steps.

8. Pick your battles. Try to keep focused on the issues that are really important or relate to your child's safety. Allow your child to make mistakes and learn from them. This can be frightening for the parent. Ask yourself, "What is the worst that can happen if I do not get involved?" may help you decide where to step in. Hair, clothes, and personal hygiene are areas where other people may solve your concern. Drugs, speeding, delinquency, risk taking, and abusive behavior need to be addressed.

9. The world of impulsive children moves so quickly that they may occasionally benefit from a quiet place to calm down and regain control. A think-about-it chair may help. This is a designated chair where the out-of-control child can go, think about his behavior, consider the results, and decide what should be done next.

# Is AD/HD an Excuse for Misbehavior?

It would appear that the topic of AD/HD comes up frequently in conversation. Many teachers think that a disproportionate population of their students have the disorder. News programs blast teachers for demanding that parents get their child the "magic pill" so they can get on with the business of teaching. Then newscasters turn around and make parents feel guilty about "drugging" their child. With all the publicity given this topic, anyone who has ever had trouble concentrating might begin to wonder if he has AD/HD.

The *Diagnostic and Statistical Manual of Mental Disorders, 4th ed. (DSM IV)* lists the criteria for the diagnosis of AD/HD. It is very explicit as to when AD/HD may be present. The manual is very clear that the symptoms of AD/HD must be present in at least two other settings and *interfere with a life function*. These are the key factors that distinguish the disorder from the occasional lapses in attention we all experience.

All of us go through periods when we cannot hold thoughts or seem agitated or impulsive. Often the cause is stress. How many of you feel the stress of the holidays begin to creep in when you see Christmas trees before Halloween? By mid-December, you may feel panicked, tired, and irritable from all the pressure. You may find yourself forgetting whose present you just wrapped because you are thinking of the batch of cookies you burned while trying to find the wrapping paper. By January, however, you are back to your old self.

Individuals with AD/HD live each day at the hectic pace some of us experience from time to time. With AD/HD, this feeling of lack of control does not go away. It is a lifelong experience that interferes with the person's ability to complete a homework assignment or a business contract. It has children wandering aimlessly around the soccer field or adults roaming the grocery store. It is something that only intensifies with age if it is not diagnosed early and managed consistently.

Is the term AD/HD simply an easy excuse for misbehavior? We do not think so. The explanation we can offer for the publicity this disorder is receiving is twofold. First, extensive research is being conducted in this field. Grants and funding are available to continue the search for new information. Research centers have been established across the country for the purpose of finding out more about this disorder. One result of this research is that a large number of adults are being diagnosed with the disorder, especially females. Many researchers are publishing their findings, and AD/HD is receiving a lot of exposure.

Second, education has changed. One could conclude that if AD/HD is not outgrown and a large population of adults are getting diagnosed, then they must have had AD/HD as children. Why was this not a learning issue for them?

For many, it *was* a learning issue. Nancy's husband, David, struggled in school. He knew he was smart and could not understand why school was so difficult for him. Like many individuals with AD/HD, once he got into college and found a career path that used his skills, he excelled. As an adult, he is very successful.

More than ever, the educational system today is not set up to meet the needs of the majority of students. Individual differences are not understood and respected. Everyone is expected to master all subject areas. Proficiency tests are given to make sure this occurs. Those students who cannot pass a particular test often have their lives changed. One test has the power to invalidate four years of accomplishments. One test can determine if a student's daily efforts over four years are rewarded with a diploma.

Students today are attempting to function in a world where everyone is expected to learn and perform in the same way. This lack of tolerance for individual differences is one reason why many students struggle to find their place in today's classrooms and why those with AD/HD do not seem to fit in.

# Look for the Positive

Children caught in this struggle can quickly relate all the negative aspects of their lives. Rarely do they realize that they have positive qualities. As adults, we need to make an effort to balance the negative with the positive. At times, we may need to scrutinize the situation to come up with something positive about a child. Suggested ways of boosting the child's self-worth can be found at the end of chapter 24.

It is important to let the child know that your love is unconditional. These children are beautiful, talented creations that bring humor and sparkle to your life. We all need to receive strokes on a regular basis. Our children are no exception!

# Points to Ponder

1. The three hallmark characteristics of AD/HD are inattention, hyperactivity, and impulsivity.

2. A qualified medical diagnosis is recommended to evaluate for AD/HD and any related disorders.

3. Information from the school is an important part of the evaluation process, but school personnel should not diagnose AD/HD.

4. Ineffective parenting skills are *not* a cause of AD/HD.

5. Your child's rights are protected under Section 504 of the Rehabilitation Act of 1973 and Americans with Disabilities Act (ADA).

6. AD/HD is not outgrown, but the way it is manifested can change as the individual ages.

7. Females can effectively mask the symptoms of AD/HD and as a result often do not get diagnosed until adulthood. Do you know a young female who takes mind journeys, appears spacey, or whose grades do not reflect her efforts?

8. All children need limits and boundaries. Does your fatigue and frustration often result in giving in to your child?

9. Children with AD/HD often receive more negative feedback than positive. Find ways to emphasize the positive qualities and actions the child demonstrates.

Additional resources and information can be obtained from the following agencies and organizations:

- Attention Deficit Disorders Association, P.O. Box 488, West Newbury, MA 01985 (800) 487-2282.
- Children with Attention Deficit Disorders, 499 NW Seventieth Avenue, Suite 308, Plantation, FL 33317 (305) 587-3700.

# 12

# Tourette Syndrome

The first thing many people think of when they hear the mention of Tourette syndrome (TS) is the profusion of profanities associated with the disorder. This is an extreme characteristic affecting less than 15 percent of those diagnosed with the disorder. Most individuals diagnosed with Tourette syndrome demonstrate much milder symptoms.

## How Tourette Syndrome Is Defined

The earliest documentation of this syndrome, characterized by involuntary motor and vocal tics, was in 1825. In medical literature, a French physician, J.M.G. Itard, described the lifelong struggle of a woman with what today would be diagnosed as Tourette syndrome. Sixty years later, a French neurologist, Georges Gilles de la Tourette, M.D., became very interested in Itard's account of Madame de D. Some of his patients manifested similar symptoms to those described in the literature. The result of Tourette's work was his identification of a hereditary disorder with multiple features that today bears his name.

Tourette syndrome is defined as a neurological disorder characterized by involuntary movements (motor tics) and vocalizations (vocal tics). There can also be mental tics. These movements usually begin to appear around the age of seven. However, for some they may appear earlier and for others later.

Motor tics usually occur first. Blinking is the most commonly occurring tic at the onset of Tourette syndrome. Involuntary sounds, such as throat clearing and grunting, can also be early indicators of TS. The tics will often wax and wane. Old symptoms may disappear and new ones replace them, or a new tic may be added to the existing symptoms.

This waxing and waning may cause some people to believe that the individuals with TS can control their tics. This is not true. A child does not make the noises or gestures to annoy others or disrupt a classroom. This is a very important fact to remember. Children with TS are average to high intelligence and eager to learn. It has been documented that stress can affect the severity of the tics. Patience, understanding, and alleviating undo pressure will help minimize their severity by reducing stress.

It is estimated that one person in every 2,500 may be affected with Tourette syndrome. Some studies indicate that in males, the statistics may be as high as one in 1,000.

Tourette syndrome is often accompanied by other conditions. At least 50 percent of individuals with TS demonstrate obsessive-compulsive behaviors. About 60 percent of TS diagnoses are accompanied by a diagnosis of AD/HD. An estimated 60 percent of children with Tourette syndrome may also have a learning disability. Impulsive behaviors are an issue for 25 to 35 percent of individuals with TS. Sensory integration problems and sleep disorders can also accompany this syndrome. The severity and complexity of TS often depend upon the combination of these comorbidities.

## Other Tic Disorders That Are Not Tourette Syndrome

Vocal and motor tics are not always a sign of TS. Below are a few other types of tic disorders.

1. **Chronic motor tic disorder.** Only motor tics are demonstrated.

2. **Chronic vocal tic disorder.** Only vocal tics are demonstrated.

3. **Transient tic disorder.** May present one or more motor tics *and* one or more vocal tics. The condition lasts fewer than twelve consecutive months.

4. **Tic disorder not otherwise specified.** All other types of motor and vocal tics occurring *after* the age of eighteen. These often appear to be milder forms of TS.

# The Causes of Tourette Syndrome

Extensive research is being conducted to determine the exact cause of Tourette syndrome. What's clear so far is that TS is an inherited neurological disorder that is not outgrown. It is believed to occur because of the abnormal metabolism of the neurotransmitter dopamine. Other brain chemicals, such as serotonin, may also play a role in Tourette syndrome.

It is believed that the TS gene, or genes, is passed on to the child by either parent. If one parent has the disorder or is a TS gene carrier, each offspring has a 50 percent chance of inheriting the gene. Each child may develop TS, have a tic disorder, develop obsessive-compulsive symptoms, or have no effects at all.

Among children with the TS gene, males tend to develop TS symptoms three times as often as females. About 30 percent of females who inherit the TS gene show no symptoms of the disorder. This is true of about only 1 percent of the males with the gene. Of those who inherit the gene, only about 10 percent will ever have symptoms severe enough to require medical intervention.

In rare cases, brain damage caused by a virus, head trauma, or lack of oxygen at birth may result in the disorder.

# The Age of Onset of Tourette Syndrome

In rare cases, tics may begin in the first year of life or past the age of eighteen. According to the *DSM IV,* onset must occur before the age of eighteen for a diagnosis of TS. However, manifestations of the disorder become less likely as the child gets older. Research indicates that as individuals with TS mature, the symptoms lessen. By adulthood, as many as one-third experience a significant reduction of their tic symptoms.

According to the research provided by David Comings, M.D., in his book *Tourette Syndrome and Human Behavior,* the following patterns may be more in line with the norm for the onset of the tics.

- Twenty percent of the children experience the onset before kindergarten.

- Sixty-five percent experience onset between the ages of five and nine.

- For 15 percent, the onset is between the ages of ten and fifteen.

# How Tourette Syndrome Is Diagnosed

Early diagnosis of TS can help the child avoid years of discomfort. Before an individual can be diagnosed with TS, multiple motor *and* vocal tics must be exhibited. Motor and vocal tics are classified as either simple or complex. Simple motor tics include blinking and lip licking. Facial gestures, touching, and smelling things are more complex motor tics. Simple vocal tics include throat clearing, sniffing, and grunting. Animal sounds and the repetition of words or phrases are complex vocal tics.

Tourette syndrome requires a medical diagnosis. Neurologists, neuropsychologists, psychiatrists, clinical psychologists, and pediatricians are most qualified to make the diagnosis. The *DSM IV* outlines the criteria that distinguish TS from other tic disorders.

There are no X rays, blood tests, or other medical tests to identify TS. At this writing, the Tourette Syndrome Association is sponsoring an international consortium with the purpose of conducting extensive genetic research in this field. Researchers in nine centers located in five countries will be participating in this effort to locate the genetic underpinnings of the disorder. Perhaps this collaboration will result in something as simple as a blood test to give conclusive answers and result in earlier identification of Tourette syndrome.

At this time, extensive family histories, developmental histories, information from the school, and observation of the symptoms are the sources of data used in making the diagnosis. Sometimes a CAT scan, MRI, or EEG may be requested to rule out any conditions that may mimic the symptoms of TS. Because of the complexity of this disorder, a thorough evaluation is required to tease out all the factors involved before a diagnosis is made.

# Observable Traits of Tourette Syndrome

The waxing and waning of TS symptoms sometimes delays a medical referral. Parents and teachers should be aware of the criteria for diagnosing Tourette syndrome. Even though both vocal and motor tics must be present for the diagnosis, other tic disorders may be present and also should be addressed by a physician. Before a diagnosis of Tourette syndrome can be made, the following conditions must be met.

1.  Both multiple motor and vocal tics must be present but not necessarily appear together.

2.  The tics must occur many times a day, nearly everyday, or intermittently for more than a year, during which there is never a tic-free period of more than three consecutive months.

3.  The disturbance causes marked distress or significant impairment in social, occupational, learning, or other important areas of functioning.

4.  The disturbance is not due to drug or alcohol use or conditions of the central nervous system, such as Parkinson's disease.

5.  The onset of tics occurs before the age of eighteen.

# Strategies to Support the Child with Tourette Syndrome

Once the diagnosis has been made, a team consisting of the parents, school personnel, the evaluator, and any other professionals working with the child needs to meet to prepare a management plan. This plan will be used to support the student and create a successful learning experience. Some of the strategies suggested below may be considered in the development of the management plan.

1.  Depending on the severity of the tics and other related symptoms, medication may be recommended. The physician and parents need to make this decision together. If medication is prescribed, the school needs to be informed. (See chapter 26 for questions teachers need to ask when a student is placed on medication.) Note: As with any learning difference, medication is just one part of the management package. A multimodal, multidisciplinary approach is needed, one that combines the efforts of everyone working with the child.

2.  Children with sensory integration problems may require an occupational therapist.

3.  Know the child's rights. Students with an identified learning disability accompanying the TS qualify under IDEA and should have an IEP to address the learning disability. Under Section 504 of the Rehabilitation Act of 1973, children with TS are protected from discrimination. Classroom accommodations should be available when the disorder interferes with the child's ability to learn.

4.  Parents can be of great support to themselves, their child, the teachers, and any personnel working with their child by becoming informed about the disorder. The bibliography in the back of this book is a good place to start. Local chapters of the Tourette Syndrome Association may also offer information and support. As parents learn more, they can share information with the school and their child.

5.  Stress intensifies the tics. At school, minimize stress by allowing the child to take tests out of class, without time limits.

6.  Many children are self-conscious about their tics and struggle to suppress them. Give the child frequent breaks to release the tics

(run an errand, get a drink). The child may be more comfortable releasing the tics in a private place, such as the health room, a resource room, or the psychologist's or counselor's office. Help the child monitor his own need to leave the classroom. This voluntary time-out will help him learn to remove himself from stressful situations that may produce inappropriate behaviors or increase the tics.

7. Help educate other classmates about TS. Books, a representative from the TS Association as a guest speaker, an Everybody Counts program, or the school nurse or psychologist may be helpful resources. Informed classmates can alleviate much of the social stress felt by children with TS.

8. Help the child come up with ways to handle socially offensive tics. For example, the child who spits involuntarily may need to carry a tissue at all times.

9. Because many children with TS have poor handwriting, a scribe or a word processor may be helpful. (See chapter 10 for more suggestions on easing the stress of handwriting.)

10. Allow students to leave the classroom a few minutes before the bell rings to avoid crowded hallways during the changing of classes.

11. Tic symptoms may worsen at the end of the day. Whenever possible, try not to schedule academic-intensive courses at the end of the day. Older students may want to try to plan their schedules accordingly.

12. Have the child sit up front on the school bus to alleviate stress. Educate the driver about the child's condition.

13. Give positive feedback often. Remember that the tics are beyond the control of the child. This behavior is not done to annoy or disrupt the family or the classroom. The more the child tries to suppress something his body is doing naturally, the more stress will occur. The more stress, the more intense the tics. This becomes a vicious cycle.

# Points to Ponder

1. Tourette syndrome is an involuntary action that involves both motor and vocal tics.

2. Not every tic is a sign of TS.

3. Stress may increase the number and intensity of the tics.

4. The waxing and waning of tics may give the appearance that the child has control over his actions. This is not true!

5. TS is primarily inherited and affects more males than females.

6. Other disorders may accompany TS. Obsessive-compulsive disorder, AD/HD, oppositional defiant disorder, and learning disabilities are common comorbidities.

7. Learners with TS are protected under IDEA and Section 504 of the Rehabilitation Act of 1973.

8. A multimodal, multisensory management plan, of which medication may be a part, is needed to support the learner with TS.

For additional resources and information, contact: Tourette Syndrome Association, 42-40 Bell Boulevard, Bayside, NY 11361-2874 (718) 224-2999. The e-mail address is tourette@ix.netcom.com and the World Wide Web site is <http://neuro-www2.mgh.harvard.edu/tsa/tasmain.nclk>.

# 13

# Obsessive Compulsive Disorder–Rituals and Obsessions

Matthew sat at his table in the kindergarten class meticulously coloring on his paper. Over and over again he colored in the same spot. A task that should have taken less than ten minutes was nearing thirty minutes for Matt. As the teacher gently urged him to leave the task and join the rest of the class for a story, he became quite agitated. In frustration, the teacher left him to his work. When, by the end of the morning, he was still coloring the same paper, the teacher had to take it away and prepare him for his ride home. At this point, Matthew threw a tantrum and was still screaming when his mother arrived at the door.

By the time Matthew reached second grade, things had gotten worse. With a need to make every letter perfect, he erased the same letter over and over again. Often frustrated that the quality of work still did not meet his standards, he would begin to cry. By the end of the morning, Matthew, striving for perfection, often had not completed any of the morning tasks. No amount of urging from the teacher could get him to move along and get his work finished. She was confused because the work he did manage to complete was flawless. She did not understand for what he was striving.

When Matthew was in kindergarten, his parents consulted a physician about his need for perfection. They were concerned that need to have everything perfect was interfering with his ability to relax and enjoy being a child. At that time, Matthew was diagnosed with AD/HD and monitored for obsessive-compulsive disorder. The physician wanted to observe whether the AD/HD might be causing Matthew's perfectionism. By the end of second grade, as rituals began to appear, clear indicators resulted in his being diagnosed with obsessive-compulsive disorder, or OCD.

# How Obsessive-Compulsive Disorder Is Defined

In his book *Compulsive Behavior,* psychologist Richard Sebastian, M.A., defines OCD as "a psychological disorder typically marked by uncontrollable, repeated thoughts and recurrent, 'driven' patterns of ritual-like behavior." Judith L. Rapoport, M.D., a leading researcher in this field, refers to OCD in her book *The Boy Who Couldn't Stop Washing* as the doubting disease. She states that individuals with the disorder do not trust their senses. They do not seem to "know" the things that most of us take for granted. Rapoport states that being asked questions such as "Is the grass really green?" or "Are my eyes blue?" continues to amaze her.

Actions that many of us take for granted, like locking the door and turning off lights, individuals with obsessions and compulsions need to constantly check and recheck. Children with OCD do not realize that their thoughts and behaviors are senseless and unrealistic. They often feel guilty or ashamed. Adults with OCD are the first to admit their behavior is irrational, but this realization does not allow them to stop. They continue to second-guess their decisions and never consider their accomplishments good enough.

The involuntary behavior of OCD is embarrassing and uncomfortable for those who suffer from the disorder. They do not want to behave as they do, yet they have an internal need to fill. Telling a child with OCD to stop is like trying to stop a car without brakes that is speeding down a hill. It cannot be done!

Because of the embarrassment caused by their compulsions and obsessions, many children affected with OCD go into hiding. Their feelings of guilt, shame, or fear result in ingenious ways to mask the symptoms. In Rapoport's book, she shares some of the astounding strategies her clients have used to hide their OCD.

Because so many become experts at covering their disorder, the number of individuals affected is unclear. Studies conducted by the National Institutes of Mental Health (NIMH) indicate that approximately 3 percent of the U.S. population—that is, about five million Americans, have OCD. Of that number, an estimated one million young people are affected. These figures are probably very conservative. According to Rapoport, the majority of her OCD patients are not only successful in their everyday lives but amazingly resourceful at hiding their disorder.

## Types of OCD

OCD can range from very mild to very severe. Some people have only persistent, unwanted thoughts called obsessions, others perform only compulsions or rituals, and some have both. Like the tics associated with Tourette syndrome, the obsessions and compulsions of OCD can wax and wane.

OCD can be manifested in several ways. The symptoms of episodic OCD recur for limited periods of time. This type does not cause much interference in daily functioning and usually does not need to be addressed medically. Continuous OCD produces severe episodes during stressful times and often interferes with the individual's functioning outside the home. The individual may benefit from medical intervention. The third form is deteriorative OCD. This is quite serious, in that the symptoms become so severe that the individual cannot function. The performing of rituals consumes all of the person's time. He could spend an entire day straightening a drawer or cabinet.

# The Causes of OCD

OCD is thought to occur because of a chemical imbalance within the brain. Brain scans provided by positron emission tomography (PET scans) reveal that the basal ganglia area is most affected in OCD. The neurotransmitter serotonin appears to be involved. PET scans indicate that a deficiency in serotonin may result in the obsessions and compulsions of OCD. Researchers agree that serotonin is the major neurotransmitter involved but suspect that others may also play a part in the onset of OCD. Being a neurological disorder, it is not outgrown.

Because of its neurological aspect, OCD is considered a genetic disorder. Studies reveal that 20 percent of individuals with OCD have a relative with the disorder. Children of a parent with OCD have a 25 percent chance of inheriting the disorder. It has been documented that in some families, four or more generations have been affected, though all may have displayed the traits differently.

There are several related, or comorbid, disorders. Tourette syndrome is closely related to OCD. The same part of the brain is involved in both disorders. More than 50 percent of all individuals with Tourette syndrome also have the characteristics of OCD. Likewise, many people with OCD manifest tics. Tourette syndrome and OCD tend to run in the same families.

Epilepsy, Sydenham's chorea, severe nail biting, and trichotillomania are also related to OCD. Sydenham's chorea causes involuntary rapid, jerky movements, primarily of the arms and legs. About one third of individuals with this disorder also have OCD.

Trichotillomania is the need to pull out one's hair, whether on the head or elsewhere on the body. Many researchers believe this to be a subtype of OCD. It often begins around the age of twelve or thirteen, resulting from a stressful event in the life of the affected person. This condition runs in the families of persons with OCD, and many of the affected individuals have OCD symptoms. The National Institutes of Mental Health estimates that between four and eight million people suffer from this condition. Ninety percent of them are females.

Individuals with OCD may also have AD/HD and learning disabilities. Because of the propensity of these related disorders, a careful, expert evaluation of the individual is crucial, especially if medication is indicated. Some medications, like Ritalin, can exacerbate OCD.

# The Developmental Differences of the Child with OCD

About half of all people with OCD experience the symptoms in childhood. Among children, twice as many boys as girls demonstrate the characteristics of OCD. For others, the disorder begins in adolescence or early adulthood. Interestingly, by adulthood, the male-female ratio is fifty-fifty.

It is believed that a traumatic or stressful event triggers the onset of the disorder. While the role that stress plays in the manifestation of symptoms is still unclear, it is agreed that the predisposition to OCD must be present in the individual. In other words, without the gene(s), stress would not trigger the onset of OCD.

The symptoms of OCD may be present in young children without being noticed. An important part of early development is the establishment of rituals and routines. They give structure and continuity to the child's life. Bedtimes and mealtimes are established early. Children become collectors of "treasures" and enjoy group, rule-oriented activities. They quickly learn the routine of the school day and find comfort in its consistency. These are all part of the developmental patterns of childhood. Children learn how to interact and fit into their social environment through structure and routine.

In children with OCD, the need for rituals tends to intensify. Onset of the disorder is usually around the age of seven, but it can begin in adolescence or adulthood. The rituals are compelled by an inner force that makes the individual uncomfortable and unhappy. Rather than helping him function in society, the rituals isolate the child. Getting an evaluation as soon as the disorder is suspected can alleviate much of the child's stress, guilt, and anxiety.

# How Obsessive-Compulsive Disorder Is Diagnosed

Ideally, an evaluation should be conducted before these behaviors become intrusive and interfere with the individual's ability to function. Controlling the symptoms depends on early diagnosis and treatment. Because OCD is a neurological disorder, it requires a medical evaluation. Psychiatrists and clinical psychologists generally diagnose the disorder.

There are no blood tests, X rays, or other medical tests for OCD. Usually OCD is diagnosed by identifying the situations causing the obsessions and/or compulsions and rating how anxious the patient becomes if the ritual is not performed. Several measures are used to gather this information. One such tool is the Yale-Brown Obsessive-Compulsive Scale. Another is the Leyton Obsessional Inventory.

The results of these measures, along with interviews, data from the school, and family and developmental histories, give vital information to the evaluator. The criteria used in the diagnosis of OCD can be found in the *Diagnostic and Statistical Manual of Mental Disorders*.

# Observable Traits of OCD

The two major indications of OCD are obsessions and compulsions, neither of which are particularly pleasurable for the individual. One or both may be present in individuals with the disorder. A parent's or teacher's awareness of the signs may result in early identification and care of the child.

1. **Obsessions** are unwanted or meaningless thoughts, ideas, impulses, or images that persist in the mind of the individual. These thoughts may be unpleasant or repulsive, such as
   - Fear of dirt, contamination by germs, poisons, secretions.
   - Fear that something is wrong with their body in shape or function.
   - Fear of bringing harm, injury, or death to self or others.
   - Worry that something is not done properly (e.g., turning off water).
   - Needing to have objects in a particular place or order.
   - Forbidden sexual or blasphemous thoughts.
   - Worries about safety of relatives or friends.

2. **Compulsions** are the urges one gets to perform certain behaviors in response to the obsessions. These rituals seem to lessen the anxiety caused by the obsessions.
   - Excessive cleaning of objects. Handwashing is most common. Some children will wash up to 150 times a day to rid themselves of germs. This can result in chapped or bleeding hands.
   - Repeated checking to make sure an item is in its proper place.
   - Arranging objects in a specific position or order.
   - Repeating actions. Writing and erasing words or touching things an exact number of times.
   - Hoarding objects. Fears that something valuable will be lost.
   - Counting repeatedly to a specific number.
   - Nail biting.
   - Thumb sucking or knuckle cracking.
   - Hair pulling.
   - Self-touching and touching other people and things.

3. Individuals with OCD do not want to perform these actions but are unable to stop until an inner sense relays the message that the action can be halted. They have no apparent control over the stopping and starting of obsessions and compulsions.

4. OCD individuals tend to be serious and structured personalities.

5. They often appear cold and detached.

6. Friendships and social interaction are difficult to initiate and maintain because of the need for perfection.

7. They seek to control.

8. They exhibit extraordinarily slow completion of tasks or tests because of their need for perfection.

9. They make numerous erasures, causing holes in the paper.

10. They may refuse to turn in work because they need to check it one more time.

11. They may have difficulty with note taking because they want to write down every word and do it perfectly.

12. They may make frequent trips to the restroom to hide the rituals.

# Strategies to Support the Child with OCD

Once the diagnosis of OCD is made, a management plan should be developed by a collaborative team. Everyone involved with the child and the parents should work together to make the child more comfortable and learning more successful. Some of the following suggestions may be beneficial to the learner with OCD.

1. Understanding and patience from those working with children with OCD is essential. The learners cannot control their obsessions and compulsions and are uncomfortable that they are occurring. Do not insist they try to suppress them. This only causes shame, guilt, fear, and embarrassment.

2. Teachers and parents need to recognize the symptoms of OCD and get a qualified evaluation as soon as possible.

3. Providing extended test time, out of class, may be helpful.

4. Teachers consider giving objective tests where answers are circled or short answers given.

5. Teachers giving consideration to reducing the number of questions to be answered on essay or long answer tests.

6. Word processing may better suit the perfectionistic standards of the student. Allow the use of the computer for essay tests.

7. Teachers should allow the learner to use a tape recorder during lectures so the need for complete and perfect note taking does not interfere with learning.

8. Teachers and parents can set time limits for the child. Explain to the child he has ten minutes to complete the task before the work is collected. Set a timer if necessary.

9. Teachers should consider reducing the amount of work expected. Given the child's limitations, assign what can be accomplished in a reasonable period of time.

10. Teachers should reduce the amount of copying necessary whenever possible. For example, copy or reproduce math problems for the child so only the answers need to be written.

11. Parents and teachers should resist the urge to tell the child to get back to work. Instead, try giving step-by-step instructions to break the cycle of behaviors: "Pick up your pencil. Now find number one. Now answer the question."

12. To break the repetitive cycle, change the environment, redirect attention, or assign a physical activity. This will help neutralize the cycle of repetitive thoughts.

13. Set up a communication system between yourself and the child so he can relate the severity of his obsessions/compulsions at any given moment and when he needs your help. Use a "fear thermometer"—a rating scale that indicates the intensity of the OCD. For instance, 0 to 30 might mean, "I can handle it." Seventy to 100 could mean, "I'm really stuck and need your help!" Or use a color coding system. A red card indicates that the child is all right and wants you to stay away. A yellow card means you should stand by; your help may be needed. "Please come help me" may be indicated by a green card.

14. Medication is often part of the management plan. Inform teachers of possible side effects. They can provide valuable information while medications are being monitored for the desired results.

15. Therapy is also recommended for most patients with OCD, especially when the disorder is interfering with their ability to function.

16. Become informed about the disorder and share that information with others on the child's team.

17. Know the child's rights, so you can advocate for services.

# Points to Ponder

1. Obsessive-compulsive disorder is an uncontrollable need to perform rituals that alleviate the stress brought on by intrusive thoughts, ideas, images, or impulses.

2. The obsessions and compulsions are uncomfortable and unwanted by the individual.

3. The rituals are performed until an inner sense of comfort is reached by the individual.

4. Despite a strong desire to stop or control the obsessions and compulsions, they do not cease until the body gives the signal.

5. Awareness of the warning signs of OCD can result in early diagnosis and treatment. This can save years of anguish for the child.

6. Medication and therapy are successful methods used to support the child with OCD.

For additional resources and information contact:

- Obsessive/Compulsive Foundation, P.O. Box 70, Milford, CT 06460-0070 (203) 878-5669. E-mail: jphs28a@Prodigy.com. Web site: http://pages.prodigy.com/alwillen/ocf.html.

- Obsessive-Compulsive Information Center, Dean Foundation, 8000 Excelsior Drive, Suite 302, Madison, WI 53717-1914 (608) 836-8070.

- Trichotillomania Learning Center, 1215 Mission Street, Suite 2, Santa Cruz, CA 95060 (408) 457-1004.

# 14

# Sensory Integrative Dysfunction

As an infant, Megan appeared hypersensitive to touch. Whenever she cried and her mother tried to soothe her, she would scream more intensely. She appeared more uncomfortable when wrapped in a blanket than when clad only in a diaper.

As she grew, she rejected many foods and became a very picky eater. It took her forever to learn to ride her bicycle, and she hated her swing set. Megan's mother was concerned that she appeared less coordinated than other children her age.

When Megan began school, new problems arose. She became so upset when riding the school bus that her parents gave up in frustration and drove her to school. Lunchtime was a nightmare! She cried and refused to enter the lunchroom, much to the dismay of her teacher.

Megan was also struggling academically. Following directions was difficult. She had trouble expressing herself. Her handwriting was almost illegible, and she often reversed letters and words. She appeared so distracted that her teacher suggested to her parents that they consider an evaluation for AD/HD.

Socially, Megan was not well accepted. Her lack of coordination and fear of getting hurt kept her from participating in many sports. At recess, her discomfort on the playground equipment kept her isolated. She was often ridiculed and ostracized, and frequently in tears.

Megan was experiencing a sensory integrative dysfunction. With the proper diagnosis and therapy, many of the sensations she was encountering could be modified.

# How Sensory Integrative Dysfunction Is Defined

The child with sensory integrative dysfunction (SID) may appear irritable, controlling, whining, clumsy, hypersensitive, lazy, or unmotivated. It takes a trained eye to connect these behaviors to SID. Because sensory integration dysfunction has been researched for only a few decades, many parents, educators, and professionals do not recognize the symptoms of this disorder.

In the late 1960s, A. Jean Ayers, Ph.D., an occupational therapist doing research at the University of Southern California, defined sensory integration as "the process by which the brain organizes sensory information for appropriate use." According to Ayers, sensory integration allows our brain to sort, order, organize, and process all of the sensory information our body receives from its contact with the world so that we can interact effectively with our environment.

Sensory integrative dysfunction is thought to occur when the central nervous system does not respond appropriately to the incoming stimuli. Ayers explained this as a traffic jam that occurs during rush hour. Most of us are able to process sensory information smoothly, and our responses are automatic. In 5 to 10 percent of the population, however, sensory input gets jammed, and the central nervous system cannot clearly interpret the information it receives. This usually results in an inappropriate response by the individual. The response can take three forms: flight, fright, or fight.

The flight response is a form of avoidance. The child moves away from the uncomfortable situation. He may quietly withdraw or become the class clown to mask his pain. He may constantly fidget in his seat or make frequent trips to the bathroom or water fountain. Such children have learned how to control their environment to avoid uncomfortable situations. Some choices bring desirable results, but usually the child's behaviors are considered bizarre and inappropriate.

Fright is the second form of response to a distressing situation. Children who use this option often appear shy and uncommunicative. They may hide behind their mother, clinging to her. They are so focused on the potential dangers in life that they appear distracted and detached from the world around them. "I can't" and "I'll get hurt" are responses frequently heard from these children, who fear for their safety in an unfriendly world.

A third response is fight. These are the children who respond aggressively. They may become physically aggressive or utter unkind remarks that alienate them from peers and adults. They are often labeled as behavior problems. Their bodies have difficulty discriminating between an innocent nudge on the arm or tap on the shoulder and an aggressive shove. Unable to discriminate between playful gestures and those that threaten, they react inappropriately by lashing out at those around them.

Adults can help the child modify his responses once they have an understanding of the sensory systems involved and the functions they perform. A continuous flow of sensory input comes from all over the body and from their environment. Integrating this monumental amount of information is an overwhelming job for the brain. To begin to understand it, it's helpful to look at each of the major sensory systems individually. It is important to keep in mind, however, that each area works in conjunction with the others to help us interact successfully with our environment.

# The Sensory Systems Affected in Sensory Integrative Dysfunction

The central nervous system processes the information about our world that it receives through the receptors in our sensory systems. When there is interference within these systems, the central nervous system does not get the information it needs for an appropriate response. Because sensory integrative dysfunction ranges from mild to severe, any combination of the following sensory systems may be affected.

Tactile—The sense of touch. We can learn about our world through the sense of touch. This sensory system helps us interpret descriptive information, such as temperature, texture, size, and shape. It allows us to identify objects without seeing them. Without looking, our tactile sense helps us to distinguish between a fork and a spoon or between macaroni and spaghetti.

Tactile awareness also enables us to sense danger. It helps us discriminate between the feel of a bee on our arm and the tickle of a feather, or a playful nudge from an aggressive shove.

Children who are tactilely defensive have an exaggerated sense of touch. They are not always able to distinguish between harmful and harmless messages. They may overreact to one type of touch, such as a light or unexpected touch, and block out other, often painful, types, such as a bee sting.

Children who overreact may be characterized by abnormally responding to touch, especially unexpected touch. They can appear very ticklish when lightly touched. Being cuddled, hugged, or even gently touched on the shoulder can startle the child, causing him to withdraw. Or the child may react aggressively if brushed against while standing in line.

Such children may appear to be picky eaters because they avoid certain foods with unpleasant textures. They may also react to the texture of certain fabrics. They may need tags and labels removed. Refusal to go without shoes or to wear shorts or sleeveless blouses can also indicate that the child is tactilely defensive. These sensitivities can interfere with learning. A child wearing a tight collar is more concerned with being uncomfortable than with what is going on around him.

Children who are tactilely defensive may respond abnormally to self-care tasks. Washing the face, brushing the teeth, and washing or combing the hair can be major ordeals. They may even respond adversely to the temperature of the bathwater.

Anything that involves getting his hands dirty or messy can cause great distress for the child. Finger paints, clay, glue, and paste are just a few of the mediums that are avoided by the child who is tactilely defensive.

Conversely, some children who are tactilely defensive underreact to touch. Such a child often feels minimal pain. This can be a potentially dangerous situation. If he is unable to sense danger, he can put himself in situations that are harmful and not realize it. This child can have frequent accidents and may not feel the pain caused by the bruises or abrasions he sustains.

Because they often experience poor discrimination of touch, children who are underreactive to touch demonstrate poor fine motor skills. Finding pencils, pens, markers, and crayons that fit the hand comfortably is important. Since not all writing implements are the same, finding one that the child can use comfortably may be a challenge.

Children who are underreactive to touch may need to touch. They are often the children who cannot keep their hands to themselves. They touch everybody and everything. Unintentional pain may be inflicted on others by children who do not know how to gauge the intensity of their touch. They may be more forceful than they realize.

**Vestibular system—The sense of movement.** This system gives the brain information about our orientation in space and changes in our head position. It helps keep us tied to the ground by coordinating the movement of our head, eyes, and body and giving us a sense of balance. Receptors in the inner ear tell us whether we are moving, the direction in which we are moving, and how quickly we are moving.

The inner ear helps us maintain a sense of balance against the force of gravity. Movements such as swinging back and forth, climbing up and down steps, going in circles (as on a merry-go-round), and hanging upside down are all stabilized in the inner ear. This sense of balance helps guide our movements so that we can avoid crashing and bumping into people and objects.

The vestibular system also provides the muscle tone needed to stand and hold our head upright. Children with poor muscle tone may be more comfortable leaning against something than standing upright. Every classroom has at least one child who appears to fatigue easily and lays his head on his desk or uses his hands to prop it upright. Other children who slouch in their seats or sit in contorted positions may lack the muscle tone needed to maintain a sitting position. For these children, sitting can be more fatiguing than standing or running.

Bilateral tasks such as using scissors, rowing, and riding a bike are possible because of the vestibular system. We use this system to discriminate left from right and to perform other tasks that require the integration of both sides of the body. "He has two left feet!" we say when a person has difficulty coordinating such movements.

Children with a dysfunction in the vestibular system may also demonstrate language disorders. Their language development may be delayed. They may not have the ability to organize and express their thoughts in such a way as to be clearly understood. Pragmatic language skills may also be affected, which further complicates social interaction.

Children can also have an underactive vestibular system. As extreme risk takers, they often place themselves in unsafe situations. They appear to have no sense of fear whatsoever and go out of their way to seek new and more intensive movement experiences that defy the laws of gravity.

The proprioceptive system—Awareness of body position. This system usually coordinates with the vestibular system to help us locate our body in space. The proprioceptive system relates the position of our body through the receptors in our muscles, joints and tendons. Receptors from these areas help the brain know where each part of the body is at any given time and how it is moving.

When this system is functioning properly, we do not have to think about where our hand is and what it is doing. We have the ability to guide it without having to visually monitor each action. The brain tells the muscles when to stretch or contract to complete a task. Likewise, the joints get the message to extend, bend, pull, or compress.

Tasks like tying shoes, buttoning or zipping a jacket, or writing become difficult when children must watch every action. The child who tries to coordinate listening to the teacher while copying the assignment and watching her fingers write does not work effectively. Because these can become very intensive tasks, the child may avoid them.

The receptors constantly relay messages to tell the brain about where our body is in space. Our muscles, joints, and tendons adapt and readapt to the continual shifts in the position of the body. When the receptors in these areas tell a part of our body what to do, it adjusts accordingly. That is how we know when to shift our weight to compensate for pushing, pulling, or carrying heavy loads. Our body position may be very different, depending on whether we're carrying a twenty-pound turkey or a roll of paper towels.

Children with a dysfunction in this system do not readily adjust to changes in body position. They do not know where their hands and feet are located. They are clumsy and awkward, often tripping over their own feet. They appear to be lost in space.

**The visual sense.** Some children are oversensitive to light. Variations in lighting may be disturbing. They may prefer hats and sunglasses in bright sunlight. Dim light may be more calming and relaxing. Colors can also affect children with a visual defensiveness. Bold, bright colors may be more irritating and overstimulating than more muted shades.

The visual senses can also be affected by the degree of visual distraction that is presented. Cluttered classrooms with busy bulletin boards and objects hanging from the ceiling can be a nightmare for visually defensive students. Messy or chaotic workplaces can distract the child. When trying to function in such an environment, the child may appear hyperactive and distracted.

**The auditory sense.** An abnormal sensitivity to sound can be characteristic of children with an auditory defensiveness. Areas where noise levels are elevated may be distressful. The lunchroom and gym are two such areas within a school building. The rhythm of sounds may also be a factor. Some children respond more adversely to fast rhythms; others to slower beats. The sound level also can be a factor in distracting the child's attention. Some children learn best in an environment where noise is minimal. For other children, the quiet is so distracting, they cannot concentrate. They need some background noise.

Praxis—Motor planning. The integration of all these sensory systems help us plan our movements to get the desired response. Motor planning relies on prior knowledge about how the body moves and incorporates this information to develop new plans of action to complete unfamiliar tasks.

Good motor planning begins with an idea about what to do. The actions are organized and sequenced, then executed. This process will occur automatically after the actions have been repeated a couple of times. For example, a child who learns how to get on and off a bike has a plan he can use anytime he encounters another riding toy. He does not have to stop and think about the process, because it has become second nature. For the child with poor motor planning, riding a bike at preschool may pose a problem because he cannot adapt to the difference from his bicycle. He may know what to do, but cannot devise a plan to do it.

Motor planning also helps us organize our thoughts and ideas and express them clearly. This is an important aspect of communication. Children with poor motor planning often have a language disorder. They may not be able to make themselves understood and send the appropriate nonverbal messages.

All of these systems send vital information to the brain about the world around us. How the information is processed determines how we respond. For most of us, the responses are smooth and effortless. However, for others, the world is not a friendly place, and stress and anxiety are around every corner. How severely limited the child with SID is depends upon the involvement of the sensory systems.

# SID Levels of Severity

Three levels are identified by Patricia Wilbarger and Julia Wilbarger in their pamphlet *Sensory Defensiveness in Children Aged 2–12*. Each level is identified below.

1. **Level I (Mild)**

   Picky, oversensitive, slightly overactive, and resistant to change.

   Exert enormous effort and control to succeed.

2. **Level II (Moderate)**

   Two or more aspects of the child's life affected.

   Problems with social interactions—too controlling, too aggressive, or may isolate self.

   Difficulty with self-care—dressing, bathing, combing hair, brushing teeth.

   Attention or behavior problems may begin to surface.

   Fearfulness of new situations may interfere with exploration and play.

3. **Level III (Severe)**

   SID disrupts every aspect of the child's life.

   Usually diagnosed with other comorbidities (AD/HD, autism, developmental delay).

   Strong avoidance of some kinds of sensations or may seek strong sensory input.

   May interfere with normal development.

# The Causes of Sensory Integrative Dysfunction

As mentioned, the integration of sensory information takes place within the central nervous system. This is also the center for learning, behavior control, vital body functions, and motor skill performance. If there is a breakdown in one area, the other functions are affected.

The brain receives sensory information from all over the body. The nerve cells on the skin send information about touch, pain, temperature, and pressure to the brain for interpretation. The inner ear maintains our sense of balance, movement, and head positioning. Our sense of body position can be determined by our muscles, joints, and tendons. By receiving sensory input from receptors all over the body, the central nervous system helps us interact and respond to our environment. A malfunction in any of these areas can result in sensory integrative dysfunction.

There are several reasons a malfunction may occur. A high percentage of premature births result in SID. These infants have fragile, easily stimulated nervous systems that can make them hypersensitive to the stimuli in their environment. A lack of oxygen at birth or other delivery traumas may also result in sensory integration problems. Prenatal exposure to crack and alcohol may put infants at risk. Limited research is indicating that there is a high incidence of sensory deprivation in children growing up in orphanages in countries such as Russia and Bosnia. There is little interaction with the children, who are usually confined and seldom touched.

Brain injuries and strokes can interfere in the brain's ability to integrate sensory input. Aging causes our sensory processes to become less efficient and reliable. The occurrence of these conditions is not necessarily a result of the genetic composition of the individual.

It is believed that in many cases SID is inherited. Research shows that 50 percent of children with SID have parents with similar characteristics. Males are affected five times more often than females. Most individuals with SID are of average to above average intelligence. While the disorder does not affect intellect, it can interfere with learning.

Sensory integrative dysfunction is usually accompanied by other disorders. Many children with SID are autistic or have other developmental disabilities. As many as 70 percent of children with SID also have learning disabilities. A large percentage of children with SID also have AD/HD. Communication disorders are a common occurrence in children with sensory integrative dysfunction.

There are several secondary effects of SID and these comorbidities. These children tend to be at risk for substance abuse and exhibit behavior disorders. They often have a difficult time controlling their stress and anger. Early identification of SID is important to help alleviate the child's discomfort and possibly avoid the onset of these secondary effects.

# The Developmental Differences of the Child with SID

Some types of sensory integrative dysfunction can be detected at birth. Parents usually sense that something is not right. Since the disorder is not outgrown, the characteristics remain but the tolerance level changes. The two-year-old who screams at the barbershop may not seem as socially inappropriate as the eight-year-old who exhibits the same behavior. As the child grows, certain signals may alert parents and professionals to the possibility that he or she is experiencing some sensory integration issues.

### Infancy.

- Premature babies are at particular risk. They tend to be more restless, sensitive, and disorganized when body position is changed than full-term infants.
- Lifting the head, rolling over, crawling, and walking may be delayed.
- Child may dislike lying on stomach, preferring to sit or stand.
- Holding and cuddling may distress the infant or make her more irritable.
- Infant may require little sleep and have difficulty settling into a feeding and sleeping routine.
- Feedings may take an unusually long time.
- Baby may avoid putting things in mouth.
- Child may reject foods with certain textures.
- Child may avoid eating with fingers and get upset if hands get messy.
- Parents often sense that something is not right as behaviors and reactions appear extreme.

Toddlers.

- Speech is often delayed.
- Child may avoid new textures, such as the sandbox, wet grass on bare feet, or a fuzzy teddy bear.
- Child may be uncomfortable on swings, slides, merry-go-rounds, and other playground equipment.
- Child may avoid crayons, markers, pencils, and any form of writing or coloring.
- Child may have difficulty manipulating utensils and feeding himself.
- Washing, brushing, combing, and other self-care procedures may be a struggle.
- Child may have a strong preference for certain textures of clothing, and tags and labels may annoy him.
- Child may appear uncoordinated and spill often.
- Child may have difficulty with gross motor activities, such as running, jumping, and kicking a ball.
- Child's movements may appear awkward and clumsy. He may trip over his own feet.
- Child may appear to be more irritable, controlling, manipulative, and uncooperative than most children his age. Temper tantrums may be more extreme.
- Child may have difficulty following simple directions.
- Child may have difficulty maintaining eye contact.

The preschool-age child.

- Learning to work shoelaces, buttons, and zippers may be difficult.
- Child may still avoid playg        _nces.
- Child may have difficulty wo    ᵎ puzzles.
- Earlier behaviors appear more extreme and inappropriate at this age.

- Child plays with toys but might not progress beyond the pounding, dumping, throwing, and banging stage to more complex play.

## The school age-child.

- Child may be unhappy and frustrated and demonstrate disruptive behaviors.
- Child may have a difficult time paying attention.
- Child may have a difficult time staying in a chair.
- Child may be socially ostracized because he does not participate at recess or in organized sports.
- Child may have difficulty following directions with multiple steps.
- Child may have problems with auditory processing of information.
- Child may have difficulty expressing thoughts and feelings.
- Reading and writing problems often interfere with learning.
- Child may fatigue easily.
- All aspects of the child's life seem to be affected. Academic, social, family, and recreational interactions are all stressful and demanding for the child. A trip on the school bus can be excruciating for the child with SID.

## The adolescent.

- Child is usually doing poorly in school.
- Child feels frustrated and overwhelmed.
- Child may have difficulty fitting in socially. He may do poorly in academics or sports and have a hard time finding a place to shine.
- He may begin to demonstrate the secondary affects of SID, such as substance abuse or delinquent behaviors.

## The adult.

- He may have difficulty performing in the workplace.
  Being socially inappropriate may interfere with personal relationships.
  He may have severe mood swings and be abusive.

- The most effective way to avoid a life of discomfort and fear is to get an evaluation as early as possible. With occupational therapy, the prognosis for the management of SID is excellent.

# How Sensory Integrative Dysfunction Is Diagnosed

An occupational therapist (OT) who has sensory integration training needs to be consulted about an evaluation. The assessment process has many different components. The OT will evaluate to determine the neuromuscular status, sensory processing, independent living skills, and cognitive and perceptual skills of the child. Evaluative instruments are available to assess individuals from infancy to adulthood. Using this data, the OT can determine the specific areas of sensory dysfunction.

These tests, in addition to family and developmental histories and documentation of other related disorders, are important components of the assessment. Together, the data give a composite of the whole child.

Once the evaluation has been completed, the course of therapy is determined. It was once believed that occupational therapy was only effective with young children. Many therapists believed that the "window of plasticity" had closed by the time the child reached puberty. Recent research shows that the brain is constantly regenerating and restoring itself. New sensory channels are constantly being constructed. While early diagnosis and intervention is the ideal, adolescents and adults can gain remarkable results from occupational therapy. Clients who understand their reactions to their environment can better adjust to any residual problems. Therefore, it is never too late to ease the discomfort caused by a sensory integrative dysfunction.

# Observable Traits of SID

Because there are a number of different areas where SID may be manifested, it might be more helpful to look at some of the identifying symptoms in each category. It is important to keep in mind that more than one area may be affected. Only a thorough evaluation by a qualified occupational therapist can determine if a sensory integrative dysfunction is present.

1. Tactile defensiveness
   - Child dislikes having others touch him, especially unexpectedly. He may prefer to touch rather than be touched.
   - Child may become aggressive if accidentally bumped or pushed, as when standing in line.
   - Self-care functions are stressful.
   - Labels in clothing are annoying. Clothing that fits tightly or is restrictive—such as buttoned collars, ties, turtlenecks, and necklaces—can cause discomfort.
   - New clothes can be uncomfortable. Certain fabrics or textures can cause distress.
   - Child dislikes crowds or being in the middle of groups.
   - Child avoids going barefoot. Prefers to keep his body covered, no matter what the temperature.
   - Child dislikes finger painting, mud, clay, or getting hands messy in any way.

2. Oral defensiveness.
   - Child is sensitive to the texture of food. This makes him appear picky in food selections.
   - Foods may be too spicy or not have enough flavor.
   - Child does not put objects in mouth.
   - Child dislikes brushing teeth.
   - Trips to the dentist are unusually stressful.

3. Visual defensiveness.
   - Child may avoid sunlight or bright lights.
   - Child may insist on wearing hats or sunglasses outside.
   - Child may avoid making eye contact.

4. Auditory defensiveness.
   - Child is easily upset by loud noises.

- Large, noisy places, such as the lunchroom, playground, or gym, can be irritating.
- Child may make noise when he hears loud noise. For instance, he may scream when the vacuum cleaner is running.
- Child may be oversensitive to certain rhythms or beats.
- Some children need complete silence to concentrate. Others must have background noise.

5. Sense of gravity and movement.
   - Child may be uncomfortable when his feet are off the ground.
   - Swinging, sliding, merry-go-round, and amusement park rides may be disturbing.
   - Turning upside down may be frightening.
   - Learning to ride a bike may be delayed.
   - Child may have difficulty coordinating both sides of the body in activities such as rowing, jumping rope, and using scissors.
   - Child may be disturbed by riding on the bus, especially if his feet dangle over the seat.
   - Child may slouch when sitting and lean when standing.
   - Child may have difficulty holding his head up, so he may look at the floor or use hands as a prop.

6. Sense of body position.
   - Child may have difficulty with buttoning, zipping, tying shoes, or putting on jacket.
   - Handwriting is difficult.
   - Child may rock to calm himself down.
   - Child may exhibit autisticlike behavior, such as feet banging or excessive jumping.
   - He may fall out of chair often.
   - He may constantly move to find a comfortable body position.
   - He may be more comfortable kneeling, standing, or assuming a contorted position.

7. Motor planning may be disrupted.

8. The child may be overly fearful or exhibit extreme risk-taking behaviors.

9. The child may be inattentive, impulsive, and/or hyperactive.

10. Learning disabilities or language disorders may be present.

11. The child may appear lazy and unmotivated.

12. He may have poor peer relationships.

13. He may respond with either flight, fright, or fight.

# Strategies to Support the Child with a Sensory Integrative Dysfunction

With the assistance of the occupational therapist, a "sensory diet" should be prepared for the child. A sensory diet provides nourishment for the body's sensory system, helping it stay alert, adaptable, and skillful. This is accomplished by teaching the child how to cope with the daily obstacles that will make them uncomfortable. Children on a sensory diet often feel more calm, alert, and organized throughout the day. Together with the therapist, the child selects the activities that will empower him to stay in control of uncomfortable situations. As with any course of treatment, modifications to the diet are an ongoing process.

The components of a sensory diet may include the following:

1. Specific time-oriented activity routines, such as jumping on bouncy surfaces or climbing and crawling for specified periods of time.

2. Deep touch pressure and joint compression before stressful events, such as bathing or hair washing.

3. Adapting the environment so that the child can learn to meet his sensory needs. Create a hideout where the child can go to regain composure when he's overstimulated. This can be a quiet corner with pillows or a beanbag chair, or a space under a table or desk. The child's play area can be adapted to include old

mattresses for jumping, swings made from old tires suspended from tree branches, or large appliance boxes to use for tunnels.

4. Other play and leisure activities that improve the child's sensory input include horseback riding, snow sports, swimming, gymnastics, karate, Tae Kwon Do, and learning to play an instrument.

Other accommodations that may make life more comfortable for the child with SID are suggested below. Work with the occupational therapist to find those that are most effective for the child. The child never should be forced to participate in any activities that will increase stress or discomfort. Begin slowly and build as the child feels more confident. Your child needs your patience and understanding.

1. Tactile defensiveness.
   - Remove tags and labels from clothing.
   - Slowly introduce the child to new textures and sensations. Begin with a pan of sand and work up to the sandbox.
   - Provide brightly colored modeling clay, a rolling pin, and cookie cutters for the child to explore. Add rice or legumes to the clay for texture.
   - Include the child in cooking activities that required ingredients of various textures. (Children tend to eat and enjoy their own creations.)
   - A "feely box" with many different textures can be effective. The game of identifying what they are feeling or describing how the object feels appeals to many children.
   - A firm touch will be less disturbing that a light touch.
   - Get in front of the child, at eye level, and let him know of your presence and desire to touch before doing so.
   - Teachers who use a light tap on the shoulder as a signal for inattentive children need to realize this could be threatening to the tactilely defensive student.
   - Place the child at the front or end of the line or on the perimeter of the group when everyone is sitting or standing together.

- Carpet squares can keep other children in their own space.
- Keep the child out of the middle of a crowd. Seat him at the end of a row, away from a heavy traffic pattern.
- Practice different kinds of touches and talk with the child about which are harmful and which are not, which is a playful gesture and which is aggressive. Discuss when and where these touches may occur. It is natural to get bumped in a crowd, and rarely is this contact intentional.
- Allow children to wear their favorite clothes when around peers.
- Teachers may allow children sensitive to touch to wear a jacket or sweater in the classroom.
- Pick your battles, and unless the child is in danger, save the power struggles for more important matters.

2. To develop a sense of movement and gravity.
   - Practice walking up and down steps, along the curb, over ramps, across balance beams.
   - Climb the hill and roll back down.
   - Carry the child piggyback.
   - Provide opportunities to explore playground equipment and experience the body in different positions.
   - Give the child opportunities in creative play to pretend to be an airplane, elephant, or ice skater.
   - Rocking back and forth may be a calming technique used by the child.
   - Encourage the child to lie on his stomach and hold up his head while playing a game or watching TV.
   - Limit the amount of time needed to stand and wait.
   - Break activities into small chunks and give frequent breaks to avoid fatigue.
   - Go fishing and let the child row around the lake.
   - Rent a paddleboat for the child to maneuver with his feet.

- Teachers need to find ways to help the child to socially interact during playtime.
- Be alert to the need for a break when the child becomes restless or overactive.
- Allow frequent restroom and drinking-fountain breaks for this child.
- Consider allowing the student to test and prepare assignments on the computer to reduce the demand on handwriting if keyboarding skills are proficient.
- Be sure the child has a desk that fits him. Are his knees touching the desk? Are his feet touching the floor?

3. Body position.
   - Allow the child to assume the position that is most comfortable. This may be standing or kneeling.
   - Pillows or a beanbag may be preferable to a chair.
   - Look beyond misbehavior as an explanation for why the child falls out of his chair. This could be an important warning sign.
   - Engage the child in "heavy" work. Have him carry grocery bags or a basket of laundry. Wearing a backpack will also help him learn to shift and adjust his body weight to compensate for the load.
   - Allow jumping on a mini trampoline or an old mattress.
   - Engage the child in pushing and pulling exercises using wagons or carts.
   - Urge the child to push another child on a swing or pull the merry-go-round until it spins.
   - Give bear hugs or hold the child closely and securely.
   - Hold the child's feet and have him walk like a wheelbarrow.
   - Kicking a ball, throwing beanbags in a bucket, hitting a ball off a tee are great activities.
   - Play charades, hokeypokey, tug-of-war, Twister, or Simon says with the child.

4. Motor planning.
   - Provide Legos, building blocks, and Tinkertoys.
   - Play follow-the-leader or pantomime with the child.
   - Play catch with a soft ball, a hard ball, a large ball, and a small ball.
   - Dolls that need to be dressed and have buttons, zippers, and snaps are helpful.
   - Begin with simple directions. Have the child repeat them, then carry them out in the correct sequence.
   - Give the child short tasks he can complete quickly and successfully.
   - Work from a schedule or checklist that the child can use to mark off completed steps.
   - Minimize visual distractions. Keep clutter and chaos in classrooms and workplaces minimal.
   - Assign projects that require a sequence of steps to complete.
   - Help children learn to approach tasks by breaking them down into manageable parts.
   - Provide a model such as a diagram, outline, or example. Peers can also model how something is done.
   - Engage the child in a variety of art activities that require cutting and pasting. Making a collage of pictures cut from magazines is an excellent activity.

# Points to Ponder

1. Sensory integrative dysfunction occurs when the central nervous system is unable to receive, organize, and process information from the body's sensory systems and respond appropriately.

2. The sensory systems most often addressed in SID are the tactile, vestibular, proprioceptive, visual, and auditory. Smell and taste may also be affected.

3. Motor planning or praxis relies on the integration of these systems.

4. SID may range from mild to severe.

5. An occupational therapist with sensory integration training can evaluate for SID, as well as prepare a sensory diet as part of a therapy program to ease the discomforts resulting from SID.

6. SID is a lifelong disorder and can affect the individual intensely throughout the life span.

Additional resources may be obtained by contacting Sensory Integration International, P.O. Box 9013, Torrance, CA 90508 (310) 320-9986.

# 15

# Oppositional Defiant Disorder and Conduct Disorder

All children test the limits. This is just part of normal development. It is the job of the child to see how far he can go before the adult in charge says, "Enough is enough!" The expression "terrible twos" derives from the attempts of the child at this age to recognize herself as an individual rather than an extension of her mother. With hands on hips and a stomp of the foot, the child catches most parents offguard when she utters her first defiant no. Parents need to recognize that this initial attempt to establish autonomy is very normal.

Around the age of six, most children again test the limits. They feel very grown-up as they enter school and further loosen their ties to mother and home. Friends and peers become their center of focus. Some experts refer to this period as the child's first adolescence.

As the child enters the teenage years, hormones rage, and the child struggles to cope with body changes, self-image, and the need for peer acceptance. The battle of wills between parent and child often continues until the child leaves home. This is truly the age of rebellion, as teenagers work to break out of their cocoon and fly, independent and strong. This, too, is a part of the normal cycle of development.

When acts of rebellion persist and result in antisocial behavior, concern may be warranted. Among the types of antisocial behavior that need to be addressed by a mental health professional are oppositional defiant disorder (ODD) and conduct disorder (CD). Because these two conditions are so closely related and one often triggers the other, we will address both together in this chapter.

# How Oppositional Defiant Disorder and Conduct Disorder Are Defined

In his book *Attention Deficit Hyperactivity Disorder: A Handbook for Diagnosis and Treatment*, Russell Barkley, Ph.D., clarifies some of the differences between ODD and CD. Barkley's research suggests that undiagnosed or mismanaged ODD can be the forerunner to CD. According to Barkley, oppositional defiant disorder usually first manifests itself during the preschool years. The unacceptable behavior is usually directed toward adults and peers the child knows well, and only rarely around strangers or clinicians. Thus the kindergarten terror may be absolutely angelic in the pediatrician's office for a ten-minute visit. This, of course, could delay a diagnosis.

Barkley states that the antisocial behavior of conduct disorder, on the other hand, is often directed against strangers. He also feels that CD is ODD that has gotten out of control. Children with conduct disorder often become physically aggressive, while this is not necessarily true of those with ODD. The criteria for each of these disorders is defined in *DSM IV*.

Both disorders are characterized by types of behavior that extend to the extreme limits of what is considered "normal" in a child. A child with ODD and CD, unlike his peers, does not outgrow these types of behavior. Instead, they become more intense as he gets older.

# The Causes of ODD and CD

The research is somewhat inconclusive about what may cause these two disorders. It appears that there is a strong genetic basis for both, but environmental factors may influence their severity.

Research has substantiated that children with these disorders usually have a parent, often the father, with the same behavior. A family history tends to reveal that ODD, CD, antisocial personality disorder, substance abuse, and/or major depression are present in at least one parent or extended family member. The male child of a parent with any of these conditions is five times more likely to inherit the same condition, and a female child is ten times more likely. Males are four times as likely to be diagnosed as females.

The genetic link is strengthened by the fact that children with a diagnosis of AD/HD run a higher risk of being identified with ODD and CD. Sixty-five percent of children diagnosed with AD/HD develop some level of ODD. By adolescence, 40 to 60 percent of those with AD/HD are diagnosed with CD. Of this population, the majority also have been diagnosed with ODD. Sixty-four percent of those with Tourette syndrome demonstrate ODD and/or CD. The chemical imbalances thought to be associated with AD/HD and Tourette syndrome also seem to be a factor in ODD and CD, and lower levels of the neurotransmitter serotonin have been linked to the antisocial behaviors.

Environmental factors play an important role in both disorders. The research presented in David Comings's book *Tourette Syndrome and Human Behavior* consistently states that socioeconomic status is not a cause for either disorder. The environment in which the child is reared is a stronger indicator. The research of Lee Robins, M.D., of the University of Washington School of Medicine in St. Louis, indicates that a sociopathic and/or alcoholic father is a more predictable indicator of antisocial behaviors in his child than is socioeconomic status.

Most children with ODD and CD come from homes where the discipline is inconsistent or nonexistent. There is often chaos and abuse in the home. An above-average frequency of child and/or wife abuse, illegitimacy, separation or divorce, and removal of the child from the home exists in the lives of children diagnosed with ODD and CD.

Robins's research has found that the number, not the type, of behaviors seen in childhood is a strong predictor of whether they will continue into adulthood. The more there are, the stronger is the likelihood. A sociopathic or alcoholic father can be another strong predictor when accompanied by the deprivation of love, support, and physical needs such as food and shelter. Social status is not usually an indicator.

Caution must be exerted here. No one factor can lead to the onset of ODD or CD. The genetic predisposition must be present with the environmental factors to result in either condition. Early diagnosis can often result in a child's receiving the support and management needed to control his antisocial tendencies.

# The Development of the Child with ODD and CD

The onset of ODD usually occurs during the preschool years. Developmentally, it is not uncommon for most children of this age to display many of the symptoms of ODD. This may delay an early diagnosis. However, when the symptoms persist and begin to intensify as the child gets older, a professional should be consulted as soon as possible. When an angry, hostile disposition continues to be demonstrated along with defiant and noncompliant behavior, the possibility of the presence of ODD should be investigated. This is especially true when the behaviors are usually directed toward those people who are familiar to the child.

The onset of CD is usually between the ages of six and ten for males and not until puberty for females. Often ODD is also present. Behaviors related to conduct disorder will occur in the home, school, community, and with peers.

# How ODD and CD Are Diagnosed

Because it is normal for children to be defiant and rebellious from time to time, parents should not assume from such behavior that their child has ODD or CD. However, when this behavior is pervasive and carried to extremes, and when it increases in intensity as the child matures, consulting a professional is warranted.

Psychiatrists and clinical psychologists specializing in antisocial disorders are most qualified to make the diagnosis. Using behavior rating scales, parents and teachers can provide valuable information. Family and developmental histories are important. Also, how long the symptoms have been demonstrated and their intensity are critical considerations in the evaluation. A duration of longer than twelve months, increasing intensity, and interference with the child's ability to function are strong indicators of the disorders.

# Observable Traits of ODD and CD

Awareness of the symptoms of these disorders may help parents and educators determine if the child's behaviors are extreme. The behaviors associated with ODD can appear to be the same as those exhibited by any normal developing child. In normal development, however, the behaviors are outgrown. It is when the child's actions increase and intensify that concern may be warranted. The following list of behaviors may alert parents and teachers to the warning signs for each disorder.

### Oppositional defiant disorder.
- Frequently has outbursts of temper.
- Frequently argues with adults.
- Frequently defies or refuses adult requests.
- Frequently defies or ignores the rules.
- Frequently does things to annoy and disturb adults and peers.

- Frequently blames others for own mistakes.
- Frequently oversensitive, easily annoyed, angry, resentful, spiteful, and vindictive.
- May swear or use offensive language.
- Has low self-esteem.
- Has a low tolerance for frustration.
- Often does poorly in school.

## Conduct disorder.

- Steals with or without confronting a victim.
- Lies.
- Sets fires.
- Truant.
- May break into and enter homes, cars, or buildings.
- Threatens or physically attacks people, sometimes with a weapon.
- Initiates or enters fights.
- Cruel to animals.
- Runs away from home.
- Teases people by being verbally, emotionally, or physically cruel.
- Has a violent temper.
- Is unusually loud and boisterous.
- Is menacing.
- Has severe mood swings.
- Abuses alcohol or drugs.
- Has promiscuous or abusive sex.

# Strategies to Support the Child with ODD/ CD

The management of learners with ODD and CD is often beyond the capabilities of parents and teachers. Often these are children unwilling and unable to change their behavior. Therefore, a strong collaborative team is necessary to bring about the most effective results.

1. The care of a qualified mental health professional is essential. Behavior therapy can help many individuals with ODD or CD manage their symptoms (see chapter 13). Therapy and guidance from the professional can also provide support for the parents, family, and teachers.

2. Medication may be appropriate to help stabilize the child.

3. Contracting may be a valuable tool to set expectations and consequences. Focus on positive reinforcers.

4. Model appropriate behavior. Research shows that loving, nurturing, supportive, and caring environments are most effective. Aggressive behavior teaches aggression.

5. Teach problem-solving skills to give alternative ways to handle frustration and anger.

6. Address one area of noncompliance at a time. Trying to solve the whole problem at once is too overwhelming for everyone.

7. Establish home and school rules. Set up incentives for compliance and consequences for noncompliance.

8. Do not make idle threats. Think before you speak. Make sure you can do what you say.

9. Do not state requests as a question or imply the child has an option. State the directive clearly and simply, as in "Please take out the garbage!" rather than "Would you take out the garbage?"

# Points to Ponder

1. Both ODD and CD are serious emotional disorders that should not be ignored.

2. Developmentally, it is normal for many children to exhibit the behaviors resembling ODD. It is not normal for these behaviors to increase and intensify as the child gets older.

3. It is believed that ODD often precedes the onset of CD.

4. ODD is characterized by hostile behavior directed toward parents, teachers, and peers that are known to the child.

5. CD involves more severe behavior that is directed against people in the community not necessarily known to the child.

6. Both disorders have a genetic predisposition, but the environment in which the child lives often determines the severity and extent of the disorders. Abusive, neglectful parents who have substance abuse problems can exacerbate the condition.

7. Children with ODD and CD usually become involved with law enforcement early in their lives and many die violent deaths at young ages.

8. The intensive care of a mental health professional is strongly recommended.

# 16

# Autism

Of all the disabilities discussed in this book, perhaps the least understood is autism. The child who is uncommunicative and aloof is an enigma to parents and educators. Lacking language and problem-solving skills, the child with autism often has a difficult time learning how to interact with those around him.

## How Autism Is Defined

Autism is a condition in which the individual fails to respond normally to peers and adults. In fact, contact with others is often frightening and upsetting for the child. From the Greek word *autos*, meaning "self," the term *autism* literally means "to turn inward."

This condition occurs in about five out of every 10,000 births. Males are four times more likely to have autism than females. Seventy percent of children with autism are thought to have some level of mental retardation. About 10 to 16 percent of the males have fragile-X syndrome, a form of mental retardation (see chapter 17).

Children with autism may have very sharp visual-spatial skills that allow them to notice the most minute detail. They also exhibit selective areas of high functioning ability referred to as splinter, or savant, skills. The individual may demonstrate a special talent such as perfect pitch, exceptional artistic ability, or a superior memory for certain details. A familiar illustration of a splinter skill comes from the movie *Rainman*. In one scene, Raymond, portrayed by Dustin Hoffman, was able to tell the exact number of toothpicks that fell to the floor. His brother immediately recognized this unique aptitude. Unfortunately, Raymond was not aware of this special talent. This is true of children with autism. They are unable to use or apply their special gifts to everyday life.

# Causes of Autism

Autism is an enigma to researchers. It is not clear what causes this disorder. There appears to be some abnormality in the development of the brain. Some evidence points to a genetic predisposition. Researchers suspect that an imbalance in the neurotransmitter serotonin may be involved as a cause of the disorder. Researchers are also investigating a possible connection between autism and premature births, prenatal infections, and birth traumas.

It was once believed that cold, aloof, and detached mothers were to blame. This has definitely been proven untrue. Autism is not an acquired disability. Research indicates that the condition emerges within the first three years of life and comes from biological causes. In diagnosing for the disorder, this is one fact that separates it from other conditions such as schizophrenia.

# How Autism Is Diagnosed

Evaluating a child for autism can be difficult because it mimics other disorders. A professional who specializes in working with children with autism may provide the most accurate assessment.

Beginning the diagnostic process with a thorough physical screening is important. This rules out any physical ailments. Vision and hearing should also be screened. Children with undiagnosed vision and hearing problems can appear autistic and/or mentally retarded.

The official criteria mental health professionals use for the diagnosing of autism is found in the *DSM IV*. Family histories and observable traits provide other helpful information. Intelligence scales and measures used to determine the cognitive level can be fairly accurate *if* the evaluator is familiar with autism and the tests are modified for nonverbal children. There are also specific rating scales used in the evaluation of autism.

Speech and language skills should also be assessed. Communicating effectively is an issue for children with autism. More than half of the children remain uncommunicative. Those who do talk are not effective communicators. Echolalia is a common speech pattern of individuals with autism. Like a tape recorder, the child repeats back what he has heard rather than express anything original. Therefore, an evaluation by a qualified speech and language pathologist will indicate the correct course of therapy. Facilitated communication may be an option.

## Facilitated Communication

Within the past decade, some very surprising research has emerged about the ability of individuals with autism to communicate. The use of facilitated communication is causing many researchers to question the cognitive capabilities of individuals with autism. Are they truly mentally retarded or just incapable of relating the information they know? Is the inability to communicate the source of the frustration and tantrums characteristic of autism? Many are wondering if those with autism have an inner language that can be released by facilitated communication.

Rosemary Crossley, a pioneer in the field of facilitated communication, is attempting to answer these and other questions. At her clinic in Australia, she conducts extensive research with individuals experiencing severe expressive language disorders, especially those with autism. Interested in the concept of teaching facilitated communication to individuals with autism, Douglas Biklen visited Rosemary Crossley. He is now conducting his own research in this area at Syracuse University.

Facilitated communication is a technique that uses the assistance of a trained facilitator who touches the arm, hand, elbow, or shoulder of the communicator. Using a communication board, such as the Canon Communicator, the "speaker" can type or point out the letters that relate the intended message. The facilitator physically supports the arm or hand and keeps the communicator focused. Once the individual has learned how to use the adaptive device, the presence of the facilitator is phased out.

Individuals with autism who have learned to communicate through this medium have demonstrated an ability to read, answer questions, and share their feelings on what it is like to be locked within the silent world of autism.

Skeptics claim the technique is a hoax and that it is the facilitator who is controlling what is being related, not the user. As a result, a major controversy has evolved. Most experts would agree, however, that language skills are a fairly strong predictor of how successful the child with autism will be.

Biklen and Crossley continue their research amid the heated debates. If this does prove to be a method to bridge the silent, isolated world of autism, it should be utilized to its fullest potential. Only time will tell.

# Observable Traits of Autism

Although autism is difficult to diagnose, symptoms begin to emerge within the first three years of the child's life. Recognition of these initial signs of autism is important.

In 1943 psychiatrist Leo Kanner noted five characteristics he saw consistently in the condition he named *autism*. Later, more traits were added. The characteristics are divided into three main categories. The major characteristics of autism are listed below.

1. Poor social interactions.
   - Appears indifferent toward other people. Appears not to recognize that others have feelings.
   - May not seek comfort when hurt or upset.

- May isolate himself from others and appears to be a loner. Has no friends.
- May not play with other children, preferring to be left alone.

2. Poor communication skills.
   - Avoids eye contact. Often looks past, or through, a person.
   - Does not use speech or body language.
   - Speech is abnormal in tone, frequency, and pitch (e.g., monotonous or high-pitched).
   - Repeats what he hears. May repeat the same thing over and over.
   - Cannot maintain a conversation.

3. Restricted activities and interests.
   - Demonstrates strange behaviors, such as arm flapping, rocking, or spinning.
   - Temper tantrums and inappropriate outbursts are frequent.
   - May follow strict rituals and routines. For example, must have meals at exact time each day or becomes very upset.
   - May demonstrate splinter skills by doing some things very quickly and very well.

Many children demonstrate some of these characteristics at one time or another. For the child with autism, these behaviors are extreme and intense. It is the physical and emotional detachment from other people and the severe communication difficulties that are the hallmark symptoms of autism.

# Strategies to Support for Child with Autism

Research indicates that the child with autism can benefit immensely from the stimulation of being around other children. Other strategies may also be helpful.

1. Speech and language therapy may help develop communication skills.

2. Behavior modification therapy is often recommended as a management tool.

3. Family therapy may be beneficial for managing the stress of living with a child with autism.

4. The child may benefit from occupational therapy to ease sensorimotor issues.

5. Try to keep the environment as consistent and structured as possible.

6. Speak in short, simple sentences using concrete ideas.

7. An IEP should be designed to meet the specific needs of the child.

8. Facilitated communication may help unlock the thoughts and feelings of the child.

# Points to Ponder

1. Autism is a disorder that severely affects the child's ability to communicate and to interact socially.

2. Autism appears to have genetic causes. It is *not* a result of cold, unresponsive parents.

3. Most children with autism have some level of mental retardation and severe speech and language problems.

4. Family therapy should be considered to manage the many challenges a child with autism presents.

5. Facilitated communication may provide a peek into the mysterious world of autism and allow those with autism to relate their thoughts and feelings.

For more information and resources contact:

- Autism Services Center, Prichard Building, 605 Ninth Street, P.O. Box 507, Huntington, WV 25710 (304) 525-8014.

- Autism Society of America, 7910 Woodmont Avenue, Suite 650, Bethesda, MD 20814 (301) 657-0881.

# 17

# Mental Retardation and Developmental Disabilities

When we think of mental retardation, we think most often of Down syndrome. This is a very common type of mental retardation, but the disorder can take many forms. As more is learned about mental retardation, society is changing its views and expectations of the individuals with this diagnosis.

In the past, children identified as mentally retarded were often taken from their families and placed in institutions. This is where they spent the rest of their lives. They experienced very little human interaction, and educational opportunities were not made available to them.

Rarely did they leave the facility or have much contact with the outside world.

Thankfully, today fewer children are institutionalized. Children with mental retardation reared in their homes have social and intellectual skills far superior to those placed in institutions. As researchers have learned more about mental retardation, they have come to realize that with the proper care, stimulation, and learning environment, individuals with this disability can be educated and grow into functional, independent adults. With their rights protected by federal laws, individuals with mental retardation are today less likely to be in institutions and confined to their homes and more likely to be in classrooms, community facilities, and workplaces.

# How Mental Retardation Is Defined

Mental retardation is defined as significantly below average intellectual functioning. (Average intelligence is considered to be around an IQ of 100.) This condition may be a result of injury, disease, or an abnormality that exists before the age of eighteen. The impairment interferes with the individual's ability to adapt to or function within his or her environment.

This definition would apply to approximately 2.5 percent of the population, or about six million people. The measured intelligence of individuals with mental retardation is somewhere around 70 or below. Those considered in the mild range have a measured intelligence of 50 to 70. The moderate range is 40 to 55, with 25 to 40 considered severe. Those within the moderate to mild range are often children with Down syndrome. Males with fragile X are often found in the more severe range.

# The Causes of Mental Retardation

Both genetic and environmental factors can result in mental retardation. Congenital anomalies and genetic disorders account for the highest percentage of inherited forms of the disorder. Down syndrome and fragile X both have a genetic connection.

## Down Syndrome–Trisomy 21

Down syndrome is one of the most common forms of mental retardation. This disorder was first described in 1866, by John Langdon Down. He identified the distinctive set of characteristics that individuals with the disorder exhibit.

Down was not able to determine what caused the syndrome. It was not until 1959 that Jerome Lejune discovered Down syndrome was caused by a chromosomal abnormality affecting males and females evenly. Lejune found that an extra chromosome is the cause of Down syndrome. The individual has forty-seven, rather than forty-six, chromosomes. Instead of two, there are three number-21 chromosomes. This extra chromosome prevents normal brain development in the individual. The brain is smaller and less structurally complex in babies with Down syndrome.

Down syndrome appears in about one out of 700 births. The defect occurs in the egg 85 percent of the time and in the sperm 15 percent of the time. The age of the mother appears to have significant influence on the occurrence of the syndrome. A woman between the ages of thirty-five and thirty-nine is 6.5 times more likely to have a child with Down syndrome than is a twenty- to twenty-four-year-old. Between the ages of forty and forty-four, the likelihood increases to 20.5 times.

Besides having the very distinctive characteristics noticed by John Down (see below), children with the disorder may be more prone to other health risks. They often have a higher risk than the general population of developing heart defects, intestinal problems, respiratory infections, vision and hearing problems, thyroid problems, vertebrae instability, obesity, weak ankles and flat feet, and umbilical hernias.

With early intervention and the strong support of family and qualified professionals, children with Down syndrome can grow into independent adults. This can be accomplished by early identification of the child's strengths through early intervention programs. For children up to age three, these programs have produced excellent results. Local Arc chapters or school districts can provide information about such a program for your child. Arc is a support agency. At one time it was an acronym for association for retarded citizens. This is no longer used.

## Fragile X

Fragile X syndrome is the second most commonly identified form of mental retardation. It is a sex-linked trait that is inherited from either male or female carriers. This phenomenon occurs more frequently in males than females. One in every 1,500 males is born with the disorder, while it occurs in one in every 2,500 female births.

Caused by an abnormality on the X chromosome, fragile X results in severe mental retardation in males and less severe symptoms in females. It is estimated that 6 to 14 percent of all males with severe mental retardation have fragile X. About 7 percent of mild mental retardation in females is a result of fragile X.

Limited communication skills, severe behavior problems, and poor social skills make learning difficult for the child with fragile X. Researchers find that the IQ of the individual with this disorder tends to decrease with age. At this time, no one knows why this occurs.

Children with fragile X also have accompanying health and mental problems. Ten percent of boys with autism also have fragile X. Communication and speech disorders are frequent. In 20 percent of the cases, seizures are common. Behavior problems, self-injurious behaviors, AD/HD, conduct disorder, and disciplinary problems are also typical.

Neither of these conditions is a result of anything the parents did, or did not do, before or during the pregnancy. Guilt, fear, and grief are normal feelings when parents learn their child has mental retardation. Many seek the support of mental health professionals to cope with their feelings. While parents are working through their emotions, it is important that they also get support for their child as soon as possible.

## Environmental Causes

Other factors that may result in mental retardation are congenital infections, lead poisoning, and prenatal exposure to alcohol and drugs, especially crack. Traumatic brain injury from falls or automobile accidents involving the head are the most prevalent environmental causes. Diseases affecting the brain, such as meningitis and encephalitis, rank next, with environmental toxins responsible for only a small percentage of the cases.

Recent findings have identified one other powerful influence on the mental functioning of children. This is the educational background of the mother. Research conducted by the Centers for Disease Control and Prevention's Division of Birth Defects and Developmental Disabilities shows that 22 percent of all births in this country are to mothers with less than a high school education. Mothers who have not graduated from high school run four times the risk of having children with mental retardation.

This is thought to occur because the mothers do not know how to provide the experiences and mental stimulation needed in the first three years of life. This lack of stimulation can reduce the child's intelligence level by 15 points or more. The mother's level of education, therefore, far exceeds the risk of poverty as a factor for producing children with mild mental retardation.

Intervention to help young mothers complete their education and learn how to interact with their children could reduce this cause of mental retardation. However, no matter what the age of the parent, providing the proper stimulation and support at each stage of development is extremely important.

# The Development of the Child with Mental Retardation

Children with mental retardation often show substantial delays in their development. Many children attain each developmental milestone but at a much slower rate. Mental retardation that is present at birth can result in early signs of developmental delays. Astute pediatricians will monitor the telltale indicators carefully until a conclusive diagnosis can be made.

The greatest developmental gaps appear in the first three years of life. Infants are less alert and interested in their surroundings. They often have a weak sucking reflex and are poor nursers. Because of weak muscle tone, their bodies may be floppy and maintain poor head control. There are significant delays in smiling, following objects with their eyes, and rolling over.

As the child grows, sitting, standing, crawling, and walking are also noticeably delayed. Language and communication skills are slow to develop. Once the child learns to talk, unusual speech patterns often emerge that make being understood difficult. With intervention, the child may keep progressing in the first three years of life from one developmental milestone to the next.

During the school years, the goal is to teach adaptive skills, basic educational skills such as reading and math, and vocational skills. With these skills, 80 percent of those with mild mental retardation find employment in unskilled or semiskilled jobs. Many individuals leave their parents' home and marry or live independently in group homes. With a strong support system and by remaining in the home, rather than being placed in an institution, many individuals with mild mental retardation can live a full life.

For the most favorable long-term prognosis, an early diagnosis is especially important. Some forms of mental retardation, like Down syndrome and fragile X, can be diagnosed before or immediately after birth. Other forms may produce more subtle symptoms, delaying a diagnosis.

# How Mental Retardation Is Diagnosed

Down syndrome and fragile X can be determined prenatally. Family histories are particularly important in detecting these genetic forms of mental retardation. If either disorder is suspected, physicians can detect it through amniocentesis during the sixteenth to eighteenth week of pregnancy. Another method is chorionic villus sampling, performed between the ninth and eleventh weeks of pregnancy. An ultrasound may also be used in the prenatal detection of these disorders.

The cognitive functioning level of the child often cannot be determined until around school age. Children suspected of having a developmental disability are guaranteed a free appropriate public education under IDEA (see chapter 4). Multifactored evaluations, administered by professionals who are part of a multidisciplinary team, help determine the child's level of functioning. The cognitive level of functioning is usually determined by an intelligence test, such as the WISC-R. Other measures determine the child's fine and gross motor skills, language skills, self-help skills, and social-adaptive abilities.

Once all the information has been collected and evaluated, the team of professionals and parents meets to determine the least restrictive placement and to write an IEP for the learner. Placement in inclusive learning environments has proven to be very effective and beneficial for the learner with mental retardation.

# Observable Traits of Mental Retardation

Developmental delays are the most prominent signs that a parent or professional is likely to observe initially. Especially in the first three years of life, significant delays in such developmental markers as rolling over, smiling, holding up the head, babbling, standing, crawling, walking, and talking may be clear indicators.

In children with Down syndrome or fragile X, certain physical characteristics, often apparent at birth, are distinctive clues.

1. **Down Syndrome**
   - Head is smaller than normal and flatter in back.
   - As infants, the soft spot is larger and takes longer to close.
   - The neck may appear shorter, and newborns may have loose folds of skin on the back of neck.
   - Hands are smaller and fingers shorter than normal.
   - Eyes slant upward and ears are small.
   - Face appears flat because of small nose and a flat bridge. Nasal passages are often smaller.
   - Thin, straight hair.
   - Small mouth.

- Teeth come in late and not necessarily in the sequence most babies follow.
- Low muscle tone makes the child seem floppy. This can affect the child's movement, strength, and developmental patterns.

2. **Fragile X Syndrome**
   - Elongated faces.
   - Prominent jaws.
   - Elongated ears.
   - Bridge of nose is often flattened.
   - Poor coordination.
   - Many males have enlarged testicles.
   - Mitral valve prolapse is common.

# Strategies to Support the Child with Mental Retardation

Skill development and active involvement in the developmental process is important. Many children with mental retardation may need extra support to do what most children do naturally. Through repetition and "patterning" of the skill, learning can occur.

Though children with mental retardation do attain most of the developmental milestones, it is at a significantly slower pace and with more difficulty. Strong parental interaction is imperative to the early development of the child.

1. Early diagnosis and intervention provides the most desirable results in helping the child develop and use all her capabilities. With professional guidance, parents can learn how to best support their child. Some programs are designed so that professionals come to the home, and others require that the child go to a center.

2. Parents need to work with a team of professionals involved in helping their child. This team may include the child's physician,

a physical and/or occupational therapist, an early-intervention specialist, teachers, a psychologist, a psychiatrist, a cardiologist, an internist, or an ear, nose, and throat specialist.

3. Parents also benefit from support groups where they can share with other parents.

4. Reading and talking to the infant and child are the best ways to develop language skills.

5. Be as consistent as possible, especially in your goals and expectations.

6. Break tasks into smaller units to keep from getting overwhelmed. Small steps can keep you focused on your goals and minimize frustration.

7. Repetition may be boring to you, but the child will benefit from hearing the same thing over and over until it is internalized.

8. Being patient may be your most difficult task. Look for small achievements over time. These will indicate that you are on the right track.

9. Give genuine praise and positive reinforcement often. This will encourage the child and instill a sense of pride.

10. Interaction with other children can help the child develop social and language skills. Being part of a world outside of himself is a healthy part of development.

Children with mental retardation enjoy other people and are as caring and loving as other children. They can experience life with the same exuberance as any other child. When given the opportunity and a strong support system, most children with mental retardation grow up to be adults who work hard and enjoy their independence.

# Points to Ponder

1. Mental retardation results in developmental delays and a below-normal IQ.

2. Down syndrome and fragile X syndrome are the two most common forms of mental retardation.

3. Early diagnosis and intervention provide the greatest support for the child and parents.

4. Individuals with mild mental retardation can lead productive, independent lives outside the family home.

5. Allowing the child to interact with other children is very beneficial in the development of social and language skills.

6. A team of parents and professionals working together can determine the least restrictive environment for the child. An IEP will define the appropriate placement, learning accommodations, and goals for the child.

Contact the following organizations for more information, resources, and local support chapters.

- National Down Syndrome Society, 141 Fifth Avenue, New York, NY (800) 221-4602.

- Arc of the United States, 2501 Avenue J, Arlington, TX 76011 (817) 640-0204.

# 18

# Visual Impairment Including Blindness

Children with a visual impairment depend upon all their senses to help them learn. For many, these include the remainder of their vision. Many children, classified as legally blind, can learn to use their limited vision effectively. Many read regular print materials. Others with the same impairment may function more successfully within the classroom as active listeners. As auditory learners, they acquire much of their information from what they hear. Each child with a visual impairment uses his vision differently. While some can use their vision to learn, others rely more heavily on other senses. To accommodate all the learning styles, a multisensory, multimodal approach to learning is most beneficial.

# How Visual Impairment and Blindness Are Defined

There are specific criteria that define the different levels of blindness and visual impairment. Normal vision is 20/20 with a visual field of about 105 degrees. Individuals with a visual acuity in both eyes of less than 20/200 or a visual field of less than 20 degrees with corrective lenses are considered legally blind. This terminology may be misleading. As a legal term used to qualify the individual for services, it does not mean the individual has a total absence of vision. However, individuals who are totally blind have neither vision nor light and dark perception.

Those who have a visual acuity of between 20/70 and 20/200 with corrective lenses are said to have low vision. Depending upon the degree of impairment, there is some light and dark perception and functional vision. Children with low vision have a visual impairment severe enough to qualify them for special education services.

Blindness or visual impairment occurs in about 1 out of every 3,000 children. Of these children, about 46 percent are born blind. Another 38 percent lose their vision within the first year of life.

The intelligence levels of children who are blind or visually impaired vary as much as those of other children. Many children with visual problems have normal intelligence and function very well academically with the appropriate supports and learning aides. They often do not have accompanying disabilities that can complicate the learning process. However, multiple disabilities are not uncommon among children who are blind or have a severe visual impairment. For children qualifying as multihandicapped, a wide range of support services is available to meet each of their individual needs. Early intervention programs are available to infants who have been diagnosed.

## Common Visual Impairments

The location, extent, and type of visual problem often determines the accommodations, appropriate adaptive devices, support services, and learning style of the child. Some of the more common types of visual impairments are briefly discussed below.

1. **Albinism.** This hereditary condition reduces visual acuity and is characterized by a lack of pigment in the eyes or throughout the body. Children with this condition are extremely sensitive to light and often wear tinted glasses indoors and out. Seating away from windows and using a black desk blotter may help reduce glare.

2. **Amblyopia.** Caused by a muscle imbalance, the two eyes do not work together. This reduces the visual acuity in one eye. This may result in the brain suppressing the vision in one eye and, eventually, in a permanent loss of vision. If the other eye has any other type of impairment, the ramifications could be significant.

3. **Astigmatism.** Children with this condition have blurred vision. This can cause them to become irritable or restless when working for long periods of time. Copying from an overhead projector and other activities that require frequent refocusing from far to near, or vice versa may result in adverse behaviors.

4. **Cataract.** This condition causes the lens of the eye to become cloudy, and vision is blurred. Sensitivity to light is a frequent result of cataracts.

5. **Glaucoma.** When the pressure of the fluid inside the eye is too high, glaucoma occurs. If not treated, peripheral vision is affected and an eventual loss of vision occurs.

6. **Hyperopia.** The eyeball is too short from front to back, making close objects appear out of focus. Extended periods of sitting can be frustrating and fatiguing.

7. **Macular degeneration.** A condition that results in reduced acuity and a blind spot in the central portion of the visual field. This affects detail vision, which is required for reading and writing.

8. **Myopia.** Producing the opposite results of hyperopia, this condition occurs when the eyeball is too long from front to back. Seeing objects at a distance is difficult.

9. **Nystagmus.** Small, rapid, involuntary movements of the eyeballs characterize this condition. The movements can go from side to side, in a rotary or pendular motion, or in any combination. Maintaining focus and one's place can be difficult. Windows or line markers are helpful.

10. **Optic atrophy.** A degeneration of the optic nerve that affects visual acuity. Children with this condition hold reading material close to their eyes and prefer bright light.

11. **Retinitis pigmentosa.** A heredity degeneration of the retina that begins as night blindness and gradually produces a loss of peripheral vision. Regular print, rather than large, is often more appropriate for children with this condition. Due to the loss of peripheral vision, crowds and unfamiliar places may cause anxiety.

12. **Retinopathy of prematurity.** Found in premature infants given oxygen during incubation and those with low birth weight. Reduced visual acuity or total blindness occurs, as well as other disabilities.

13. **Strabismus.** Due to an imbalance of the muscles in the eyeball, the eyes are not directed to the same object at the same time. This condition can have more social ramifications than academic. Support and understanding is needed when this condition occurs.

# The Causes of Visual Impairment and Blindness

Loss of sight can occur in any area of the eye, including the retina, the optic nerves and neural pathways between the eye and occipital lobe of the brain, the eye muscles, the lens, and the cornea.

Some conditions are inherited. Congenital influences can result in conditions such as albinism or retinitis pigmentosa. Premature birth can affect normal eye development. Infants born before the retinas have fully developed may experience retinopathy of prematurity.

Tumors and head traumas resulting in traumatic brain injury are other factors that can affect vision. Diseases such as measles, rubella, diabetes, tuberculosis, meningitis, encephalitis, syphilis, and anoxia are other causes of visual impairments. Eye infections and a vitamin A deficiency can adversely affect vision.

Many times, with prevention, this condition need not occur. Silver nitrate drops given to newborns can prevent many eye infections, and with the proper diet and immunizations many diseases that pose a risk to the eyes can be avoided.

Knowing the warning signs of a visual problem increases the chances of early diagnosis and intervention. This support is especially important for the child and the family.

# Observable Traits of Visual Impairment and Blindness

Parents and physicians who are aware the child is not responding to his or her environment in a typical manner can save valuable time in helping the child. Early warning signs of blindness and visual impairment include the following:

1. The infant does not fixate on parents or bright and shiny objects early in life.
2. Abnormal eye movements may be noticed.
3. The infant may not blink or cry when a frightening movement is made.
4. Older children may rub their eyes, squint, or cover one eye. Eye poking is common.
5. The child may hold reading material or other work close to his eyes or at a distance.
6. The child may complain that things appear blurred or that words move about on the page.
7. The child may sit right next to the television or computer screen.

8. The child may complain of headaches or say her eyes hurt.

9. Sensitivity to sunlight or bright light is not uncommon. The child may squint or close his eyes when he goes outdoors.

10. Many children avoid reading.

Children who are blind at birth or experience early blindness often have severe developmental delays. This occurs because they are limited in their ability to imitate and pick up cues that stimulate early development. A child who has never seen someone walk does not know he has that ability. Therefore, parents and early intervention specialists need to work closely with the child to teach him the necessary skills. This is accomplished through words, movements, feelings, interpretations, and opportunities to learn. Children with multiple handicaps need a thorough diagnosis so that appropriate interventions can be provided.

# How Visual Impairments and Blindness Are Diagnosed

When parents observe any signs of a visual impairment, they should consult an ophthalmologist for a thorough examination. The earlier the condition is diagnosed, the sooner an intervention program can be put in place. Early intervention can improve the long-term prognosis.

The type of examination will depend on the age of the child. Eye charts are usually the initial diagnostic tool. The Allen Kindergarten Chart is used for younger children who cannot identify letters or numbers. The chart consists of pictures of toys, animals, and other objects familiar to small children. The tumbling *E* chart is also used. The letter *E* is placed in various positions, and the child responds by pointing in the direction the legs of the *E* are pointing. The Snellen eye chart is used for older children and adults.

An ophthalmologist can also examine the front and back part of the eye for tumors or any other abnormalities that may be the cause of the visual impairment. Sometimes an electroretinogram (ERG) is requested to check the retina for damage or abnormality.

Children diagnosed with blindness or visual impairments qualify for services under IDEA and should be placed in the least restrictive learning environment. They should also be provided with an IEP stating the goals and objectives. Section 504 of the Rehabilitation Act of 1973 and the American Disabilities Act also protect the rights of these children. All this legislation makes it possible for parents, professionals, and educators to work collaboratively to support the child's learning process.

# Strategies for the Visually Impaired or Blind Child

For many individuals with vision problems, the onset and severity of the condition determines the long-term outcome. Many individuals with a mild visual impairment and no other disabilities are very successful students. They continue their education through college and have fulfilling careers. Several factors appear to enhance learning opportunities for the child who is blind or visually impaired. One influence is the child's ability to use her remaining vision in the learning process. Certain exercises have been proven to strengthen the visual acuity of the individual. Most children who can use their remaining vision can read regular- or large-print books. Another strategy is identifying the strongest modality the child uses to learn and providing appropriate educational experiences. Making use of all the resources and learning aides available for the blind can also promote a positive learning experience.

## Special Devices for the Visually Impaired

Louis Braille, himself blind since the age of three, devised a system of raised points or dots. Each letter, number, and punctuation mark is represented by the number and placement of the dots in the cell. Each cell consists of one to six dots, no more than three dots high and two dots wide. Children who do not have, or are unable to use, their remaining vision can learn to read using the braille system. A braillewriter, slate, and stylus make written communication easier.

Other supportive devices are listed below.

1. Prescription lenses. May be tinted or dark if the child has a light sensitivity.

2. Small telescopes, either hand held or in the eyeglass frame, to view distant objects.

3. Hand-held magnifiers.

4. Book stands, acetate (preferably yellow), large-type books, textbooks on tape, cassette tape recorders, and computer technology.

5. Sun visors and shields for students who are sensitive to light.

6. A Cubarithum slate or Cranmer abacus can make learning math easier.

7. Raised-line paper, templates, and braille and raised markings on measurement tools (beakers, rulers, yardsticks, etc.).

8. A closed-circuit enlargement system to enlarge printed material on the TV screen.

9. A long cane, Mowat Sensor, Polaron, or Sensory 6 to enhance mobility.

In addition to these special devices, the strategies listed below can also be beneficial.

1. Prevention is ideal. Immunizations, a balanced diet, and protection from injury are the best ways of preventing blindness and visual impairments.

2. Early intervention programs with the guidance of specialists can begin at birth. These programs will help parents learn how to support their child.

3. Teaching modalities should include the use of sight, smell, sound, and touch. The child will learn about her world through exploration of all the senses.

4. When approaching a child who is blind, identify yourself. Voices are not always recognized.

5. Discourage inappropriate mannerisms such as eye poking, rocking, drooping the head, or making inappropriate sounds or noises.

6. Using a computer may make school assignments easier to complete.

7. Preferential seating in the front of the classroom is helpful.

8. Many calculators and computer programs have voice synthesizers that open up a whole new world for the child.

9. Vision therapy can be beneficial for some types of impairments.

10. Requesting a sighted guide may be helpful in maneuvering around the classroom or school building. Working with an orientation and mobility instructor will also help the child to learn how to travel independently.

# Points to Ponder

1. Many individuals with vision problems use their remaining vision to learn. Others use other modalities such as hearing, smell, and touch. Identifying the modality most comfortable for the learner is imperative to success.

2. In many cases, blindness and visual impairments are preventable.

3. The earlier a diagnosis is made and intervention occurs, the better the prognosis.

4. Many children with vision problems also have other disabilities that need to be addressed.

5. The rights of children with visual problems are protected under IDEA, Section 504, and ADA.

6. The availability of numerous adaptive devices can make learning and daily functioning easier and more successful.

For more resources and information about blindness and visual impairments, contact the following resources.

- American Foundation for the Blind, Inc., 15 West Sixteenth Street, New York, NY 10011 (212) 620-2020 or (800) 232-5463.
- National Federation of the Blind, 1800 Johnson Street, Baltimore, MD 21230 (301) 659-9314.
- National Society to Prevent Blindness, 500 East Remington Road, Schaumburg, IL 60173 (312) 843-2020.
- Recordings for the Blind, 20 Roszel Road, Princeton, NJ 08540 (609)452-0606.

# 19

# Hearing Impairment Including Deafness

Graduation day is filled with pride and a sense of accomplishment for both parents and students. For Amy's parents, however, this was especially true. Amy, deaf since birth, graduated from the local high school at the top of her class. Amy, who has perfect speech, attributes her accomplishments to her mother's persistence and her own resourcefulness. Through the use of hearing aids and headphones, as well as by reading lips, feeling vibrations, and being a keen observer of the world around her, Amy has mastered much in her young life.

Like Amy, an estimated two million Americans are deaf. Another fifteen million persons experience some degree of hearing loss. A strong support system can help them stay connected to their world. As Amy would quickly admit, living in a hearing world poses its challenges. Perseverance and persistence are needed to achieve goals.

A hearing impairment can have devastating effects on the learning process, especially speech and language development. Children who are born deaf or experience a significant hearing loss within the first two years of life usually do not develop normal speech and language patterns. The hearing impairment interferes with the young child's ability to imitate the speech patterns of parents and those around him. The hearing child will reproduce the sounds he hears by babbling, then saying simple words, and finally talking in complete sentences. This model does not always occur for the infant with a hearing disorder.

Being unable to hear individual sounds can interfere with the child's ability to understand what is being said. In speech, vowel sounds tend not to pose a great problem for children with a slight to moderate hearing loss. Vowels are low-frequency sounds and usually emphasized when pronounced. Consonants, however, are high-frequency sounds, and they are often missed by the child who is hearing impaired. Since conversation consists of the use of high- and low-frequency sounds, the individual with a hearing loss can miss a lot of what is said.

# How Hearing Impaired and Deafness Are Defined

A hearing loss occurs when there is a malformation or malfunction, in some part of the hearing mechanism. Anywhere along the route from the external, to the middle, to the inner ear, a flaw may occur. Some children experience a unilateral hearing loss (affecting one ear), and others have a bilateral loss (affecting both ears).

Hearing loss can range from a slight impairment to profound deafness. About 40 percent of children with a hearing impairment experience a mild hearing loss. Twenty percent have a moderate loss, and another 20 percent have a severe loss. The final 20 percent have a profound hearing loss. The characteristics of each level are described below and in Figure 19.1.

## Normal range of hearing.

- (Decibels (dB) measure the loudness, or intensity, of a sound.)
- Individuals with normal hearing can hear sounds from −10 to 15 decibels.
- The normal range for children is usually between 0 and 15 decibels.
- For adults, the normal range is between 0 and 25 decibels.

## Slight hearing loss.

- Sounds must register between 16 and 25 decibels to be heard.
- May be a result of middle-ear infections.
- Vowel sounds can be easily heard.
- May miss unvoiced consonants.
- Hearing difficulty occurs with faint or distant speech.
- May miss up to 10 percent of what is said and may easily fatigue from straining to listen.
- May miss subtle conversational cues, thus appearing socially inappropriate.
- Hearing aid or FM amplification may be helpful.

## Mild hearing loss.

- Sounds must register between 26 and 40 decibels to be heard.
- Caused most often by chronic otitis media.
- Some vowel sounds and the louder voiced consonants can be heard.
- Speech and language problems are usually present.
- May cause the individual to become fatigued and appear inattentive when he attempts to follow the conversation.
- May cause the individual to miss up to 40 percent of what is said.
- May benefit from the use of a hearing aid, FM amplification system, and language therapy.

## Moderate hearing loss.

- Sounds must register between 41 and 55 decibels to be heard.
- May miss 45 to 90 percent of what is being said.
- May hear almost no speech sounds at the conversational level.
- May have a limited vocabulary.

- May make frequent speech errors.
- May experience a delay in learning.
- May benefit from the use of a hearing aid, FM amplification, speech and language therapy, and tutoring.

## Moderate to severe hearing loss.

- Sound must register between 56 and 70 decibels to be heard.
- Hearing loss usually occurs before the age of two.
- Amplification is essential.
- May hear some sounds but cannot distinguish words without amplification.
- Speech can be taught with amplification devices if condition is detected early enough.

## Severe hearing loss.

- Sounds must register between 71 and 90 decibels to be heard.
- No speech sounds can be heard at normal conversational levels.
- If hearing loss occurs before normal speech development, oral speech and language skills may be severely delayed.
- Hearing loss that occurs after speech and language skills are developed may not produce as severe an oral language deficit.
- Amplification and speech and hearing therapy are essential.
- Special classes where a total communication approach to learning is offered may be extremely beneficial to the learner.

## Profound hearing loss.

- Sounds must be greater that 91 decibels to be heard. (A rock concert registers at around 100 decibels.)
- May react to very loud sounds but is more aware of vibrations.
- Cannot comprehend speech.
- Depending on the age of onset, some individuals with profound hearing loss do speak.
- Communication is through signing and lipreading.

**Fig. 19.1. Relationship of Degree of Long-term Hearing Loss to Psychosocial Impact and Educational Needs**

| Degree of Hearing Loss Based on modified pure tone average (500–4000 hertz) | Possible Effect of Hearing Loss on the Understanding of Language and Speech | Possible Psychosocial Impact of Hearing Loss | Potential Educational Needs and Programs |
| --- | --- | --- | --- |
| **Normal Hearing** −10 to +15 decibels | Children have better hearing sensitivity than the accepted normal range for adults. A child with hearing sensitivity in the −10 to +15 decibel range will detect the complete speech signal even at soft conversation levels. However, good hearing does not guarantee good ability to discriminate speech in the presence of background noise. | | |

*(continued on next page)*

**Fig. 19.1. Relationship of Degree of Long-term Hearing Loss to Psychosocial Impact and Educational Needs,** *continued*

| Degree of Hearing Loss | Possible Effect of Hearing Loss | Possible Psychological Impact | Potential Educational Needs |
|---|---|---|---|
| **Minimal (Borderline)** 16 to 25 decibels | May have difficulty hearing faint or distant speech. At 15 decibels student can miss up to 10 percent of speech signal when teacher is at a distance greater than 3 feet and when the classroom is noisy, especially in the elementary grades when verbal instruction predominates. | May be unaware of subtle conversational cues, which could cause child to be viewed as inappropriate or awkward. May miss portions of fast-paced peer interactions, which could begin to have an impact on socialization and self-concept. May have immature behavior. Child may be more fatigued than classmates, due to listening effort needed. | May benefit from mild gain/low MPO hearing aid or personal FM system dependent on loss configuration. Would benefit from sound-field amplification if classroom is noisy and/or reverberant. Favorable seating. May need attention to vocabulary or speech, especially with recurrent otitis media history. Appropriate medical management necessary for conductive losses. Teacher requires inservice on impact of hearing loss on language development and learning. |

| **Mild**<br>26 to 40 decibels | At 30 decibels can miss 25 to 40 percent of speech signal. The degree of difficulty experienced in school will depend upon the noise level in classroom, distance from teacher, and the configuration of the hearing loss. Without amplification the child with 35- to 40-decibel loss may miss at least 50 percent of class discussions, especially when voices are faint or speaker is not in line of vision. Will miss consonants, especially when a high-frequency hearing loss is present. | Barriers beginning to build with negative impact on self-esteem as child is accused of "hearing when he or she wants to," "daydreaming," or "not paying attention." Child begins to lose ability for selective hearing and has increased difficulty suppressing background noise, which makes the learning environment stressful. Child is more fatigued than classmates, due to listening effort needed. | Will benefit from a hearing aid and use of a personal FM or sound-field FM system in the classroom. Needs favorable seating and lighting. Refer to special education for language evaluation and educational follow-up. Needs auditory skill building. May need attention to vocabulary and language development, articulation or speech reading and/or special support in reading. May need help with self-esteem. Teacher inservice required. |

*(continued on next page)*

**Fig. 19.1. Relationship of Degree of Long-term Hearing Loss to Psychosocial Impact and Educational Needs,** *continued*

| Degree of Hearing Loss | Possible Effect of Hearing Loss | Possible Psychological Impact | Potential Educational Needs |
|---|---|---|---|
| **Moderate**<br>41 to 55 decibels | Understands conversational speech at a distance of 3 to 5 feet (face-to-face) only if structure and vocabulary are controlled. Without amplification the amount of speech signal missed can be 50 to 75 percent with 40-decibel loss and 80 to 100 percent with 50-decibel loss. Is likely to have delayed or defective syntax, limited vocabulary, imperfect speech production, and an atonal voice quality. | Often with this degree of hearing loss, communication is significantly affected, and socialization with peers with normal hearing becomes increasingly difficult. With full-time use of hearing aids and/or FM systems child may be judged as a less competent learner. There is an increasing impact on self-esteem. | Refer to special education for language evaluation and for educational follow-up. Amplification is essential (hearing aids and FM system). Special education support may be needed, especially for primary children. Attention to oral language development, reading and written language. Auditory skill development and speech therapy are usually needed. Teacher inservice required. |

**Moderate to Severe**
56 to 70 decibels

Without amplification, conversation must be very loud to be understood. A 55-decibel loss can cause child to miss up to 100 percent of speech information. Will have marked difficulty in school situations requiring verbal communication in both one-to-one and group situations. Delayed language, syntax, reduced speech intelligibility, and atonal voice quality are likely.

Full-time use of a hearing aid and/or FM system may result in child being judged by both peers and adults as a less competent learner, resulting in poorer self-concept and social maturity and contributing to a sense of rejection. Inservice to address these attitudes may be helpful.

Full-time use of amplification is essential. Will need resource teacher or special class depending on magnitude of language delay. May require special help in all language skills, language-based academic subjects, vocabulary, grammar, and pragmatics, as well as reading and writing. Probably needs assistance to expand experiential language base. Inservice of mainstream teachers required.

*(continued on next page)*

**Fig. 19.1. Relationship of Degree of Long-term Hearing Loss to Psychosocial Impact and Educational Needs,** *continued*

| Degree of Hearing Loss | Possible Effect of Hearing Loss | Possible Psychological Impact | Potential Educational Needs |
|---|---|---|---|
| **Severe**<br>71 to 90 decibels | Without amplification may hear loud voices about one foot from ear. When sound is amplified optimally, children with hearing ability of 90 decibels or better should be able to identify environmental sounds and detect all the sounds of speech. If loss is of prelingual onset, oral language and speech may not develop spontaneously or will be severely delayed. If hearing loss is of recent onset, speech is likely to deteriorate with quality becoming atonal. | Child may prefer other children with hearing impairments as friends and playmates. Though this may further isolate the child from the mainstream, these peer relationships may foster improved self-concept and a sense of cultural identity. | May need full-time special aural and oral program with emphasis on all auditory language skills, speech reading, concept development, and speech. As loss approaches 80 to 90 decibels, may benefit from a Total Communication approach, especially in the early language learning years. Individual hearing aid and personal FM system are essential. Need to monitor effectiveness of communication modality. As much participation in regular classes as is beneficial to student. Inservice of mainstream teachers essential. |

**Profound**
91 decibels or more

Aware of vibrations more than tonal pattern. Many rely on vision rather than hearing as primary avenue for communication and learning. Detection of speech sounds dependent upon loss configuration and use of amplification. Speech and language will not develop simultaneously and are likely to deteriorate rapidly if hearing loss is of recent onset.

Depending on auditory and oral competence, peer use of sign language, parental attitude, etc., child may or may not increasingly prefer association with the deaf culture.

May need special program for deaf children with emphasis on all language skills and academic areas. Program needs specialized supervision and comprehensive support services. Early use of amplification likely to help if part of an intensive training program. May be cochlear-implant or vibrotactile-aid candidate. Requires continual appraisal of needs in regard to communication and learning mode. Part-time in regular classes as much as beneficial to student.

*(continued on next page)*

**Fig. 19.1. Relationship of Degree of Long-term Hearing Loss to Psychosocial Impact and Educational Needs,** *continued*

| Degree of Hearing Loss | Possible Effect of Hearing Loss | Possible Psychological Impact | Potential Educational Needs |
|---|---|---|---|
| **Unilateral**<br>One normal hearing ear and one ear with at least a permanent mild hearing loss | May have difficulty hearing faint or distant speech. Usually has difficulty localizing sounds and voices. Unilateral listener will have greater difficulty understanding speech when environment is noisy and/or reverberant. Difficulty detecting or understanding soft speech from side of bad ear, especially in a group discussion. | Child may be accused of selective hearing due to discrepancies in speech understanding in quiet versus noise. Child will be more fatigued in classroom setting due to greater effort needed to listen. May appear inattentive or frustrated. Behavior problems sometimes evident. | May benefit from personal FM or sound-field FM system in classroom. CROS hearing aid may be of benefit in quiet settings. Needs favorable seating and lighting. Student is at risk for educational difficulties. Educational monitoring warranted with support services provided as soon as difficulties appear. Teacher inservice is beneficial. |

**Note**: All children with hearing loss require periodic audiologic evaluation, rigorous monitoring of amplification, and regular monitoring of communication skills. All children with hearing loss (especially conductive) need appropriate medical attention in conjunction with educational programming.

Developed by and used with permission of Karen L. Anderson, Ed.S., and Noel D. Matkin, Ph.D. Adapted from *Relationship of Hearing Impairment to Educational Needs*, by R. J. Bernero and H. Bothwell (Illinois Department of Public Health and Office of Superintendent of Public Instruction, 1966).

## Types of Hearing Loss

There are three types of hearing loss. Conductive hearing loss can occur in the external or middle ear. Chronic middle-ear infections are the most common cause of this type of hearing loss. Ninety-five percent of children who have had such infections experience some temporary conductive hearing loss. This type of hearing loss sometimes can be corrected with medications and/or surgery. Children with middle-ear dysfunctions may benefit from having tubes surgically placed in the ear. This gives temporary assistance by equalizing the pressure in the middle ear and permits drainage of any accumulated fluid in the ear. This surgery will improve hearing.

Sensorineural hearing loss is a more severe form. This type occurs when the cochlea or auditory nerve malfunctions. Assisting this type of hearing loss may be difficult. However, cochlear implants are proving successful in helping restore some level of hearing for many individuals who are deaf. These implants are permanent and electronically "synthesize" hearing. The individual will never hear as a person without a hearing loss, but the implants do assist the deaf individual with hearinglike abilities. Hearing aids, amplification systems, and speech and language therapy are other effective interventions for this type of hearing loss.

Mixed hearing loss is a combination of both types. This may result in any degree of hearing loss.

# Causes of Hearing Impairment and Deafness

Hearing loss may occur for any of several reasons. Heredity is one factor. There are seventy inherited syndromes that are associated with deafness. One in every two thousand to six thousand children are born deaf. Ninety percent of these children are born to hearing parents with a recessive gene that they have passed on to their child.

Children born with a cleft palate are at risk for hearing loss. They are 50 to 90 percent more susceptible to middle-ear infections than children without this condition. The malformation of the palate interferes with proper drainage from the middle ear, causing more ear infections. This raises the risk of damage to the middle ear and potential hearing loss.

Other causes include head trauma and overexposure to noise exceeding 120 decibels, such as loud music or the type of job-related noise experienced by factory or construction workers. Earplugs can prevent this type of hearing loss.

Disease is another major cause of hearing impairment. Rubella in the first trimester of pregnancy, bacterial meningitis, and childhood measles, mumps, and chickenpox can all affect hearing. Immunizations for these diseases can prevent a hearing loss.

Whatever the cause, early diagnosis and intervention are imperative for the best long-term results, often dramatically reducing the effects on the developing child.

# Developmental Differences of the Child Who Is Hearing Impaired or Deaf

Throughout this book, the emphasis has been on how critical the first three years of life are to normal development. During these years, the skills needed for the rest of our lives are acquired, forming the foundation upon which we build as we learn new ways to use and expand those skills.

The early development of speech and language is often significantly affected by a hearing loss. A child who experiences hearing impairment during these developmental years will have difficulty learning to speak and communicate effectively. One-third of the more severely affected children are likely to have multiple disabilities, which may include mental retardation.

It is important to stress, however, that many individuals who are hearing impaired experience academic and career success. The prognosis is particularly good for children who experience hearing loss after speech and language have developed. These children may still have difficulty communicating and will benefit from the continued support of a speech and language therapist, but they are less likely to have academic and learning problems.

# How a Hearing Loss Is Diagnosed

Hearing loss is detected with an instrument called an audiometer, which measures the loss in decibels. An audiologist or speech-language pathologist can administer the test to children of any age. Children under six months of age are evaluated objectively with auditory brainstem response (ABR) or otoacoustic emissions (OAE) testing.

Children are evaluated to determine the amount and type of hearing loss and whether it is of high- or low-frequency sounds or both. Tests can also determine whether the hearing loss is in one or both ears.

Unless there is a family history of hearing problems or physical symptoms are apparent, a hearing loss can go undetected for many years. Generally speaking, the less severe the hearing loss, the longer it takes to get a diagnosis. For this reason, many parents are confused when their child is diagnosed with a hearing loss. They do not understand why the child did not let them know he could not hear. We must remember that the younger the child is when the loss occurs, the less likely he is to relate a problem. The child thinks everyone hears the way she does and is unaware that the distortions are not normal. That is why being aware of the signs indicating a hearing loss may lead to an earlier diagnosis.

# Observable Traits of the Child Who Is Hearing Impaired or Deaf

Early signs that something is amiss can be detected in the newborn by an astute observer. A hearing specialist should be contacted if any of these characteristics persists.

- The sleeping infant does not respond to loud or startling noises.
- Infant does not respond to mother's voice.
- Baby does not turn toward sounds.
- Speech and language development show early signs of delay (see chapter 10).

- The infant may begin by cooing and babbling but does not progress to imitating speech sounds to form syllables and words.

- The child becomes less verbal, rather than more so, and is not speaking by the age of one.

- As the child gets older, he has trouble following directions and often looks confused and bewildered.

- Lipreading and interpreting gestures may be the child's way of compensating for not being able to hear the words.

# Strategies to Support Children with a Hearing Loss

Children with a hearing loss qualify for support under federal laws and are entitled to a free appropriate public education in the least restrictive environment. For some children this may be a school specializing in the education of the deaf. Children requiring special education and speech and language services will receive an IEP. Parents should be part of a multidisciplinary team that decides the best course to follow to educate the child. The following suggestions may be included in the management plan for the child.

1. Early intervention programs provide services to children up to three years old. They often begin with the professional coming to the home and eventually have the child come to a center.

2. Speech and language therapy should be offered as soon as a diagnosis is made.

3. Surgical procedures may be indicated. Placing tubes in the ears may improve hearing for those with a middle-ear dysfunction. Cochlear implants may assist the individual who is deaf.

4. Devices such as hearing aids and FM amplification systems significantly help the hearing impaired. Lipreading may be beneficial.

5. American Sign Language and other modes of manual communication, such as Signed English, cued speech, Signing Exact English, and Pidgin English, are effective methods of communication used by the deaf community.

6. Telecommunication Device for the Deaf (TDD) is another communication tool for individuals with a severe or profound hearing loss. The teletypewriter-telephone (TTY) allows the deaf to telephone each other. Telecaption decoders can be used when watching the television. RadioMail makes use of Internet technology.

7. For some children, an interpreter is helpful and makes learning easier.

8. Hearing dogs can be trained to alert their owners and lead them to the source of the sound.

9. At times, psychological therapy can be beneficial for those who need help managing their frustration surrounding their condition.

10. For the older student, there are many colleges and universities that specialize in meeting the educational needs of deaf and hearing-impaired learners.

11. The office for students with disabilities located on any college campus will supply hearing-impaired students with an FM amplification system and someone to sign lectures for the student.

In her book *How to Survive Hearing Loss,* Charlotte Himber lists the ten commandments of living with a person with a hearing loss.

1. Be patient.

2. Accept reality. The condition usually does not go away, so focus on the child's positive qualities.

3. Speak slowly. Allow the child time to process information.

4. Do not shout. This does not help. Speaking distinctly is more beneficial.

5. Reduce distractions and background noises when talking to the hearing impaired.

6. Face the person to whom you are speaking. He needs to see your face to read your lips and see your gestures.

7. Do not walk away while you are still talking. Finish your thought before you turn and go.

8. Use a silent signal to indicate that the child with a hearing loss is speaking too loudly.

9. Do not get annoyed if you must repeat what you have just said.

10. Have a heart. Keep your focus on the child, not the disability. This child is full of hopes, dreams, and talents and needs your support.

Parents, teachers, and professionals must work together to help the child reach his full potential. When this happens, children like Amy find their place in a hearing world. Their accomplishments can exceed our wildest expectations. After all, deafness never discouraged Beethoven from sharing his gifts, and our world has been a more beautiful place because of him.

# Points to Ponder

1. There are several types of hearing loss, ranging from slight to profound.

2. Early detection is of the utmost importance so that normal speech and language development can occur.

3. Surgery and medications can improve some cases of hearing loss.

4. For many, hearing aids, FM amplification systems, and TDD are helpful communication devices.

5. The deaf community has its own culture and language (American Sign Language). They are proud of their accomplishments and celebrate their deafness. They are often distrustful of the hearing world attempting to impose its standards on them.

For more information and resources about deafness and the hearing impaired contact:

- American Speech-Language-Hearing Association, 10801 Rockville Pike, Rockville, MD 20852 (301) 897-5700.

- American Society for Deaf Children (800) 942-2732.

- Deafness Research Foundation (800) 535-3323.

- Deafpride, 1350 Potomac Avenue, SE, Washington, DC 20003. (202) 675-6700.

# 20

# Orthopedic Impairment

When we encounter a child with a physical impairment, we often unfairly assume that he may be mentally impaired as well. But children with visual, hearing, and orthopedic impairments span the intellectual realm. The majority fall within the normal range of intelligence.

Through the use of adaptive devices and medical technology, many children with an orthopedic impairment function very well in the classroom and their social environments. Provided with the physical space for maneuverability, these children can zip around classrooms and school buildings with relative ease.

# How Orthopedic Impairment Is Defined

Orthopedic refers to the muscles, bones, and joints that allow us to move. Thus a child with an orthopedic impairment would have restricted movement. Depending upon the degree of involvement, some children have a limited amount of restriction and others may not be able to move at all. Other children cannot control the movement of their muscles. Orthopedic impairments can be caused by a prenatal defect or an acquired source (occurring after birth, such as disease or accident).

# Prenatal Causes of Orthopedic Impairments

Orthopedic impairments that occur during pregnancy include clubfoot, spina bifida, and the absence of arms or legs. These birth defects may be inherited or occur for other reasons. Diseases such as rubella can result in a deformity when they occur during the first trimester. Certain medications taken during pregnancy can also cause abnormalities. The fertility drug thalidomide, given to women in the 1960s, is perhaps the best-known example.

Spina bifida is a malformation of the spine. Meaning "open spine" or "split spine," this condition is a result of the vertebrae, or bones, protecting the spinal cord not closing properly. In some cases, the spinal cord protrudes from an opening in the spine. About eight thousand babies are born each year with this condition.

Below the point where the opening occurs the body is permanently paralyzed. This makes the child unable to feel pain, pressure, heat, and cold. Therefore, injury may occur to this area without the child being aware. Because of the paralysis, children with spina bifida usually do not have bowel and bladder control.

Most children with this condition benefit from physical and occupational therapy. Surgery allows some children to acquire some degree of mobility. With the support of braces, splints, crutches, and walkers, many of the children learn to walk. Children needing to travel long distances (from class to class) may use a wheelchair to reduce their travel time.

According to the guidelines provided by the Americans with Disabilities Act (ADA), school buildings and classrooms must be made "handicap accessible." Most children with spina bifida, being of normal intelligence, do well in a general education classroom. Those who would benefit from special services can qualify for this support under IDEA. This legislation also protects the rights of children with an acquired orthopedic impairment.

# Acquired Causes of an Orthopedic Impairment

An acquired disability occurs during or after birth. This type of impairment may be caused by an illness or a disease, such as poliomyelitis, bone tuberculosis, or multiple sclerosis, or by an accident or injury, such as brain trauma (see chapter 21), cerebral palsy, amputations, or burns.

Caused by a virus that attacks the central nervous system, poliomyelitis, or polio, is a disease that rarely occurs anymore, thanks to the work of doctors Jonas Salk and Albert Sabin. Through their discovery of a vaccine, polio has been preventable since the 1960s.

Multiple sclerosis, one the other hand, is still incurable. This progressive disease of the central nervous system can lead to numbness and weakness in the limbs, a loss of balance, and usually paralysis.

Cerebral palsy is characterized by a lack of muscular coordination, shaking, or unclear speech. *Cerebral* refers to the location in the brain and *palsy* means "paralysis or muscle weakness." Cerebral palsy occurs in one out of about every five hundred births. The most common cause is a lack of oxygen at birth. There is a high incidence of cerebral palsy and mental retardation.

There are two types of cerebral palsy. The spastic type is the most common. Children with this type of cerebral palsy have stiff muscles that are difficult to move. The rigid muscles often pull the limbs into contorted positions. The second type is ataxia. This form is characterized by muscles that are rigid one minute and floppy the next. This lack of muscle coordination makes the child's movements appear clumsy and jerky.

Many children with this condition can learn to walk with the help of canes and walkers, and many rely on a wheelchair to transport them quickly from place to place. Because many children with cerebral palsy are prone to scoliosis, a curvature of the spine, therapists and physicians try to limit the time they spend in a wheelchair.

The child can often function well in a general education classroom with the appropriate adaptive devices. For many children with cerebral palsy, the computer is the most effective learning tool. The children who have the coordination to use a keyboard can do all of their written work on the computer. A pen with a light can be added to a computer and used by the child as a pointer. Some adaptive devices are so sensitive that eye movements, a wrinkled forehead, or a raised eyebrow will activate the computer.

Many children with cerebral palsy have unclear speech. In these children, the disorder has affected the muscles of the mouth and vocal cords. Facilitated communication using augmentative devices, such as speech and voice synthesizers, communication boards, talking notebooks, and page turners can be used to help the child communicate effectively. Speech and language therapy will also benefit the child whose speech has been affected.

# Early Intervention

Intervention therapy should begin as soon as any of these conditions is diagnosed. Public agencies provide these services. Each school district has a person in charge of programs for infants and toddlers with special needs. Contact this individual to find out which agencies have services to meet the child's specific needs.

For most children with an orthopedic impairment, the condition will remain lifelong. However, with early intervention and therapy, many become mobile and lead full lives with successful careers. Participation in most sports, independent living, driving, and marriage are all within the realm of the individual who does not feel limited by his disability. One of our most impressive presidents, Franklin Delano Roosevelt, was himself orthopedically impaired.

# Points to Ponder

1. Orthopedic impairments result when there is a restriction of movement or lack of coordination of the muscles, bones, and/or joints.

2. The impairments may occur as a result of a birth defect, disease, illness, or injury.

3. Most children with an orthopedic impairment are of normal intelligence. Many, with the support of physical and occupational therapy, as well as adaptive and augmentive devices, are mobile and learn effectively.

4. Children needing support services usually qualify under IDEA or Section 504. Ramps, elevators, and special transportation make the learning environment accessible, as provided by ADA.

5. Early intervention brings the best results in helping the children learn to function effectively and reach their full potential.

For more information and additional resources, please contact the following agencies.

- The National Easter Seals Society, 70 East Lake Street, Chicago, IL 60601-5907 (312) 726-6200.

- National Multiple Sclerosis Society, 205 East Forty-second Street, New York, NY 10010 (800) 344-4867.

- Spina Bifida Association of America, 4590 MacArthur Boulevard NW, Suite 250, Washington, DC 20007-4226 (202) 944-3285.

- United Cerebral Palsy Association, Inc., 1522 K Street NW, Suite 1112, Washington, DC 20005 (203) 842-1266.

# 21

# Traumatic Brain Injury

Of all the disabilities discussed thus far, this is the most preventable. Each year, approximately two million Americans sustain a brain injury. According to the Brain Injury Association, that equates to an astounding one every fifteen seconds. The National Pediatric Trauma Registry reports that more than one million of these injuries are sustained by children, thirty thousand of whom experience permanent disabilities.

## How Traumatic Brain Injury Is Defined

Traumatic brain injury occurs when an insult to the brain is severe enough to cause a change in the level of consciousness, and/or an abnormality in the structure of the brain impairing cognitive abilities or physical functioning. The injury is the result of an external physical force, not a degenerative or congenital condition.

Males are two times more likely to be injured than females. At greatest risk are males between the ages of fourteen and twenty-four, followed by infants and the elderly. The brain injuries sustained by males tend to be more severe. Their life-styles and increased exposure to risks make males more vulnerable to this type of injury.

Children are most likely to incur brain injuries in the spring and summer months and on the weekends, usually between noon and midnight. Traffic accidents account for 46 percent of the injuries, while 34.3 percent occur at home and 6.6 percent in recreation areas.

## Types of Traumatic Brain Injury

There are two types of injury that can be sustained by the brain—open head injury and closed head injury. Both can result in severe brain injuries and permanent neurological damage.

Open head injury occurs when the head hits or strikes a stationary surface or is hit by a moving object. The force of the impact can result in scalp injuries and skull fractures. Blood clots beneath the surface of the skull, and contusions or bruising may also develop from the force of the impact. This type of injury is usually located at a specific place in the brain. Therefore, the results of the injury will produce very specific problems. For example, there may be a loss of sight or ability to speak.

Closed head injury is more widespread. Inertial forces cause the brain to undergo a violent back and forth motion as it bounces off the inside of the skull. Nerve fibers and blood vessels may tear from the violent force. Often this injury involves the brain stem, which connects the large areas of the brain to the spinal cord. Injury to this area may result in physical, intellectual, emotional, social, and vocational impairments. The entire personality of the individual may be permanently altered.

# Causes of Traumatic Brain Injury

In the general population, more than 50 percent of the traumatic brain injuries are a result of traffic accidents. Falls are the second leading cause, accounting for more than 20 percent of the injuries. Firearms result in 12 percent of the injuries, and sports and recreational activities account for 10 percent. Alcohol is a factor in 50 percent of all the cases. The remaining 8 percent are from causes such as cardiac arrest, strokes, or any loss of oxygen to the brain (anoxia).

In young children, abuse is the leading cause of this type of injury. Sixty-four percent of children under the age of one year who are physically abused sustain traumatic brain injuries. Shaking the infant is a very common cause. In children under the age of five, 50 percent are injured as a result of falls they have sustained. In school-age children and adolescents, motor vehicle and biking accidents and attempted suicides are the major causes. With the increase in violence, firearms are rapidly becoming a frequent cause of brain injury in children and youth.

# How Traumatic Brain Injury Is Diagnosed

Following an injury of the head or brain, some patients may fall into a period of unconsciousness called a coma. The duration of the coma can be just a few minutes or a prolonged period of time. The length and severity of the coma is usually an indication of the extent of the injury. The Glasgow Coma Score is one scale used to determine the severity of the coma. The scale is administered within the first six hours following the injury. It evaluates the degree to which patients can open their eyes, and their motor and verbal responses.

A CT scan is another tool often used to determine a trauma to the brain. An X ray of the skull may be helpful if a fracture is suspected. Observation of the patient can be another clear indicator that a severe injury has been incurred.

# Observable Symptoms of Traumatic Brain Injury

Frequently referred to as the silent epidemic, the symptoms of traumatic brain injury can be deceptive. Sometimes very specific changes occur that can be observed after a head injury has been sustained, and other times the symptoms are less visible. Because head injuries tend to worsen over time, it is always prudent to have a physician examine the child even if no evidence of injury is present. If after a head injury any of the following warning signs appear, your child should receive immediate medical attention.

1.  The more visible signals indicating an injury might include the following:
    - The child becomes lethargic.
    - Appears confused.
    - Becomes irritable.
    - Develops severe headaches.
    - Experiences changes in speech, vision, or movement.
    - Bleeding occurs.
    - Begins to vomit one to two hours after the injury.
    - Has a seizure.
    - Falls into a coma.

2.  More subtle or hidden, symptoms could include changes in the following areas:
    - Long- and short-term memory difficulties.
    - Difficulty concentrating.
    - Slowness in thinking.
    - Difficulty maintaining attention.
    - Perception is distorted.
    - Difficulty communicating in either oral or written language.
    - Poor planning, sequencing, and/or judgment capabilities.
    - Changes in mood, personality, or emotional status.

3. Some affective behaviors that can arise long after the initial injury could include the following:
   - The occurrence of eating disorders where the individual eats and/or drinks excessively.
   - Verbosity (excessive talking).
   - Excessive pacing and restlessness.
   - A gradual decline in behavior that may include seizure disorders.
   - May flee an uncomfortable situation that may result in getting lost or disoriented.

# Support Strategies for the Child with Traumatic Brain Injury

Depending on the extent of these symptoms, traumatic head injuries can result in major neurological changes and even death. For most patients, rehabilitation is begun immediately after the injury, even while in a coma. The rehabilitation is focused on the areas of functioning most affected. Physical therapy may be needed for motor deficits. Occupational therapy may help in relearning self-care skills and sensory integration problems. A speech and language pathologist may be required if communication skills have been affected. Psychological and family issues may best be addressed in therapy with a mental health professional.

Because traumatic brain injury is now included under IDEA, special education accommodations may need to be established if cognitive and learning skills have been impaired. An IEP should be written to accommodate for the special needs. Parents, professionals, and educators need to work as a team to educate and reorient the injured child back into the learning environment.

# Preventive Measures

Traumatic brain injury is a preventable disability. By using caution and the appropriate safety measures, many accidents can be avoided. The following safety devices will protect not only the child but the adults as well. Adults need to be good role models.

1. When biking or riding a motorcycle, wear a helmet. In many states, helmets are mandatory. The incidence of head injuries is reduced by 85 percent, and brain injuries by 88 percent, when a bicycle helmet is worn.

2. Buckle up each time you get into the car, and place the child in a seat belt, or restraint, appropriate for the age of the child. Statistics prove that seat belts save lives. They are 57 percent effective in preventing fatalities and traumatic brain injuries.

3. Air bags also prevent many head injuries when a collision occurs. (At this writing, there is controversy over the safety of air bags for children. At present, it appears the child is much safer when secured in the backseat of the vehicle.) The overall statistics still maintain that together, seat belts and air bags can be a lifesaving combination.

4. If you must drink, do not drive. Have a designated driver whose job it is to get you and your passengers home safely. Many parents of teenage drivers are contracting with their child to call them if the child has been drinking. Local chapters of Mothers Against Drunk Drivers (MADD) are targeting the teenage population, but no one should drink and drive.

5. Speeding is another preventable factor. For every 10 miles per hour over 50 miles per hour, your chances of being killed or seriously injured in a traffic accident are doubled.

6. Each year eighty-two thousand Americans receive brain injuries as a result of sports and recreational activities. Contact sports have a higher rate of injury than individual sports.

7. Injuries and deaths caused by children and youths handling firearms are increasing. Adults need to insure the child's safety by keeping firearms inaccessible.

# Points to Ponder

1. Disabilities that result from a traumatic brain injury can be prevented.

2. Children who sustain head injuries should be examined by a physician, even if no adverse signs are observed.

3. Most traumatic brain injuries are permanent and cause disabilities in many major areas of functioning.

4. Children with this type of injury are now protected under IDEA.

For more information and resources contact The National Brain Injury Association, 1776 Massachusetts Avenue NW, Suite 100, Washington, DC 20036 (800) 444-6443.

# 22

# Environmentally Induced Impairments

Most of the disabilities discussed so far have resulted from circumstances beyond the control of the parents and the child. Most have a genetic predisposition, and many are a result of prenatal or birth complications. But three health impairments that evolve from environmental sources—lead poisoning, fetal alcohol syndrome, and prenatal exposure to drugs—can have devastating effects on learning. Awareness may help prevent these impairments.

# Lead Poisoning

Lead poisoning is one of the most common preventable diseases in the United States and Canada. Repeated exposure to low levels of lead can result in learning problems. The brain is most sensitive to lead exposure during the first six years of life, because this is the period of rapid growth and development of the nervous system. Lead is able to pass the placental barrier, exposing the fetus to the lead in the mother's bloodstream.

Mouth-to-hand behaviors and crawling on floors increase the young children's risk of ingesting lead from dust, soil, and other environmental contamination. The child's smaller body size results in a higher dose of lead per exposure than an adult might experience. Robert Tuthil, from the University of Massachusetts, writes that children absorb a greater proportion of ingested lead than adults. The child's lead clearance mechanisms are not as well developed, so the body's concentration of lead builds up more readily in a child.

Exposure to large amounts of lead causes severe lead poisoning and symptoms such as abdominal pain, headaches, vomiting, confusion, muscle weakness, seizures, hair loss, and anemia. These recognizable symptoms lead to appropriate medical treatment. However, because lead accumulates in the body, repeated exposure to small amounts can also cause lead poisoning. Unfortunately, there may not be any visible symptoms to alert parents of the need to seek medical attention. The symptoms of low level poisoning are lowered IQ scores, decreased attention span, decreased hearing, speech delays, and other developmental delays.

## Where Are the Hot Spots of Lead?

The most common source of lead is paint. Dust and soil may become contaminated with lead paint through home remodeling and sanding. When lead paint chips or peels, young children may pick up the chips and place them in their mouths. Toddlers, who continually put things into their mouths, are especially at risk.

Another source of lead in the environment is imported plastic mini-blinds, to which lead has been added to stabilize the plastic. As the plastic deteriorates lead dust forms on the surface of the blinds.

Lead is still found in low levels in some drinking water, the result of lead-based solder on old water pipes. This is of particular concern if water is used to reconstitute powdered infant formula. Lead-glazed pottery that has not been properly fired can also allow the lead to leach into whatever is put in the container. Although unleaded gas has reduced the amount of lead in the air attributed to automobile exhaust, low-income children living in highly congested urban environments have higher rates of lead poisoning. However, no socioeconomic group, geographic area, or racial or ethnic population is spared the potential risk.

## Should My Child Be Screened?

In 1991, the Centers for Disease Control and Prevention identified the following as reasons for testing a child for lead poisoning.

1. The child lives in or regularly visits a house with peeling or chipped paint that was built before 1960.

2. The child lives in or regularly visits a house that is being renovated and was built before 1960.

3. A sibling, classmate, or playmate is being watched or treated for lead poisoning.

4. The child lives with an adult whose hobby or job includes exposure to lead. Examples include furniture refinishing, making stained glass, making pottery, using indoor firing ranges, and working in industries such as storage batteries; automotive repair; and bridge, tunnel, and elevated-highway construction.

5. The child lives near an active smelter, battery recycling plant, mine tailing pile, or other industry likely to release lead.

6. The child received medical treatment for removal of a foreign body from the ear, nose, or stomach.

7. The child has the habit of swallowing nonfood substances.

8. The child is less than six years old and has an unexplained developmental delay, hearing defect, irritability, severe attention deficit, violent tantrums, or unexplained anemia.

Children who remain at high risk for lead exposure should be tested for lead at least every year until their sixth birthday.

## Treatments for Lead Poisoning

Intervention is dependent upon the amount of lead in the blood. A screening is sometimes performed by taking a capillary blood sample by pricking the finger. Should this sample test high in lead, a venous sample will usually be required before chelation agents are given. The American Academy of Pediatrics has issued treatment guidelines for lead exposure in children. Interventions vary from mild environmental modifications to aggressive environment changes. Sometimes taking a chelation agent is indicated. This medication binds with the lead and carriers it out of the body. The best intervention, however, is to be aware of your environment and protect children from the sources of lead poisoning.

### Further resources.

- *Getting the Lead Out.* Food and Drug Administration. Superintendent of Documents, Consumer Information Center, 3C. P.O. Box 100, Pueblo, CO 81002.

- *Home Buyer's Guide to Environmental Hazards.* Environmental Protection Agency. Superintendent of Documents, Consumer Information Center, 3C. P.O. Box 100, Pueblo, CO 81002.

- *Important Facts About Childhood Lead Poisoning Prevention.* Center for Disease Control and Prevention, Lead Poisoning Prevention Program, 1600 Clifton Road, Atlanta, GA 30333.

- *What Everyone Should Know About Lead Poisoning.* Alliance to End Childhood Lead Poisoning. For individual copies, write to 600 Pennsylvania Avenue SE, Suite 100, Washington, DC 20003.

- *What You Should Know About Lead-Based Paint in Your Home.* U.S. Consumer Product Safety Commission, Washington, DC 20207.

# Prenatal Exposure to Cocaine

Although initial studies of drug-exposed infants predicted a gloomy future for them, newer reports indicate children exposed to cocaine in utero are resilient. Despite low birth weight, differences in long-term development are difficult to find.

LeAdelle Phelps, professor of counseling and educational psychology at the State University of New York at Buffalo, reports that "the postnatal environment can either attenuate or exacerbate the risk factor of such exposure." She suggests that the real problem behind the previously reported slower-than-average progress has more to do with poverty than with exposure to drugs.

Abigail Cohen and her colleagues at Temple University found the same results in children they studied. Research has shown an increase in premature births associated with cocaine. The exposure to cocaine results in a greater need for medical care for infants and a higher frequency of low birth weight. "While preterm birth puts an infant at risk for negative developmental outcomes, the environment to which the child returns after birth appears to be the most significant variable to impact on those risks," Cohen said. "While cocaine-exposed infants are at risk for developmental problems, this can be ameliorated by positive enriching environments after birth. Exposure does not have to result in negative long-term outcomes for this group."

# Fetal Alcohol Syndrome

It has been over twenty years since the first baby received a diagnosis of fetal alcohol syndrome (FAS). Children with FAS are a specific subgroup of children born to alcoholic mothers.

There is a wide range of abilities and disabilities in the diverse population of children with FAS. IQs range from 45 to 110. The majority of children have mild to moderate behavior problems.

Characteristic of FAS are growth deficiency and specific physical anomalies, including characteristic facial and central nervous system (CNS) dysfunctions. The CNS manifestations include delayed development, hyperactivity, motor incoordination, learning or attention problems, seizures, mental retardation, poor sleep or eating patterns, and/or microcephaly (small head). These symptoms may even be evident in children with FAS who have normal intelligence.

As the child reaches adolescence, physical features associated with FAS may change. However, the CNS problems continue, especially attentional and social problems.

Interventions such as structuring the environment, providing consistency, teaching learning skills, and acknowledging the role of the sensory systems will help the child cope with these problems. These interventions can be designed by looking at the symptom that is most problematic for the child. Typewriters, computers, or note-taking partners may be used to remove the hurdle of writing by hand. White noise can help block out distracting noises.

The easily distracted or hypersensitive child may benefit from activities and an environment that filters out distractions or from keeping outside stimuli to a minimum. The texture, temperature, and feelings of food and utensils may cause children to play with their food or chew over and over without swallowing. Children may also benefit from sensory integration therapy, which desensitizes the child to touch, sound, and light. A child may react to sensory overload by throwing a temper tantrum or shutting down. At such times it is important to reduce or remove the stimulation and help the child use a calming technique, such as listening to quiet music, sitting in a rocker, or taking a warm bath. (See chapter 14 for more information about sensory integrative dysfunction.)

Children with FAS often need to be taught how to learn. Even the most basic skills must be carefully taught. Role playing can help the child with FAS understand consequences and appropriate behavior. Breaking tasks into small steps, using concrete examples, and rewarding for each step achieved are other suggestions.

Many children with this dysfunction also benefit from consistency in the responses and behaviors of people in their world, especially teachers and parents. Clear, consistent, concrete, and explicit communications and discipline guidelines are often beneficial at home and school. The structure helps reduce "surprises" that are difficult for the child to adapt to and lessens frustration.

A good resource for parents of a child with FAS is the book *Fantastic Antone Succeeds!*, by Kleinfeld and Wescott. The interventions in this book were developed not from research but by parents and teachers who have worked and lived with children with FAS. The strategies focus on the specific CNS impairment that affects the intelligence and behavior of the child.

Professors Lyn Weiner and Barbara Morse write that children with FAS may be inappropriately placed within the school systems "if their condition has not been accurately diagnosed or if there is a misunderstanding of FAS by the school systems." They report that learning and behavior patterns of the children are often inconsistent, masking their educational needs and making it difficult to determine if they qualify for special education classes. Children who are aggressive or have temper tantrums can also be labeled as bad or malicious, complicating and compromising appropriate interventions.

Many children with FAS are placed within the foster/adoptive care systems. Without knowledge of FAS, support families may terminate their responsibility for these children. Therefore, the CNS problems these children experience may be complicated further by the insecurity and instability of their home lives.

For more information or resources contact the National Clearinghouse for Alcohol and Drug Information, Department PP, P.O. Box 2345, Rockville, MD 20847-2345.

# Points to Ponder

1. The older mental retardation model is not representative of all children with FAS. Children fall within a wide spectrum of abilities and disabilities. Not all children with FAS are mentally retarded.

2. Be a detective and identify the developmental and/or learning disabilities for clues to successful, creative interventions.

3. FAS is preventable. Curtailing alcohol use during pregnancy does improve the chances of a healthy outcome. To reach this goal, the U.S. government initiated two policies: The 1981 surgeon

general's warning against drinking alcoholic beverages during and when planning pregnancy, and Public Law 100-690, enacted in 1988, which mandates labeling of alcoholic beverages with a warning about the risk of birth defects associated with alcohol use during pregnancy.

4. Prevention is best. Remove potential lead hot spots from the child's environment.

5. The postnatal environment can attenuate the risk factors of prenatal exposure to cocaine.

# 23

# Deficits in Organizational Skills

The world around us is ordered and sequenced into neat patterns. Most of us follow a morning routine to assure we get off to work on time. A series of steps allows us to start our car and drive to work. At the workplace, schedules and structure guide us through our workday.

How closely we can adhere to our daily routine often determines the tone of our day. If the alarm fails to wake us, we may find ourselves scrambling all day to make up the lost time. Elusive car keys make us frantic and upset the whole household. An unscheduled meeting or appointment may be a source of further havoc in our routine. By the day's end, we find ourselves tired, irritable, and unproductive.

What has occurred is an upset in our organizational patterns. Our sense of order and routine has been interrupted. Yet, millions of people struggle every day to fit into the world's predetermined structure. These individuals always appear to be at loose ends. They often scramble at the last minute and leave a paper trail behind them as they rush to make deadlines. For these individuals, struggling to function in a world that values order can become very stressful.

In the classroom, organizational skills are also stressed and appreciated. Neat desks and lockers make educators happy. Notebooks with the pages securely attached rather than jutting out loose in all directions make studying more effective. Coming to class prepared means books, assignments, and supplies arrive with the student. "A place for everything and everything in its place" is the motto of teachers everywhere.

Teachers use baskets, trays, drawers, and folders in an attempt to organize their students. They work long hours on outlines, assignment sheets, study guides, and notes to help condense and organize information. Tests, term papers, and reports are scheduled in advance to help the students plan for long-range deadlines. Teachers urge parents to buy folders with pockets for each subject to keep the learner organized. Some folders even zip or Velcro shut to ensure the safety of the contents.

Despite all these efforts, there are students who can never find the study guide, do not have a clue that a ten-page paper is due tomorrow, and ask, "Test? What test? Nobody ever told me about a test!" These are the same students who always come to class late and unprepared.

Such learners may become even less organized as they get older and have to be responsible for more materials and assignments. The increase of long-term assignments is a particular source of distress for this student. Unless effective time-management and study skills are established, being disorganized can cause the student's life to snowball out of control by seventh or eighth grade.

Two types of organizational problems can interfere with every aspect of the school curriculum and the student's ability to function within his environment. They are spatial-materials organization and temporal-sequential organization.

# Spatial-Materials Organization

Students lacking organizational skills are constantly struggling for survival within an ordered environment. It's a real challenge for parents to get them out of bed in the morning and out the door with everything they need for the day before the school bus leaves. Invariably, they forget something and need to make a phone call home.

This scenario describes Debra, a fourth grader. "She is so disorganized!" is the familiar comment her parents have heard from teachers since preschool. Debra rarely has her assignments. Yet Mom insists she watches her complete the tasks. This is true. Debra does complete the assignments she has written in her plan book. It is the omitted entries and the materials left at school that cause the problems.

The assignments that are completed are often not of the quality expected from a fourth grader. Words run together, lines are skipped, margins are ignored, and often the paper is turned upside down with the holes on the wrong side. The appearance is messy and difficult for the teacher to read.

Similar problems occur in math. Problems are seldom lined up so that columns are straight. This affects Debra's math grade. She often gets the problems wrong because of incorrect copying and spacing.

At home, things are not much better. Her lack of organization often causes conflict within the family. Her parents always seem to be nagging because seldom are her responsibilities completed, and her belongings are all over the house. Her bedroom is a disaster. Toys, books, clothing, and papers are everywhere. In a hurry, Debra will grab something to wear from a pile of tangled clothes on her floor.

Interestingly, while it may appear chaotic to anyone with a sense of organization, Debra's environment does have its own structure. Within the boundary of her bedroom, Debra can find almost anything. If the room is cleaned and straightened, she becomes very upset because *her* organizational system is in chaos. However, anywhere else in her world, no structure is apparent.

# Observable Traits of a Spatial-Material Organizational Disorder

1. Child has a difficult time physically organizing information on paper.
   - Margins are askew or nonexistent.
   - Spacing between letters in words and words in sentences is irregular or nonexistent.
   - Child has little sense of top and bottom of the page.
   - Notebook paper may be backward, with holes on the wrong side.
   - Child may confuse left-right orientation.
   - Centering titles and information on page may be difficult.

2. Work is often messy. Teachers have difficulty reading it, and child is not proud of the finished product.

3. Child leaves school without books or materials to complete homework assignments.

4. Assignments may be incomplete because of errors or omissions in copying.

5. Child usually cannot find completed assignments.

6. Child often scrambles to find papers, notebooks, supplies, textbooks, shoes, or lunch.

7. Child has difficulty in following routines or following through with tasks. (It is important to understand that forgetting to do something because of a lack of organization is very different from choosing to ignore a request.)

8. Child has the "Pigpen syndrome." Desk, locker, workplace, and bedroom are messy. Personal appearance is often disheveled. However, in some situations, the child appears to have his own system of organization.

9. Child has difficulty organizing notebooks or assignment books.

# Strategies to Support a Learner with a Spatial-Material Organization Disorder

1. To assist with the spatial organization on paper.
   - Give cues or reminders to check for location of holes, as well as the wide spaces that indicate the top of the page or the margins.
   - Cue that colored lines down the left side of the paper indicate the starting place for the left-right orientation. A star or another symbol on paper without this line will serve the same purpose.
   - Being allowed to use a word processor whenever possible will alleviate many of these issues and produce a clean, organized product of which the student can be proud.

2. To help with spacing of math problems.
   - Use graph paper to help keep the columns straight.
   - Turn notebook paper sideways so that lines and spaces run down the page instead of across.

3. Use line markers, cover pages, or "windows" to mark the place and help prevent copying errors and omissions.
   - Have someone copy math problems.
   - Ask teacher to copy pages out of books so that only answers need to be entered.
   - Reduce the writing requirement by allowing student to write only the answer rather than copy a sentence or question. For example, if copying sentences from a grammar book is required before circling the nouns, allow the child to just write the nouns in each sentence.

4. To organize school materials.
   - Color code. Use one color per subject area. All book covers, notebooks, and folders pertaining to that subject should be the same color. The student then grabs by color on his way to class or home at the end of the day.

- Ask the teacher to assign a "study buddy." This is a classmate who can assist the student in getting together everything needed to go home.

- A few extra minutes at the end of the day may give the student an opportunity to get her thoughts together, check her plan book, and grab the necessary materials.

- School supplies stores have plastic locker organizers. They are shelves designed to fit into any standard-size school locker.

- Give opportunities to have desks, workplaces, and lockers cleaned out often.

5. To assure the assignment book is correct and complete.

- Extra time should be given to get the assignments entered. Last-minute assignments after the bell has rung will not assure proper entries. An assignment written on the blackboard, a weekly assignment sheet, or a monthly syllabus is ideal.

- Have the student get his plan book initialed by the teacher at the end of each class. This will ensure complete and correct entries.

- Parents can initial the plan book in the evenings to indicate the assignments have been completed.

- A homework folder or envelope may assure assignments get back to school.

6. To help organize the child at home.

- If morning routines are difficult, try having your child become his own disc jockey by talking himself through the routine between his favorite songs. For example, "By the time this song is over, I'll be out of bed and in the shower." This great idea, shared by Sam Goldstein, Ph.D., in his tape Why My Child Won't Pay Attention, is a favorite with children.

- Hang a large calendar in a prominent place. Color code each family member and write in his or her scheduled activities. Everyone can see the daily commitments at a glance.

- Design a family schedule and make every attempt to maintain it. This might include mealtimes, family time, story time, homework time, television time, and bedtimes. This will help develop a sense of routine.
- Try to have a specific place for things: a toy box, bookshelves, a basket with school supplies.

7. Make lists, lists, and more lists. Writing things down may help the child remember to do what is expected of him. Crossing off the accomplished task will help remind him of what to do next. For example, clear the dinner dishes off the table, take out the garbage, feed the dog.

# Organizing Homework

Homework can be a time of stress and aggravation for the whole family. Parents often relate that their child's homework causes them more anxiety than it causes the child. Students with learning differences often return home after a day in school tired and mentally taxed. Trying to function, pay attention, and stay focused for an additional six hours is very stressful. Asking them to work in the evening seems unfair and unreasonable. What educators seldom understand is that for children struggling with learning issues, they fatigue much faster than their peers. What might be a twenty-minute assignment in the teacher's mind could be two or three hours' worth of work for the disorganized student.

The following tips may help parents organize their children so that homework time may be used more efficiently.

1. Establish a homework time. This should be the same time each day. It could be right after school, but the child may need a break. Early evening after dinner may be the best time, or splitting the time before and after the dinner hour may work. When homework is completed is not as important as the consistency of having the same schedule every day.

- Even if no homework is assigned, maintain this time and use it as quiet time or to work on upcoming assignments or tests.
- Try to select a time when everyone can be quietly working. Dad may be catching up on office business or reading the newspaper. Mom might be reading to a younger brother or sister.

2. With your child, examine the homework assignments.
   - Look through the assignment book. Check for teacher signatures indicating accuracy and completeness of entries.
   - Allow your child to select what she wants to do first, second, and third. Guide the selections so that pencil/paper tasks alternate with studying or reading tasks.

3. Make a schedule of each task. Have your child check off each assignment when completed.

4. Clear the workplace of everything except what is needed to complete the task.

5. Have a basket or tub for supplies (pens, pencils, markers, erasers, scissors, a ruler, and a calculator) at the workplace.

6. Ask your child to explain the assignment and his plan to complete it. This may reduce questions and avoidance tactics before the assignment is finished.

7. Check the finished task to see if the work has been copied accurately (as in math problems or spelling words) and completed.

8. Have your child put the completed paper in an assignment envelope or notebook.

9. Clear the workplace and move on to the next task.

10. When homework is completed, all books, notebooks, folders, and homework envelope should go into a schoolbag. Place the bag at the door ready for the next morning.

11. When the duration of the homework time becomes excessive, discuss this with the child's teacher. Modifying the assignments may be appropriate. For example, if it takes an hour for the child to complete fifteen math problems, perhaps the teacher would require the child to complete only the odd or even problems.

# Temporal-Sequential Organization

A second type of organizational problem many students encounter is called temporal-sequential. Sequencing, completing long-term assignments, having a sense of time, and understanding and following directions can be affected by an impairment in this area.

Almost every task we do involves some sort of a sequence. From getting dressed, to following a recipe, to starting a car, a step-by-step procedure must be followed. Knowing the sequence and being able to follow it to completion result in the desired outcome.

For students who are unable to recognize the step-by-step plan required to master most academic skills, school can be very overwhelming. Confusion can arise anytime the child is required to learn things in a specific order. The memorization of the alphabet, telephone numbers, seasons of the year, or multiplication tables can be trying. Knowing which letter follows another determines whether a word is spelled correctly. Therefore, not being able to remember the sequence of letters in a word can interfere with the correct spelling of words. Letter order is also necessary for word recognition in the reading process. In written language, word order and a sequential organization of thoughts is necessary for clear expression. Science lab experiments can have very different results if the steps are performed out of sequence. In math, explicit steps must be followed in sequence before a long division problem can be solved or an equation answered. One step out of order and the whole problem is incorrect.

Directional concepts such as *before/after, soon/later, over/under, on top of/beneath, more/less* may be difficult to master. The child needs a clear understanding of these concepts before she can follow directions. Serious learning difficulties can arise if these terms are not understood.

Concepts of time are also difficult for the child with this type of organizational dysfunction. Learning days of the week, months of the year, and how to tell time can be very confusing. The ability to manage time can also be affected. Completing long-term assignments can be very challenging. The learner usually waits until the last minute before starting the task, then panics as he races against the clock. The final product is usually incomplete and of poor quality.

Because the child has little concept of time, she can easily lose track of it. Ten minutes or two hours has little meaning to this child. Sometimes this interferes with the child's ability to adapt the pace of her work, especially in a testing situation.

Knowing where to begin a task also can become an issue. The student may sit for a long time before starting an exercise. He may appear to be goofing off or wasting time. In reality, he may literally need for someone to show him where to begin the assignment. He needs clear instructions as to what to do first, second, and so on.

## Observable Traits of a Temporal-Sequential Organizational Disorder

1. Child has difficulty with anything requiring a specific order or sequence.
2. Child has difficulty with handwriting.
   - Copying is difficult and labored.
   - Words in sentences are often out of meaningful order.
   - Sentence order is confused and jumbled.
3. Child tells jokes or retells stories out of sequential order.
4. Concepts of telling time are difficult and confusing.
5. Spelling is difficult.
6. Memorization of math facts can be problematic. The pressure of time tests adds to the stress.
7. Delays in learning to hop, skip, jump rope, or ride a bicycle may occur.
8. Child has little comprehension of time.
   - He procrastinates.
   - He has a difficult time completing long-term assignments.
   - He has poor time-management skills and finds it difficult to estimate how long an exercise should take to complete.
9. He has a difficult time following multistep directions.
10. He confuses directional words.

## Strategies to Support a Learner with a Temporal-Sequential Organizational Disorder

1. Writing out directions that need to be followed in a specific order may help.

2. Help teachers understand that this learner may have difficulty memorizing long lists, specific steps, or math facts. If after a reasonable period these skills have not improved, accommodations should be considered, such as the following:

   • Calculators or a matrix to help with the math facts in problem solving.

   • Cue cards listing the steps required to complete a math problem (reasonable for the student who understands the concept behind how to solve the problem but makes calculation errors because of the sequencing problem).

   • Alternative ways to evaluate students other than through rote memorization of lists.

3. Find ways to ease the stress of handwriting, so thoughts and ideas can be shared.

   • Develop keyboarding skills and use a computer for writing assignments whenever possible. Spell check and grammar check ease the writing process.

   • Design a step-by-step approach to writing (see chapter 10).

   • Get a note buddy or arrange to have class notes supplemented.

   • Reduce the demand of copying from blackboard or overheads by providing the student with the written form of the information.

4. Ease the stress of spelling.

   • Consider alternative ways to give spelling tests.

   a. Give a multiple-choice test and have the student recognize and select the correct spelling of the word. This can be done by keeping the words within the context of a paragraph.

   b. Reduce the number of required spelling words. Give ten instead of twenty.

    c. Keep the words in the spelling list related to a single spelling or phonics rule. For example, all the words have the ea combination, as in meat, beat.

    d. Consider allowing the student to take the spelling test on the computer. This will eliminate the handwriting issue and allow the child to focus on spelling the word.

- On work accomplished in class, where the time element is a factor, consider several options.

    a. Eliminate the pressure of spelling and have the learner focus on content.

    b. Give two grades, one for content and one for spelling. Average the two for the final grade. Or allow the learner to edit the spelling and adjust the grade accordingly.

    c. Give adequate time for the student to go back and edit the work. This may mean the assignment needs to be completed in two stages—first the writing, then the editing.

    d. Allow the student to use the computer to complete the assignment so that spell check can be used to correct any errors.

- For assignments that are completed at home or without a time restraint, correct spelling should be expected.

    a. The student needs to learn proofreading skills to recognize spelling errors.

    b. Dictionary skills need to be learned early.

    c. Have the child keep a log or personal dictionary at home and school where the child's frequently misspelled words can be entered and referred to when necessary.

- Use flash cards or computer software that will help the child recognize correct spelling. This will improve his proofreading skills.

5. Easing time management woes.

- Teach the child how to use a calendar early in life. Remember, children with temporal-sequential organization deficits have little concept of time.

a. Allow young children to select or make their own calendar. If they choose to make one, have them do so month by month. Provide the grid and allow them to decorate it. If possible, allow them to write in the days of the week and the name of each month, and to number the days.

b. Enter special days, such as birthdays, parties, and holidays.

c. If a calendar is purchased, point out the days of the week and the months of the year.

d. Older children should have their own calendars to keep track of events in their lives.

e. A large calendar, hanging in a prominent place, will keep the family organized. Color code each member's name.

f. A large desktop calendar should be available to older students. For long-term assignments, divide the task into manageable chunks, and mark when each task is due in a block on the calendar. The child can see at a glance each deadline. This alleviates the feeling of being overwhelmed and the last-minute rush to do the whole thing.

• Assignment books and daily planners should be introduced as early as possible.

• Provide a daily schedule for the child to help her get through the day.

a. Set up the schedule with your child to include half-hour increments.

b. Include the parts of your daily routine: when to go to bed and when to get up, mealtimes, piano lessons, soccer practice, homework, playtime, television time, family time, quiet time.

c. Have your child place the schedule in a visible location.

• To develop a concept of time.

a. Children who work too slowly or rush through their work can benefit from learning to estimate time intervals. Give numerous opportunities to develop this skill.

    b. Ask the child, "How long do you think it will take you to empty the garbage and feed the dog?" Record his answer, then set a timer and see how close he comes to his estimate.

    c. Children who labor over completing assignments may be asked to estimate how long they think the task should take. Set the timer and see if they can finish within their estimated time. If necessary, continue to set the timer with a new estimate until the work is completed. (Caution, this idea should be used with the understanding that the quality of the work must be maintained.)

    d. Children who rush through their assignments need help slowing down so that they use the full time on the clock. Urge them to use the extra time to proofread their work.

6.   Following multistep directions in sequential order can be difficult for the child with a sequencing problem.

- Try writing down the directions.

    a. Have the child number each step required.

    b. Highlight each step using a different color.

    c. Mark key words in the directions. Put a circle around the word circle, or underline the word underline.

- Try to limit oral directions to no more than two or three steps.

    a. Ask the child to repeat what you've said, keeping the steps in order.

    b. Use words such as first, second, next, then, last, or finally to indicate more than one step.

    c. If possible, he may say each step as he does it. "I am putting the place mat on the table. Next I am putting the plate on the mat. Now I am adding the silverware."

7.   Provide opportunities to follow recipes, make models, or do other activities that require a sequence to successfully complete.

8. Ask your child to relate the order of events in a family outing, e.g., "We went to the zoo. First, we saw the lions, then the seals."

9. Take pictures of events and ask your child to put them in the order they occurred.

10. After reading a story, ask the child, "What happened first? What occurred next? After the wolf blew down the house of straw, where did he go?"

11. Practice directional concepts.
    - Use terms such as *beneath, over, above, under, on top of* often.
    - Give your child opportunities to hear and practice these concepts often, with such instructions as, "Put the napkin under the fork," and "Can you crawl under the table and get the ball?"

# Points to Ponder

1. We function in a world that demands order. When we cannot find our place in this order, we are said to lack organization.

2. Not everyone's organizational style is the same. Some people are neat and tidy, and others find order in chaos.

3. A child lacking organizational skills can find school a very unfriendly place. Everything from putting a name on paper, to lining up math problems, to turning in assignments requires specific organizational skills.

4. Spatial-material organization is how we organize ourselves in space. Placement of words on the page and being able to find books, assignments, and car keys fall into this category.

5. Temporal-sequential organization is the ability to follow a sequence, as in directions, spelling a word, writing a sentence, completing a task, retelling a story, or effectively managing time.

# 24

# Multiple Disabilities and Severe Emotional/ Behavioral Disorders

As we conclude this long list of disabilities that can interfere with learning, two categories remain. Perhaps it is these categories more than any other that bring home the point that the information in this section should not be oversimplified. Our concern is that by presenting each disability in isolation we may unintentionally convey the message that children with learning issues can be placed in nice, neat packages. This is not true. The issues are very complex.

It is our hope that we have explained carefully that there is a major overlap of all of these disabilities. This is one reason why so many categories have been included in the federal legislation under IDEA. In this tangled web of issues that interfere with learning, very rarely is just one factor disrupting the child's ability to learn. This is especially true of the learning differences that have genetic and/or neurological origins. It is our genetic composition and neurological wiring that make us unique.

We must therefore be very cautious not to pigeonhole children with disabilities. Nor should we allow their differences to become an excuse for their failure to learn. Every child, no matter how complex his learning issues, has strengths that must be identified and reinforced. It then becomes the responsibility of educators and support professionals to teach to the child's strengths. In doing this, they maintain the child's dignity and spirit. As has been mentioned so frequently in this handbook, differences should be celebrated, not discouraged. It is through those differences that we have the music, art, literature, and inventions that make our lives easier and more enjoyable. We must be careful, therefore, that we do not get so caught up in what the child cannot do that we lose sight of the child. It is with these thoughts in mind that we discuss two final areas of disability.

# Multiple Disabilities

This classification includes children with a combination of two or more disabilities. These might include deafness, hearing impairment, blindness or visual impairment, mental retardation, orthopedic impairment, serious emotional disturbance, or speech and language impairment. Children with multiple disabilities usually exhibit moderate, severe, or profound deficits in socialization, communication, and/or adaptive abilities.

When the individual impairments are complicated by the involvement of additional disabilities, placement in a program designed for just one of the disabilities may not be appropriate. Therefore, children with multiple disabilities are usually placed in learning environments that can address all of their disabilities.

A multifactored evaluation is performed to identify the various disabilities involved. The results are then discussed by the multidisciplinary team, of which the parents are a part, and an IEP is written for the child.

Although the criteria listed for this category are specific, it is important to point out that the learner may also have any of the other disorders presented in this section. For example, AD/HD is frequently exhibited in children with multiple disabilities. Unfortunately, it is not always diagnosed. Likewise, children whose vision or hearing is impaired are often thought to be mentally retarded. Children with autism are particularly difficult to diagnose. Because of the complexity of each of these disorders, identifying the dominant obstruction to learning can be very difficult. A team of qualified professionals should be in constant collaboration with the parents.

For many of the children with these disabilities, behavior is a major issue. Too often it seems easier to dump them into a class for severe emotional and/or behavioral disorders than to examine the underlying causes of the child's behavior and find ways to modify it so that learning can occur.

# Severe Emotional/Behavioral Disorders

We have saved this category for last because we believe it is the least understood. Behavior and discipline problems frequently accompany each of the disorders discussed thus far. Children with learning differences are easily frustrated and have a lower opinion of themselves and their capabilities. The more frustrated they become, the more they act out.

The terminology identifying this category may differ from state to state. It may be called severe behavior handicap, severe behavior disability, or severe emotional disturbance. For our purposes, we have chosen to identify this section as emotional/behavioral disorders. Of the many factors that can influence a child's behavior, this area is the most nebulous and difficult to diagnose and address.

We would like to begin by stating that there are those who truly benefit from placement in a special class for children with unacceptable behaviors. The guidance they receive often helps them understand and manage their behavioral issues.

However, it has been our personal and professional experience that the classification of emotionally and behaviorally disturbed given to many of the learners is inappropriate. Too often these are children who have not been properly diagnosed, and are therefore being mismanaged in the learning environment. In other words, these are children who are frustrated and failing and do not know why.

As an example, a first grader is having difficulty learning to read. He cannot understand the words; he has problems decoding and is embarrassed. No one else around him appears to be having the difficulties he is experiencing, so he assumes he must be stupid. By the end of September, he is throwing a tantrum every day during reading time.

As the demand for reading increases throughout the year, he becomes more and more difficult for the teacher to handle. The teacher also notices that he is responding inappropriately to his classmates. His temper is short, and he lashes out at the slightest provocation. Convinced he is a behavior problem, the teacher refers him to an intervention assistance team for an evaluation.

Surprisingly, the multifactored evaluation shows the child has a reason for his behavior. The reading specialist suspected a hearing problem when she evaluated him. She consulted with an audiologist, who discovered that the child had a moderate hearing loss. Learning to read was difficult because he could not hear the sounds and words well enough to make the necessary discriminations. He also was having difficulty hearing his teacher and classmates. A combination of speech and language therapy, special tutoring, and a hearing aid enabled the child to become more comfortable in the learning environment, and the behavior problems diminished.

This is not an isolated scenario. As a learning specialist, Nancy sees children every day whose behaviors are misunderstood. When behavior becomes the issue, Nancy begins to look for underlying problems. More often that not, the behaviors have emerged because the child is frustrated.

No matter how hard he or she tries, nothing seems to work, and the child just gives up. This allows plenty of time to find negative ways to work against the system.

# Factors Affecting the Emotional/Behavioral Status of the Learner

There are children whose personalities are prone to true emotional and behavioral disturbances (see chapter 15). Several factors may explain why some children develop antisocial personalities. It is important to note that rather than a single clear-cut indicator it is a combination of factors that interferes with the child's ability to learn and function appropriately in the family and community.

## The Genetic Factor

There is strong evidence that many children are born with a genetic predisposition toward emotional or behavioral disorders. The first indicator can be in the temperament of a newborn. In about 10 percent of newborns, very specific behaviors can alert parents and professionals to potential emotional problems later in life.

Newborns who are highly emotional are easily identified. They are more irritable than other infants; they are not easily comforted; and many demonstrate extremely fearful reactions to sudden changes.

Along with being more emotional, these infants appear to have an elevated activity level. They are always moving. As they become more mobile, they need to be constantly monitored because their activity level often puts them in dangerous situations. As older children, they also have a difficult time settling down and concentrating for an extended period of time.

The third indicator in the temperament of newborns is their unsociable nature. They show little interest in human contact and are often unresponsive to the attention of others.

Later in life, many of these children are diagnosed with the emotional and behavioral disorders identified in the *DSM IV*. About 70 percent of the children who display conduct problems are diagnosed with a psychiatric disorder. About 5 to 30 percent of all school-age children meet the criteria for at least one disorder in the *DSM IV.*

Thus far, we have pointed out the more aggressive type of emotional and behavioral dysfunctions. A passive type is also included in this category. Fears, phobias, depression, and eating disorders are also emotional/behavioral disorders.

Anxiety disorder is the most frequently diagnosed of all the disorders. It occurs most often in females and tends to diminish in frequency with age. The next most common overall are conduct disorder, oppositional defiant disorder, and AD/HD. These tend to increase in frequency with age, being most prevalent in adolescents.

Many of the parents of the children with these disorders also have the same conditions. The data show that children of depressed mothers often are depressed, and fathers with a conduct disorder tend to have children with the same characteristics. The majority of the disorders discussed in this section have a strong genetic thread woven between parent and child.

One point needs to be made very clear. Being born with a predisposition toward emotional and behavioral disorders does not necessarily mean these tendencies will evolve into an actual disorder. Even though the genetic pattern is present, a strong supportive environment can teach the coping skills needed to avoid many of the antisocial behaviors. Also, learning environments designed to meet the needs of children with disabilities reduce the chances of frustration and failure. This decreases the frequency of negative behaviors and emotional upsets.

## Family Dynamics

Speaking from experience, we would be the first to attest that living with a child with a disability is extremely stressful. As infants, they can be demanding and require much more care than tired, anxious parents can provide. Parents take time from other siblings and from each other to care for them. This lack of attention may cause the siblings to react with negative behaviors. Many parents begin to feel isolated and overwhelmed. These feelings often cause parents to ignore the difficult infant and develop negative feelings toward him. This reinforces the negative behaviors.

Strong evidence indicates the dynamics of the family environment are a powerful indicator of the emergence of emotional and behavioral problems. Children reared in homes where the parents are supportive and caring of each other and their children are less likely to develop problems as they grow. Parents who have a strong support network of extended family, community resources, and mental health professionals learn coping skills they can teach their child. However, when the child becomes emotionally separated from the parents and when the parents pull apart the potential for future problems becomes greater.

## The Effects of Life Experiences

Many families are pulled apart because they cannot cope with the stress of rearing a child with a disability. Conflict between parents can be very traumatic for the children. Research shows that parents in constant conflict who stay together "for the sake of the children" may be doing more harm than good. Understandably, the divorce or separation of parents can have a dramatic and powerful effect on the emotional stability of any child. However, it is not so much the separation as the conflict that threatens the emotional equilibrium of the child. Children living in homes with constant strife are more likely to develop emotional and behavioral disorders than children living in situations without conflict.

Other factors that may result in emotional stress or inappropriate behaviors include the serious illness or death of a family member or someone close to the child, the birth or adoption of a sibling, and moving to a new living environment.

## Reinforcing Negative Behaviors

Many parents unintentionally reinforce negative behaviors because it is easier to give in than to deal with the situation. Children in these circumstances quickly learn how to manipulate their parents to get their way. For example, if Brian does not like what is being served for dinner, he may demand that Mother fix him something special. If Mother refuses to do so, Brian may throw a tantrum and ruin the meal for everyone. He learns that if he screams loud enough, someone will meet his demands. This reinforces the inappropriate behavior and causes additional stress and friction within the family.

Another way that the negative behavior is reinforced is by giving attention to it alone. When the positive things the child does are not noticed and reinforced, he learns very quickly that negative behaviors make people sit up and take notice. In the classroom, Karen may have shared her crayons with another child and no one noticed her kindness. However, when she grabbed a paper away from a child, the teacher quickly pointed out what she did wrong. Karen, who wants and needs attention, learns that negative attention is better than no attention at all. Thus, the message that is being reinforced is that only when she does something wrong is she noticed. Each time Karen gets this message, the negative behavior is strengthened.

## Community Factors

There are also community factors that can influence the emotional development of the child. Single parents, working long hours to make ends meet, struggle just to provide for the physical needs of their children. Finances are tight and time is limited as many single parents, often mothers, try to provide for their children. Without a strong extended family and social network to help, the parent and the child often do not get the emotional nurturing they need. This can put both of them at risk.

# A Vicious Cycle

Trying to sort out all of these factors can be overwhelming. Each seems to be woven into the next. A temperamental infant causes stress within the family who then withdraw and do not give the nurturing needed for healthy emotional development. The added stress may cause conflict between the parents, which pulls the family further apart, adding to the emotional upheaval. Separation or divorce may occur, which results in single parents who struggle financially and emotionally, withdrawing still further from their child. The parents acknowledge only negative behavior, thus reinforcing it.

At school, the same cycle may occur unless someone takes the time to get to the source of the disturbance. Many children come to school so emotionally bound that learning becomes secondary. A child worried about where he will be sleeping at night could care less about his spelling assignment. Just trying to survive is his number one goal.

These are children who need mental health professionals to help them manage their emotional distress. They need patience and understanding. Educators who persist in placing academic demands on these children push them further away. The additional stress increases the likelihood of an adverse reaction.

For this reason, the behavior of children in our classrooms must be examined closely. Inappropriate behavior could be a telltale sign that the child is in distress. With few exceptions, children want to please. When given no other options, they will do what any human fighting to survive does—they will rebel. They begin to think, "OK, if you think I'm a screwup, then I'm going to be a screwup!" In other words, they begin to live up to our expectations, positive or negative.

Sometimes it is easier to place the child in a class with other children who have similar problems than it is to examine why the behavior is occurring. What is the child's physical condition? Is there a psychiatric disorder present? Has something changed in the home? Is the child's learning environment supportive or frustrating? These and other questions need to be asked until the source of the disturbance can be located. Placement in a class for children with severe emotional and behavioral disturbances must be done with extreme caution. If it is the wrong placement, it can send a message that we have given up on the child.

Before the child can change his behavior, the caretakers must change the way they approach the child. Modeling and teaching the appropriate behaviors will help the child become more socially accepted. This is not easy to do and requires the efforts of a strong support system of mental health and school professionals working with the family and extended family. Understanding how the child learns is a crucial part of this effort; so is knowing what his capabilities are. Providing the support services and accommodations that make learning successful is important. Once the frustrations are alleviated, many of the behaviors subside, and the vicious cycle may be broken.

# Management Strategies

Emphasizing the positive behaviors of the child is a good way to begin. It is important to remember that the child who is the hardest to love is the child who needs our love the most. Perhaps one of the following suggestions may help you keep your focus on the positive actions of the child. These and other suggestions are explained in more detail in our book *Parenting a Child with Attention Deficit/Hyperactivity Disorder*, chapters 7 and 9.

1. A "positive book," or "brag book." This is a simple notebook that the child can make and decorate. Daily entries are made by the teacher, parent, and child indicating at least one positive event that occurred during the day.

2. "Sharing a positive" is another way to keep the focus on the behaviors we want to reinforce. The teacher can go around the class, or the family around the dinner table. Each person shares at least one good thing that happened to him or her during the day.

3. A "random acts of kindness" program in the classroom or home encourages the child to secretly do a kindness for someone each day, with the understanding that this gesture should give a personal sense of satisfaction.

Other suggestions that may help in managing the child with emotional and behavioral problems are the following:

1. Set rules and try to maintain routines. The child needs to know the boundaries and expectations.

2. Use scripts to practice how to behave in various situations—for example, in church, a mall, or a restaurant. Explain beforehand the consequences if these behaviors are not followed.

3. Say what you mean. Do not make threats you cannot carry out. When you have to give in, you will reinforce the negative behavior.

4. Give choices, to reduce power struggles. The choice can be the lesser of two evils.

5. Contracting with older children is sometimes successful. Sit down with the child and write out the conditions, expectations, and consequences.

6. Prioritize concerns. Do not try to resolve all the issues at once. This is too overwhelming and defeats the purpose.

7. Develop a strong support network for the family. Do not allow yourself to become isolated from social contacts or the extended family. Seek immediate support when the child begins to cause conflict between you and your spouse.

We have explored a wide range of disabilities that can interfere with the child's ability to learn. No matter how mildly or severely the child is affected, the inability to achieve academic success can alter how the family functions. Everyone in the family experiences a vast array of feelings when a child is identified with a learning problem. Many parents experience a sense of loss. The idea that their dreams and expectations for their child will never be realized triggers depression and grief.

The next section of the book addresses the grieving process, as well as ways to focus on the talents and strengths of the child. With a wide range of resources and supports available at both the national and local levels, the prognosis for the child's future can be very promising.

# Points to Ponder

1. Emotional and behavior problems may have a genetic origin.

2. The family environment is a critical factor in whether the problems emerge and to what degree.

3. In families that are pulled apart by demanding children who are difficult to manage there is a strong likelihood that the child will have an emotional or behavioral problem.

4. Families with a strong support system are more likely to meet the child's emotional needs.

5. Understanding the cause of the child's behaviors is important. Emotional distress may interfere with learning. Sympathetic teachers can be supportive by alleviating the academic stress until the crisis has passed.

6. Special placement in a class for emotional/behavioral disorders may not be appropriate. A careful examination of why the inappropriate behaviors are occurring may reveal that accommodations in a less restrictive environment could bring favorable results.

7. Remember to focus on the positive. This can be very difficult when we are working with children who are determined to live up to our negative expectations. It is these children who are difficult to love that need our compassion the most.

# 25

# Accepting Your Child's Differences

How well you cope with having a child with any of these learning differences will depend on many things. One variable is your knowledge about the causes of learning differences. Throughout this book, it has been stressed that learning problems are neither anyone's fault nor an indication of a moral deficit in the child. Still, some parents wonder if they could have done something different—spent more time with their child, sent him to preschool, read to him more, and so on.

No matter how well developed your coping skills, it is nearly impossible not to experience some grief over lost expectations. Of course, having a learning problem doesn't have to mean reduced expectations. What it usually does mean is discovering a new and different way of achieving. This can be scary and challenging. We may grieve over the difficult road ahead for our children and for the challenges they will face. Things probably won't come easy for them, and they and we will certainly become discouraged.

Although we may rarely think of it or recognize its effect, grief is a familiar companion. Its banner encompasses many aspects of our daily life. Losing a job, failing a grade, or finding out your child has a disability and learns differently are just a few of the situations that precipitate a grief response.

Elizabeth Kübler-Ross, M.D., describes the five stages of grief in her book, *On Death and Dying*. Initially, these stages were observed in dying patients, but they apply to other life situations as well. The process of working through them is not linear. Not every person experiences every stage, and some steps may be revisited. Understanding the grieving process helps families of children with learning disabilities move ahead and focus on creating interventions or remediation. The five stages of grief follow.

**Denial.** This is the "There is nothing wrong with my child" stage. Teachers and counselors express amazement that some parents would rather their child be labeled as lazy than have him evaluated for a learning disability. Perhaps this is because in their minds there is still a stigma attached to the term *learning disabilities*. Parents hear the term and associations such as "retard" and "dumb" replay in their heads. Denial is sometimes our temporary friend and allows us to sneak up on acceptance. It is how we cope with information that is too scary or painful with which to deal. For most families, at least partial acceptance comes fairly quickly. Sometimes how much denial appears to be present in a family will depend on the situation and who is present. If teachers, one's spouse, or the child's grandparents don't believe the child has a learning problem, parents may shut down or keep their suspicions to themselves. What may appear to be denial is actually protection from another's denial. Grandma might inform them, "There has never been any of *those* in our family. I don't want to hear that kind of talk. There is nothing wrong with that child. All you need to do is spend more time with him." On one level, Mom might realize that her child has a problem with learning, but faced with such vehement denial (which is often based on misunderstanding), she may hesitate to follow up on recommendations.

Levels of denial vary from family to family. Sometimes acceptance is quick, and is immediately followed by a desire to develop a plan for remediation and interventions. Other families experience denial and refuse testing for the child. This is best dealt with by demystifying the evaluation process and by identifying the child's strengths along with his weaknesses. Since learning differences tend to run in families, one parent may have experienced many of the same problems as a child. This parent can help others in the family break through any denial and be an advocate for the child.

**Anger.** As parents, most of us have high expectations and big dreams for our children. Perhaps we visualize them as lawyers, professional athletes, famous musicians, or in some other high-profile and high-paying position. Then someone tells us our child has a learning difference. Instead of worrying about what college he or she will attend, we discover ourselves wondering whether the child will graduate from high school or pass the proficiency test. Parents may find themselves asking, "Why me and why my child?" We angrily listen to other parents discuss their all-star child, who never studies and still makes the honor roll. We may be angry at God, the school, our parents, our spouse, or the neighbor with that perfect child. It doesn't seem fair that our child has to work so much harder than our neighbors' and never has seen the honor roll and is the object of scorn in the classroom, instead of joy. This focus on the negative is to be expected in the beginning. Focusing on the strengths of your child and family will get you back on the right path.

Siblings may also express anger toward the child with the learning difference. He demands a great deal of attention from parents and may also be less socially adept and embarrass siblings with, as one sister so kindly put it, their "dorkiness."

**Bargaining.** The word *bargaining* most often brings to mind talks with our higher power and promises to walk the straight and narrow if only this burden will be lifted from our life. We'll practice reading with our child every night if only the school psychologist will call and say he made a mistake. If a child's disability is not properly demystified he may attempt to bargain his way out of remedial reading or math or attending tutoring sessions, as in "I'll complete all my schoolwork, I'll do better and get better grades if only you don't make me go to the learning van." It is very important to reassure children that they are not bad, lazy, or dumb and that remediation is not a punishment.

**Depression.** Children with learning differences may be prone to depression if their learning differences have a negative impact on socialization. Parents may isolate themselves from neighbors and friends because they, too, are depressed. As other parents brag about the achievements of their offspring, parents of children with learning differences may feel awkward and uncomfortable. Constantly hearing negative comments about the child can intensify the parents' depression.

**Acceptance.** This is the goal. We firmly believe the shortest path to acceptance is demystification and strength identification. The more positive things we discover about ourselves as children or parents, the more motivated we are to try. We gain more confidence in our ability to overcome.

# Children Grieve, Too

Perhaps the most important contribution Kübler-Ross made is the lesson she taught us about listening. Her ability to listen and hear, really hear, what her patients were saying is a model for anyone working with children who experience problems learning. This is the gift we can give these children.

Understanding and validating a child's feelings and fears is very important. Parents cannot cure their child's learning problem, but they can be there to support them. They can listen and talk with their children about what is bothering them. They can provide a safe, loving place, where it doesn't matter how fast you read, whether you learned your multiplication tables, or the level of your fine motor skills.

Sometimes well-meaning parents avoid discussing the child's learning problems with him, feeling that the child is too young to understand or that such talk will undermine the child's self-esteem. They feel they are protecting their child. In cases like this, it is good to remember the advice of Fred Rogers of *Mr. Rogers' Neighborhood:* "Anything human is mentionable, and anything mentionable can be managed." Children need to talk about their experiences with learning and how they feel. Even when we feel powerless to help our child, we can do something very powerful and positive. We can really listen and talk and just be there for our children.

Ann's son came home from the first day of school and announced he was no longer going to the reading van. "They said the van is for dumb kids like me," he cried. "I hate school!" Unfortunately, this type of occurrence is not common among children with learning differences. Even when the school intervenes, it may be difficult if not impossible to completely protect your child from these experiences.

Mary Ann Healy-Romanello, Ph.D., writes that there are nine major themes observed in her support groups at Fernside: A Center for Grieving Children in Cincinnati, Ohio. Even though these themes come from children who experienced a death in their family, many easily transfer to struggling with and accepting a learning difference. These are especially important to remember when working with or parenting children with a disability.

1. Children feel defeated when teachers ignore or criticize their grief process (using a mask).

2. Children go back and forth in their development as grieving people.

3. There is no time limit on the struggle that children with learning differences experience, or their grief.

4. Help can be provided by simple acts of caring and by making the school environment a place of comfort, security, and acceptance.

5. Children are capable of "teaching" about their grief if they are encouraged to express their feelings in a safe environment.

In the book *Hyperactive Children Grown Up,* Gabrielle Weiss and Lily Trokenberg Hechtman document reminiscences by Ian Murray, a young man they followed for several years. Ian poignantly describes the sadness and grief children experience. This grief is compounded by not knowing what is wrong with them. Left to their own devices, their imagination takes off, and the results are often overwhelming. In the following excerpt, Murray describes his feelings at the end of another bad day. It is lucky for us that he is able to put the feelings of his childhood experiences into words for us to reflect upon.

> I realized as never before that I did not fit in, not at home, nor at school. For the first time, that night I began to swell up inside with sadness, a kind of remorse. What was the matter with me? I didn't look different. I wasn't missing an arm or leg. Maybe I was just dumb. You'd think with all those tests . . . they would have discovered something and fixed what was wrong. I hadn't heard from them for a long time so I guessed there was nothing more to be done. So if that's it, I am just plain stupid, there was no way I would let on to anyone that this was the case. I promised myself never to cry in front of others again. If only I could make a couple of friends, I'd be alright . . . I knew that none of the kids would dare tease me about my stupidness for fear of being punched . . . For now I would have to get by with that.

This small excerpt of Ian's story very eloquently teaches us why it is so important to teach children their strengths and help them understand their deficits or disabilities. For the most part, children will be unable to express these feelings. It's up to us to help them find the words and to be on the lookout for behaviors that indicate the presence of grief.

A child's response to grief may take longer to emerge than an adult's. Explaining the child's disabilities to him in simple and direct terms and giving examples of individuals who have succeeded in spite of disabilities can help.

## Masking the Feelings

Children may go to extraordinary lengths to hide their learning differences. Sally Smith, the founder of the Lab School of Washington, a school for children with severe learning disabilities, identified over a dozen masks that children (and adults) wear to cover up their inability to accomplish the simplest of academic tasks. Below are a few of the more common masks we have encountered.

**Mask of being bad.** This student would rather be thought of as bad than dumb. These students may be hiding feeligs of frustration and anger, or worse, take it out on teachers or other students. Being sent to detention or to the principal's office may accomplish his goal of getting out of class, where his deficits can be discovered and his feelings of inadequacy validated.

**Mask of boredom.** This student constantly complains that the work or task is too boring. But does he complete it anyway? Not usually. This mask may also be hiding an attention deficit disorder. Many children report being bored when they cannot stay focused in class. Boredom covers for frustration and the inability to perform the task at hand.

**Mask of the clown.** This student may be the life of the party or the class cutup. He may divert attention from his academic skills, or lack thereof, by making others laugh. He may have good verbal skills but be unable to do math or read or write.

**Mask of apathy.** "I don't care." "I'll never need that dumb stuff anyway. It's a waste." Students with this kind of defense keep others at a distance. They don't care because caring would make them vulnerable. If they care and try and fail, then others might know they are dumb. More importantly, it might validate their worst fears about themselves.

**Mask of helplessness.** This person refuses to risk any failure. He may use pity to get others to help him with his work. Comments like "I don't know," "I can't do anything," and "I'm dumb" are common.

**Mask of invisibility.** This is the low-profile student who sits in the back of the room. She never makes waves and avoids calling attention to herself.

**Mask of seduction.** This student may use feminine or macho wiles to get students of the opposite sex to do for them what they can't do for themselves.

Smith writes that once the students reach a certain comfort level, when they realize they are not unintelligent but learning disabled, they can begin to drop the mask, which so often interferes with their learning. "There is enormous relief that comes from knowing what you know, knowing what you don't know, and understanding why you don't know it," Smith said.

# Grief: Our Constant Companion

In his book *Getting Through Grief,* Ron Sunderland writes that grief is our constant companion. "Bereavement is the most obvious and widely recognized form of grief—but it is only one form grief may take," Sunderland writes. Another form is the loss parents feel when they discover their child has a disability or learns differently. Even after we have adjusted or accepted the loss, there may be times when grief unexpectedly creeps up and stabs us in the heart.

Darlene's family knows this only too well. Her daughter, Nicole, became sick when she was six years old. After several weeks of flulike symptoms, and despite doctor visits and blood tests, she had a grand mal seizure and was rushed to Children's Hospital. Tests in the emergency room revealed the pressure on her brain was nearly twice normal. After the child had spent several days in a coma, doctors approached Darlene and her husband with a decision. Even though they had seen some minor and gradual decreases in the pressure, it was too dangerous to continue to do spinal taps to monitor the pressure. They were planning to drill a hole in Nicole's skull and implant a pressure monitor there. They had given a probable diagnosis of viral encephalitis.

It's pretty hard to deny there is a problem when your child is in a coma, and we were too scared to be angry, but our bargaining was an ecumenical process. Friends, family, and friends of family in churches and parishes in Ohio, Kentucky, and Pennsylvania prayed for the child's recovery. The morning they were to place a pressure monitor in her skull they measured her spinal pressure one last time. As we entered the intensive care unit we were prepared for the worst, but to our surprise, no surgery had been done. Miraculously, that morning her spinal pressure was back to normal. The surgeon shook his head, shrugged his shoulders, and raised his eyebrows. He couldn't explain it, but the surgery was canceled, and Darlene's daughter, with a little divine intervention, started to recover.

When she started first grade, it quickly became apparent that her learning would be impacted by her illness. She had trouble memorizing, her fine motor skills were a disaster, and she was very sensitive to outside stimulation. Noise or distraction in the classroom, in the hall, or on the street distracted her, and she was often "off task." Darlene received the phone call at work regarding the psychological testing. Nicole's school psychologist gave her the news. Nicole had normal intelligence, but she had severe learning problems. Her best chance for remediation was at a special school for children with learning disabilities. There she would also get the occupational therapy she needed to help strengthen her motor skills. As they set up an appointment to review the test, she focused on the good news, and Darlene quietly thanked her. Numbly, and feeling like she'd just been kicked in the stomach, she left for lunch and walked the three blocks from the office to St. Louis Church and crept down the steps to the basement chapel. Why her beautiful daughter with the bouncy curls, sparkling green eyes, and innocent heart? No longer able to contain the grief, she sobbed in the soft candlelight of the chapel. After several minutes, her crying subsided. She wiped her dripping nose and blew into the ragged tissue, then got up and went back to work.

From that day, she didn't cry over school problems or the unfairness until Nicole was in high school. Then grief revisited. It was such a little thing. Nicole had struggled with religion the entire year. She had done her homework, completed all projects, but struggled with memorizing dates and failed several tests. By the end of the year, Darlene knew it would come down to how Nicole did on the final exam. The last day of the school year, she got the news from her teacher. Sometimes the best a child can do is not good enough. The teacher was sorry but she could not make any exceptions. Nicole had scored a yearly average of 69.25. Passing was 70. Intellectually, Darlene understood, but the unfairness and absolute craziness of the situation angered her. Now her tears were not ones of sorrow but of anger. No one could have worked harder, put in more effort, and not reaped the benefits. The injustice was too much. To many, this may seem crazy and totally illogical, but who said grief was a logical process?

Nicole made up the credit over the summer with a private tutor. She took it with a grain of salt, but Darlene was angry the entire summer. She was still in the early process of learning to be an advocate. Inside she fumed—over interventions not done (maybe there should have been alternative types of testing), the school's lack of flexibility and its igno-rance concerning Nicole's problems with memorization. She fumed over the fact that although she had paid school tuition all year she had to pay additional money for a tutor to get credit for the class. Besides, who cared, in the real world, who was pope way back when? I bet it never comes up in a job interview, she fumed. It's not as if it was English or math.

All Darlene's fuming did not change anything, but she did learn never to leave anything to chance. She learned to insist on what she felt her children needed to be successful students. She learned to be an advocate (known in some circles as a pain in the posterior).

Grief is our constant companion. This doesn't mean we constantly mope around with sad faces, lamenting our fate. It means there will be lots of good days and bad days. A favorite teacher or counselor leaves and you have to start all over. Your child becomes a teenager and doesn't want to get remediation or take medication because it's not cool. She wins an award or gets asked out on a date. She participates in a sport and gets cut from the team. So grief is like a mountain range: You reach great heights and then tumble to the valley in despair. We can hope the climb up the next peak is easier and the next valley not so deep. As with life itself, it is an ongoing and mysterious journey. Figure 25.1 illustrates this.

# Identifying Resources and Supports for the Family

The eco-map is a nifty tool developed by family therapist Ann Hartman for studying families in their environment. It offers a way for practi-tioners and families to assess and plan interventions. During this exer-cise the practitioners or family actually draw a map that shows all the major systems of the family's life—the groups, organizations, and indi-viduals with whom the family interacts.

To make an eco-map, draw a circle in the middle of a large, blank sheet of paper. This central circle represents the particular family the eco-map will explore. A number of other circles are then drawn around the central circle. These circles represent the other systems the family inter-

**Fig. 25.1. Peaks and Valleys of Grief.**

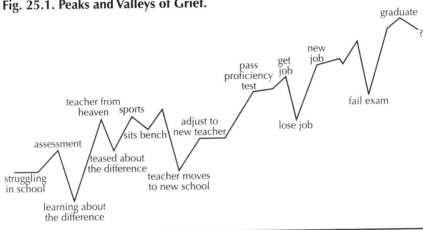

acts with. Depending on the relationship with the primary system (our family), different types of lines are used to connect the systems to the family. Interestingly, one system may have a strong relationship with one family member and a tenuous relationship with another. The eco-map helps explore and define these relationships. It is a visual way to see where your strengths, resources, and supports are and where bridges need to be built and interventions developed. The identifying connectors are:

Solid line: strong resource or relationship.

Bold solid line: very strong resource or relationship.

Dotted line: tenuous resource or relationship.

Solid crossed lined: conflicted resource or relationship.

Also helpful are directional arrows that indicate the flow of energy into or out of the family. If the relationship is mutual, there will be arrows pointing in both directions. An arrow pointing to the family means that energy is flowing in. An arrow pointing only to another system means energy is flowing out. The lines can be used to define the relationships between systems or to identify times when relationships between systems differ between family members.

In our hypothetical family, Joey Bush is an eight-year-old with a reading disability, memory problems, and AD/HD–combined type. As Figure 25.2 shows, Joey's mother has a tenuous relationship with her son's school. She is able to communicate with the staff, and Joey is getting a lot of support from the school counselor, but he is experiencing some social and academic problems. As they have increased, his relationship with his primary teacher and the school administration has become conflicted. The family is getting support from the extended family and a local support group. Joey's uncle also had difficulties in school and is a support for Joey and his family. Stressors on the family include a terminally ill relative and major debts for medical and remedial expenses for Joey's treatment. Also, Joey's siblings sometimes feel left out because so many of the family's emotional and financial resources are focused on him.

Figure 25.2 illustrates how the eco-map for this family might look. Don't forget to include formal organizations such as schools, mental health organizations, and support groups. Even if the family is not currently receiving support from these sources, include them in your eco-map. The object of this exercise is to identify both real and potential supports for the family, along with areas of stress or weaknesses in the family's surroundings.

# Stressors on the Family

**Family roles and the expectations of others.** Parents often find themselves torn between their own obligations and the expectations of others. Grandpa might believe all mothers should stay at home, but financial reality may dictate that Mom must work full-time. This means family members must refine and redefine their roles. Full-time work hours and mandatory overtime often leave parents with little energy to help with homework, let alone remediate problems. When life is so hectic, who goes to school conferences and cooks dinner? Sometimes one parent will have too many roles pulling him in different directions. This leaves him unable to satisfy anyone. No one could!

Children with learning problems may find themselves compared with older, more successful siblings. The third child in a particular family to attend a given school may encounter suspicion that he is failing

**Fig. 25.2. Eco-map for Bush Family**

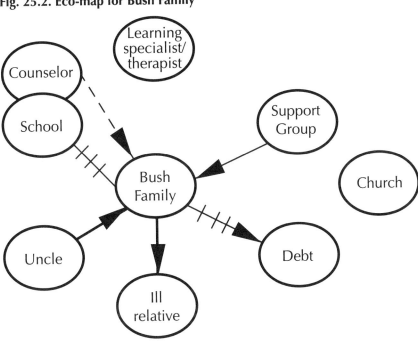

because he chooses not to learn. "We know he's smart. The only thing wrong with him is he doesn't care," comments his teachers.

**Financial pressures.** Educational testing and tutoring are usually not covered by insurance policies. Therefore families can find themselves overwhelmed with expenses for services such as tutors, testing, remediation, counseling, skills building, and language therapy.

**Siblings.** As mentioned above, siblings of the child with a learning difference can be expected to experience stress too. At times, siblings will resent or be embarrassed by the sibling with the learning difference. Parents may feel guilty that they are not giving equal time to their children. Children realizing this may try to manipulate parents or take advantage of the parents' guilt.

**Stigma and oppressive school climate:** *Webster's* defines *oppressive* as "overwhelming or depressing to the spirit or senses." This sometimes describes the school environment for the child who has a learning difference. Although he has average intelligence, he may not be perceived as intelligent. His peers see him as an "LD" or a "dummy." Teachers and advisors may have low expectations of him in regard to learning, and he may not be encouraged to experiment or develop bypass strategies. Despite the current emphasis on understanding disabilities through programs such as Everybody Counts, many families and children do suffer injustice. They feel the odds are stacked against their success because they have qualities that fall outside the ideal of our Eurocentric society. We do live in a society where perfection and success are respected and rewarded. It is important to acknowledge how overwhelming to the spirit this experience can be.

**Feeling powerless.** Basically, Joey's family (our hypothetical family) is pretty functional, but the stress of his school problems on top of the other family stressors is just too much. Sometimes symptoms of depression or grief result from stress that exceeds a person's ability to handle it. Joey's mother, for instance, hesitated to answer the phone in case it was another teacher detailing all her son's defects. The family was really pretty stable, and their responses seem very appropriate for the amount of stress they were under.

Joey desperately needs to feel OK. He knows he's different. This is certainly reinforced often enough. His school counselor or family can use storytelling to help Joey understand that his difficulties are not abnormal. They can read stories from the book *Keeping a Head in School,* by Melvin Levine, M.D. As Joey's parents become educated about his developmental variations, they can learn how to communicate with the school. This knowledge empowers the family, and relationships with the school become less conflicted.

## *Stressed* Backward Spells *Desserts*

**Can we talk?** Listen to what children say about themselves and their environment. Observe behaviors. A loving and supportive response to children's concern about their abilities is important. We adults also need a listening ear. Seek out supports for yourself.

**Ask for help.** Find and join support groups. Use your eco-map to develop a network of family and friends who can support you and your family when events knock you down and sorrows creep in. Let relatives, the kids, or their friends help with chores or car pooling. You don't have to do it all.

**Healthy activities.** The whole family needs to express their feelings through positive, healthy activities. Often this doesn't happen because of lack of time or opportunities. Physical activity is necessary and worth the effort, lest children find unhealthy ways, such as substance abuse, to escape awkwardness, loneliness, and other painful feelings.

Physical activity can produce a satisfying, natural, healthy "high" that can be created almost anytime and anyplace. Darlene organized this chapter while swimming laps. It's amazing the problems you can work out in a half mile of very slow freestyle. One family reported using Richard Simmons's exercise video tape. They reported the music and Simmons's quirky style made the activity fun. They didn't worry about doing the exercise right or how many repetitions they did. They didn't have to worry about the time of day or the weather. The focus was on moving around and having fun. You don't even really need Richard. Turn on the radio and make up your own exercise program or have an *American Bandstand* or *Soul Train* afternoon. The kids can teach you the Macarena or the Train, and you can teach them the twist, jitterbug, mash potato, or whatever the craze was during your generation. Learn to line dance!

**Laugh.** When is the last time you had a good belly laugh? If you can't remember, then you're in trouble. Play a game of Twister with the kids. Read a funny story or watch a comedy.

**Pat yourself on the back.** Our guess is that you are doing a remarkable job already. Get up and look in the mirror and remark on the dynamic person you see there. No one is perfect or has all the answers.

**Just desserts.** Too often today we are scolded or warned about using food to pacify us or soothe stress. Of course we need to be sensible. We shouldn't eat an entire chocolate pie or a pan of lasagna. We shouldn't rush home and head for the fridge every time we have a bad day. Still, food is necessary, and many cultures confirm that eating and preparing good food can be a spiritual experience. Have you ever made an angel-food cake, pizza, bread, or pancakes from scratch? Have you ever eaten homemade cannoli, sweet potato pie, or fried polenta or hominy dripping with maple syrup? Well, then, what are you waiting for? Go explore ethnic cooking. (It can be low-fat.) Your family will have fun, be proud of their creations, and enjoy eating the mistakes too!

# Points to Ponder

1. Grief is a normal response to discovering your child has a learning difference or disability. How do you cope with such information? Is it working?

2. The entire family experiences grief in an attempt to adjust to the demands placed on them. How this grief is expressed may differ from member to member, depending on age, developmental stage, family roles, and coping skills. What behaviors do you observe that could be attributed to a grief response?

3. Many things in the environment can precipitate a grief response. What is happening in your child's ecosystem that might impact his success or compound the grief? What is the school environment? Are there supports in the community? Are resources grudgingly provided for children? Are interventions designed to be one size fits all? Is diversity honored within your child's school?

4. Stress and grief can be managed. Look for the light side of life. Enjoy friends and family. When was the last time you laughed, made pancakes or a pizza together, or looked at the positive qualities in your child and family?

# 26

# Management
# Approaches

It is easy to understand why children with learning difficulties need academic remediation. Poor grades on the report card, phone calls from the teacher, and unsatisfactory work are all red flags that indicate a child needs academic remediation. However, these children may experience skill deficits in areas that are not evident at first glance. They may be inefficient in using cognitive strategies, have trouble solving problems, and struggle with social skills and personal relationships. This lack of skills affects both social and academic areas.

It's a question of coping. Most of us have strategies that help us deal with everyday stressors and small crises. Still, everybody needs somebody, sometimes, to help him sort out problems and find new ways of coping, or just to listen.

Families may struggle with accepting the child's disability or experience difficulty coping with the school. Children may be reluctant to receive remediation for fear of being labeled stupid, or they may become frustrated by the tremendous effort it takes to achieve. Therefore, a variety of approaches to management might be needed.

Just browsing through the Yellow Pages for assistance can cause confusion and anxiety. The telephone book contains an abundance of therapists, whose specializations include behavior modification, cognitive therapy, solution-focused therapy, and family therapy, to name a few. The choices are overwhelming. How do parents know what is the best intervention? Who will understand your problem and relate to your child? Who will tell you if professional intervention is even necessary?

Most therapists are proficient in a variety of therapeutic techniques and may use a mixture of them to design an intervention program specific to the child's or family's needs. (We use the term *therapist* in a generic sense. The person working with your family could be a social worker, psychologist, counselor, family therapist, or psychiatrist.)

The following is a general guide to management. These strategies are not limited to use with children who experience difficulty learning. However, it is important that the therapist you work with understand learning disabilities and their impact on the family. The family's culture, ethnicity, and goals for the family and child must be considered. Also the relationship between the family, child, and therapist is important if change is to take place. There is no cookie-cutter therapy or skills-building program that works with all children or families.

Whether you manage your child's difficulties with therapy, academic remediation, skills building programs, or medications will depend on what is most problematic. It only makes sense to identify what symptoms, learning problem, or skill deficit is causing the problem before you search for an intervention.

It is possible that a cluster of symptoms is causing the problem, and if so, you may find it difficult to determine where to start. For example, children with learning disabilities or AD/HD may experience problems with skills such as planning, organized search, flexibility of strategies, impulse control, and self-monitoring. In all cases, it is best to prioritize your concerns and begin with the behavior or situation that is causing the *most* stress or problems for your child.

The problems of children or families with AD/HD seem especially extensive and persistent. In addition to the three main criteria of impulsiveness, hyperactivity, and inattention, children may experience academic underachievement and peer rejection.

Along with medication, behavior management is the most used intervention for these children. Integrating cognitive problem-solving and behavior modification is helpful. Again, define your child's needs before beginning. A good place to start is to determine the who, what, and where of the problem.

**Who.** Who wants the change? Is the school demanding a change? Are parents dissatisfied with a child's progress or behavior? Is the child upset about school and peer problems?

**What.** What is the presenting problem? Are most difficulties with academic problems or behavioral issues? Are difficulties the manifestation of skill deficits? Does the child have self-concept or self-esteem issues? Are the parents struggling with accepting the child's difficulties?

**Where.** Where is the problem occurring? Is more structure needed in the home? Is the problem occurring on the school bus, during gym classes, during reading group?

In this chapter we will describe several types of therapy or skills-building interventions, beginning with cognitive-behavioral therapies.

# Cognitive-Behavioral Therapies

Cognitive therapy is based on the assumption that behavior is adaptive and that there is a relationship between thoughts, feelings, and behaviors. Cognitions are a body of knowledge or beliefs and a set of strategies used to adapt this information. Cognition also refers to a complex system that includes one's thoughts, perceptions, appraisals, attitudes, memories, goals, standards, values, and expectations. It also refers to the way information is represented in memory and how information is used. Cognitive skills include problem-solving or coping skills, communication and linguistically based knowledge, and interpersonal skills. The goal is not to label the child but to identify instructional goals, methods of intervention, and the efficiency of these interventions. Critics of this model express concern that its success depends on the cognition or intelligence of the individual. However, this idea is challenged by the results of an anger-management program at a school for developmentally and emotionally disabled high school students, as documented in *Adolescence Journal*. This program demonstrated that adolescents with diagnoses such as developmental delay, mental retardation, and autism can benefit from a cognitive-behavioral approach if it is modified to meet their special learning needs through the use of role play, group reinforcement, and other skills-building activities. Short sessions with frequent repetition and reinforcement were key elements of success.

Before any strategies or interventions can be created, it is important that an assessment of the student's needs be completed. This assessment should identify basic skills students have and how they solve problems. Not every student with a learning difficulty experiences problems that respond to cognitive therapy.

## Common Problems Associated with Learning Differences

**Attention.** It has long been known that most children with learning disabilities have an underlying attention problem. Such children may spend less time engaged in task-oriented behaviors, and teachers often rate them as less attentive than their peers. They may have trouble choosing what to pay attention to. These children do not give self-instruction or use verbal rehearsal as often or as efficiently as do peers without learning problems.

**Memory.** Memory deficits may be manifested as a problem with reading, language, spelling, or another content area. It is often cited as the most frequent characteristic observed among students with learning problems. Research suggests that memory problems in children with learning disabilities derive from their "inefficient use of strategies, such as rehearsal, organization, as well as limited motivation for engaging in intentional mental efforts."

**Metacognitive abilities.** Even when a child has developed memory or attention strategies, he may fail to recognize situations or tasks where it is appropriate to use them. Some researches feel students with learning difficulties lack an awareness of their own cognitive process. They are inefficient learners.

**Personal control.** Children with learning disabilities may believe there is little they can do to influence outcomes. When they are successful, they may be at a loss to understand why or how it happened. When they fail, they don't usually believe it is because they didn't try. When students don't believe they can succeed, they may become passive learners. They make fewer attempts to succeed or to find solutions.

## The Course of Cognitive-Behavioral Therapy

1. The therapist obtains information regarding the presenting problems as well as antecedent events. It is preferred to gain information from several sources. When working with a child with a learning problem, the therapist might ask for data from the teachers and parents and discuss the problem with the child.

2. The underlying beliefs, assumptions, and self-statements or automatic thoughts are identified, and the child learns to monitor these negative thoughts.

3. Specific behaviors or skills deficits are identified.

4. Other resources that support the child and his family are identified (see Figure 25.2).

5. A goal is set, and intervention is agreed upon.

6. Homework is assigned. The child and/or his family practices the technique during the sessions, and the goal is summarized to be sure it is understood by everyone and that the client is motivated to achieve it. Factors that might interfere with completion are identified and addressed.

7. At the next visit, the effectiveness of the intervention is evaluated.

## Components of Cognitive Behavior Therapy

**Cognitive-behavior modification.** This approach involves the detailed practice of a sequence of behaviors necessary to accomplish a task. The idea is to connect thought to behaviors through use of self-talk or self-instruction. Students are supplied with strategies for learning.

**Cognitive training.** This emphasizes self-regulation by helping the student become an active learner and helping him learn how to think.

**Self-instruction training.** Children are taught to verbalize their cognitive process, and this guides their academic and social behavior. Children learn to question themselves about the problem and how to address it. They give themselves instructions about performance, as well as reinforcement and corrective feedback.

**Self-monitoring.** Through self-assessment children learn to pay attention to how (or how often) they complete a task—for instance, by recording whether they are paying attention at specific times. Research shows that paying attention to your attention increases on-task behaviors. A caution exists, however: Some research indicates this is most effective when children have the necessary skills to complete the tasks. So if the child is reported to have difficulty focusing in geometry class, make sure he isn't overwhelmed by the subject before attempting to increase on-task behavior.

Another example of self-monitoring is a "hassle log," which helps children monitor conflict and angry responses. Each time the child is involved in a conflict, he must enter it in the hassle log. Information includes time and place of the hassle, who was involved, what was said and done, and what wasn't said or done. The log is then reviewed with the therapist or counselor, and alternative ways of handling the hassles are examined.

Children learn to rate their success in handling hassles. If they only rate themselves a 3, they can then use problem-solving strategies to identify what they could do to increase their score to a 4.

**Problem solving.** This involves teaching the child rules, a model, or techniques that will enable him to engage in problem solving. These may be task-specific, e.g., how to complete a certain long-term project, how to reach a particular goal, how to ask someone out on a date. Below is an illustration of how this simple model might look when the problem is anger management:

1. Define the problem. What caused the conflict?

2. Brainstorm a variety of solutions. Complete a checklist of both negative and positive solutions so you can analyze the how, where, and what of anger control problems.

3. Evaluate the ideas and decide which is the best one. Think about what has worked in the past and what has triggered loss of control.

4. Plan to implement the solution. Decide who will do what and how or who will monitor the success of the solutions.

5. Evaluate the success. On a scale of 1 to 10, how successful was the intervention? Could you have done anything differently?

**Mix and match strategies.** Keep in mind that to be effective, strategies must consider the strengths, learning style, and creativity of the child. A strategy might include self-monitoring, problem solving, and self-talk. It may also be reinforced using behavioral techniques such as home-school notes or token economy. Figure 26.1 is from the book *Cognitive Therapy with Children and Adolescents* and was designed to assist a child with independent management of assignments. The therapist used a self-monitoring checklist and a personally relevant mnemonic, "Back off," to instruct the student in the steps to complete the task.

---

**Fig. 26.1. BACK OFF: Cognitive strategy for independent management of assignments**

| | |
|---|---|
| B | Bring completed assignments in the assignment folder. |
| A | Ask questions about assignments that were difficult. |
| C | Copy down new assignments in the assignment book. |
| K | Keep the assignment book, assignment folder, texts, and important papers in a backpack so assignments can be completed at home. |
| O | Organize and prioritize assignments at home. |
| F | Finish all of the work as copied in the assignment book. |
| F | File the completed assignment in the assignment folder and bring it with you the next day. |

*(continued on next page)*

**Fig. 26.1. BACK OFF: Self-monitoring checklist for independent management of assignments, *continued***

| Date of Week | Mon. | Tues. | Wed. | Thurs. | Fri. |
|---|---|---|---|---|---|
| **B** Did I bring all my finished assignments with me today? | Y N F | Y N F | Y N F | Y N F | Y N F |
| **A** Did I remember to ask questions about assignments that were difficult? | | | | | |
| **C** Did I copy all of my assignments accurately in the assignment book? | | | | | |
| **K** Did I keep the assignment book, folder, and texts needed to complete in my backpack so I was prepared to complete assignments independently? | | | | | |
| **O** Did I organize and prioritize my work so that I had time to complete my work? | | | | | |
| **F** Did I finish my work? | | | | | |
| **F** Did I file all the completed assignments in the folder so that I was prepared for the next day? | | | | | |

*Key*: Y=Yes, N=No, F=Forgot. Time when completed:

Source: Reinecke, M.A., Dattilio, F.M., and Freeman, A. (Eds.), *Cognitive Therapy with Children and Adolescents,* p. 270. Copyright 1996 Guilford Publications. Reprinted with permission.

# Behavioral-Modification Therapy

Behaviorist theory is based on the belief that all behavior is learned. It only follows that if behavior is learned, it can be unlearned or changed. Often behavior can be changed by introducing positive or negative reinforcers or consequences.

Psychologist Russell Barkley has developed a program detailed in his book *Defiant Child*, which many clinicians use when working with children with AD/HD. Barkley recommends teaching both parents and teachers to use behavior-management techniques. He points out that training should include education about the child's disorder, in addition to behavior-management techniques. His approach involves increasing positive rewards, such as attention and praise or privilege, communicating more effectively, making consequences relevant and immediate, and changing the environment so compliance is more likely.

## The Course of Behavior Management

Children comply with requests because they have learned appropriate behavior and are in an environment that invites such behavior. The question that remains is, How do you create an environment that will invite compliance? Educator David Almeida suggests a five-step plan for managing the behavior of children in the classroom. These five Cs outline a clear course to follow when developing a behavior-management plan for home or school. The five Cs are clarity, consequences, consistency, caring, and change.

Clarity. Be clear. All students must have a clear understanding of what is acceptable and unacceptable. These behaviors must be described in the most concrete terms possible.

Consequences. Behavior management is a balance between rewards and consequences. Rewards can be intangible, such as compliments, or tangible, such as a day at the movies. Consequences should not be physically harmful or shame the child. They should be along the lines of "If the room is not cleaned, you can't go to the movie," and "If homework is not completed, you can't talk on the phone."

Consistency. Be consistent in following your plan. Pay attention to appropriate behavior and deal consistently with inappropriate behavior. The closer to the time the behavior occurs, the more effective the reward or consequences. If rewards or consequences prove ineffective, consider altering them.

Caring. It is sometimes difficult to accept that children aren't being stubborn or insubordinate. This is especially true for children who struggle with inconsistent performance. As we see sparks of the child's ability, it is easy to assume that the child has the ability but doesn't want to change. This is rarely true. If we demonstrate that we truly care about the child, we are more apt to engage him in change.

**Change.** As we attempt to create an environment where change can take place, we may discover that we (parents and educators) must also be willing to change. Structure and routine are important for any child, but flexibility must also be present when working with children with learning difficulties. Adapt the environment or task to the child's abilities.

## Components of Behavior-Modification Therapy

**Home-school note program.** Home-school notes are communiqués between parents and teachers that keep parents informed of a student's progress, or advise parents of upcoming assignments and tests. They serve the purpose of engaging parents by raising their awareness; no more surprises on the report card. Parents are advised of problems early enough for intervention and improvement. The notes are also a great way to validate a student's efforts and achievement. The frequency of the notes can be varied to the child's need for reinforcement. In early grades, students might take home daily notes. As the student becomes more successful in achieving his goals the frequency can change to weekly or monthly.

Often these notes are used to document the child's progress in achieving "target" behaviors. The "target" behaviors must be described using *positive* observable actions the child must complete (e.g., completing 80 percent of his work, participating in class, or raising his hand before speaking). Ratings for behaviors may be subjective (e.g., okay, good) or numerical (1–5). Avoid words like "will not" when defining behaviors. Remember, we are trying to tell the child what we want from him, not all the things he does wrong.

When a child successfully achieves the targeted behaviors, he may be rewarded by selecting treats or activities from a reward menu. Rewards might include both activities that are routinely available and those that aren't, such as an extension of curfew for one night or a special trip to a soda shop to share an ice-cream treat. Rewards are most successful when the child helps design the reward menu.

Home-school notes are also terrific communication tools and do not need to be tied to a token or reward system to be effective. Figure 26.2 is an example of home-school notes used by Darlene's son's high school. Each teacher reports to the tutor, who completes the note. Darlene is provided with information that assists her in supporting the student. Teachers, tutor, parents, and student are all part of the communication circle. It's very effective. If the student misses an assignment or does poorly on a test, the parent and tutor are advised in the weekly report. Interventions can then be devised before the student gets into academic trouble.

**Ignoring.** Ignoring is often used as an early intervention for mild behavior problems. It is a withdrawal of attention upon the occurrence of inappropriate behavior. It is important that this be used consistently or the child may learn that increasing the inappropriate behavior will eventually get attention.

**Modeling, or role playing.** These are ways of demonstrating desirable behavior. The therapist may model walking to the teacher's desk and asking for clarification. Children may rehearse these stressful situations so that they will be prepared to implement the desired behavior (asking for help). The therapist may model both positive and negative approaches to the problem. This can help children link behavior to consequences.

**Positive attention.** Smiles, compliments, and other positive forms of attention reinforce desired behavior, especially when given immediately following its occurrence. Praise the child frequently. Teach children how to behave by acknowledging each new step achieved in skill acquisition. Tell the child what he did that was positive, as in the following examples:

1. You did a good job making your bed.
2. I like the way you brought home all the materials you needed and finished your homework.
3. I'm proud that you remembered to call me when you were delayed at work.
4. I appreciate how promptly you cleaned up the table and did the dishes.

Positive attention can also be nonverbal, but the nonverbal messages need to match what is said. Researcher Albert Mehrabian, Ph.D., states that visual messages account for 55 percent of what is received and

**Fig. 26.2. Home-School Notes (such as the one shown here) Monitor Progress and Communicate Upcoming Assignments and Tests to Assist the Student in Planning.**

Student _____ Week ending _____

| Subject | Satis. Progress | Unsatis. Progress | Comments |
|---|---|---|---|
| English | | | |
| Math | | | |
| World History | | | |
| Science | | | |
| Keyboarding | | | |
| | | | |
| | | | |

| Upcoming Assignments | Upcoming Tests |
|---|---|
| | |
| | |
| | |
| | |
| | |

believed in spoken communication. The way you deliver a message vocally accounts for 38 percent, and the words account for only 7 percent. Nonverbal positive attention can include:

- A pat on the shoulder.
- A wink or smile.
- A thumbs-up or high-five sign.
- A hug.

To be most effective:

- Be as immediate as possible with your approval.
- Be specific about what it is you like.
- Never give a backhanded compliment.

**Time-out.** This can be an effective procedure for reducing acting-out behaviors, especially when the behaviors are maintained by siblings, peers, or adult attention. Time-out may not be effective if the behavior is due to an inability to complete the task. In fact, it might reinforce noncompliance, as the child wishes to avoid difficult situations. For example, a child who experiences difficulty might act out in a way that gets him time-out just before reading group, where he must read aloud. Thus he avoids the embarrassment of reading orally.

Several variations of time-out can be used at home and at school. One common procedure involves placing the child in a room or a place where he is socially isolated for a short time, usually one minute for each year of age. In another variation, the child uses time-out as a safety valve by going to a predetermined, supervised safe place to reflect on what happened. A think-about-it chair can also be used for time-out in the school or home.

Time-out also benefits the adult, who can use it to compose himself when faced with frustrations. The child benefits from seeing the pattern of stopping and thinking before acting modeled by the adult.

**Token economy.** This is a procedure in which tokens such as poker chips or stickers are given for desired behavior. The token can later be exchanged for desirable items or activities. The rules of the token economy—such as what number of tokens are given for specific behaviors and how items or privileges can be purchased—are established before the program is implemented.

"Response cost" is the loss of the reward or token because of inappropriate behaviors. This approach is sometimes used on long car trips. Children may start with one hundred tokens, to be used when they reach their destination. Each time the child does something inappropriate (such as punching a sibling, bouncing in the seat, or arguing), a predetermined number of tokens is subtracted.

# Family Therapy

Family therapists believe that behavior is the outcome of interaction between people and their environment. The family is a salient part of that environment. Many families of children with a learning difference do not experience problems with family functioning. However, the stress of managing and advocating for the child who learns differently may erode even the strongest family's coping skills.

There is a great diversity within the field of marriage and family therapy, and this can be confusing. Many theorists view families as rule-governing systems that can be best understood by looking at the context in which the family functions. The presenting problem often serves a function within the family and can be understood by examining family interactions. Some commonalities of family therapy are:

Deal with family hierarchy, or family roles.

Deal with communications both verbal and nonverbal.

Deal with the here and now, with some insight into what caused the problem.

Focus on what maintains the problem, not what created it.

Define boundaries between self and others and family systems and other systems.

## Goals of Therapy

The goal of all therapy is to help people change. Therapists differ in the vocabularies they use to describe change, as well as the amount of change desired, who should change, and who participates in therapy. We will include the names most often linked with each type of family therapy so you can discover more about each on your own. The list below is not inclusive.

**Bowenian family systems therapy.** In a normal family, members possess a balance between thinking and feeling. They can adapt to change, and problems exist in the whole group. They have good emotional contact with their own families of origin. Each member thinks the family is a pretty good family to live in, and members use each other as sources of feedback and learning.

Problems in a family can often be attributed to impaired relationships with the family of origin. The therapist using this model might ask a lot of questions designed to help clients think about their problems and discover how to change their role in the problem. Goals of therapy include developing a balance between thinking and emotions and learning to think about behavior instead of reacting to it. Another goal is to modify dysfunctional relationships in the family, especially within the family of origin.

**Experiential**. The normal family has high self-worth. Its members communicate in a clear, specific, and honest manner. Family rules are flexible, appropriate, and human. The linkage to society is hopeful and open. Problems in the family are a manifestation of problems with communication in the family.

**Strategic**. The normal family is flexible and has a large repertoire for developing solutions to problems and life transitions. There are clear rules and a governing hierarchy. Dysfunction is the result of unsuccessful problem-solving attempts, inability to adjust to life transitions, and malfunctioning hierarchy. The goal of therapy is to resolve the presenting problem and define a clearer hierarchy.

**Structural**. The normal family has clear and firm boundaries. There is a hierarchy with strong parents. The family system is flexible and adapts and responds to both internal and external demands. If there are dysfunctions, they are a result of imbalance in the family structure.

The goal of therapy is to reorganize the family structure by strengthening the parents, creating clear but flexible boundaries, and developing adaptive alternative patterns.

# Solution-Focused Brief Therapy

Solution-focused brief therapy was developed by Steve deShazer and his colleagues. This theory builds on the work of Milton H. Erickson, who is considered the father of brief therapy. It is built around the assumption that all clients have the strengths and resources to change and that no problem happens all the time. The focus is on not labeling, maintaining a positive perspective, focusing on the future, and promoting client strengths.

Some critics express concern that solution-focus is a Band-Aid approach, and that with so much focus on solution, client feelings are pushed into the background. Supporters say this is a pragmatic and innovative model that uses a positive focus to engage clients, even those who have been identified as reluctant participants or who have not found methods based on a medical model helpful. Matthew Selekman identifies the basic assumptions of solution-focused brief therapy in his book *Pathways to Change*.

## Ten Guiding Assumptions of Solution-Focused Therapy

1. Resistance is not a useful concept. Think solutions and change.

2. Cooperation is inevitable. Engage clients by focusing on their beliefs and strengths.

3. Change is inevitable. Use "change talk" to cocreate an environment where change is inevitable.

4. Only a small change is necessary. Each journey begins with one small step.

5. Clients have the strengths and resources to change. Focus on strength and resource identification.

6. Problems are unsuccessful attempts to resolve difficulties. Sometimes we act when we shouldn't or fail to act when we should.

7. You do not need to know a great deal about the problem to solve it.

8. Clients define the goals for treatment. There is evidence that when clients choose the action, they are more likely to follow through and succeed.

9. Reality is observer-defined, and the therapist participates in cocreating the therapy system's reality. We can't get inside of another person and know his reality. We can only observe and listen.

10. There are many ways to look at a situation, none more correct than any other.

## A Standard Course of Solution-Focused Brief Therapy

As stated above, the basic assumptions are that clients have the solutions to their problems and no problem happens all the time. The standard course of solution-focused brief therapy is as follows (the therapist guides the client through this process):

1. Client identifies his goal in coming to therapy. What is the problem, wish, or complaint? What would he like to change?

2. How is this happening now? When isn't it happening? Suppose that, except for rare occasions, Susan's family argues about her homework each night. When doesn't this happen? When Susan is allowed to sit in the kitchen when her mom prepares dinner. Exceptions can be used to create change.

    a. Is the exception deliberate? Then do more of it. Perhaps Susan cooperates because mom is near for support, or just misses her mom during the day and wants to be near. Susan could be allowed to sit in the kitchen and complete written work each night.

    b. Is this exception happening spontaneously? Find out how or why it's happening. If Susan does homework without complaint three times per week, find out what is happening on those days that make a difference.

3. When the problem is solved, what will you be doing differently? Do a small piece of that now.

4. The client is given homework.

5. The client reviews what happened that was different or better.

# Medical Management

Medications may be used to treat underlying disorders in children with learning differences. These medications may help control inattention, impulsiveness, motor activity, and mood. Some medications may lead to improvement in social interactions and academic performance. However, medication is not a cure and will not remediate underlying learning disabilities. It is just one factor in the management process. If medication is used, families must closely monitor its effects and work closely with the physician.

Because all of the disorders last a lifetime, skill development must be a part of the management plan. If medication can help ease the symptoms of the disorder, then the child can begin to learn the skills he needs.

## Points to Consider When Deciding Whether to Use Medication

1. What is your family history? Has alcoholism or depression been noted? How about Tourette syndrome? If there is a family history of Tourette, stimulants may not be recommended.

2. What symptoms are the most problematic? By prioritizing, the physician can select the medication to ease the symptoms that most interfere with the child's ability to function.

3. Will medication provide a window of opportunity for the child to develop skills?

4. Could the child's symptoms be due to other problems such as anxiety, peer problems, or increased frustrations? Has the child developed bypass strategies or skills that enable him to manage with lower doses or without medication? Note such changes when evaluating the need or effectiveness of medication.

5. What other management strategies are you using? Medication is never the complete answer. It should be used concurrently with such strategies as skill building, academic remediation, counseling, and therapy.

6. What are the possible side effects? Ask how the medication may affect your child and what changes should be reported back to the doctor. Many side effects can be eliminated by adjusting the dosage.

It is the responsibility of the physician to closely monitor medication. It is amazing how frequently teacher and parents are placed in the position of adjusting the levels of medication. This is dangerous and most inappropriate.

When medication is first administered, parents and teachers should be asked to give frequent feedback to the physician. This information helps the doctor determine the appropriate dosage for the desired results. Once the dosage has been established, feedback should continue. Children change rapidly, and this may impact the effects of the medication.

Both parents and teachers need to be aware of the following information.

1. The name of the medication, where it will be administered (home and school?), how often, and when it will be administered.

2. Any possible side effects that could affect the child's health, behavior, or performance in school.

3. How the medication will be monitored (checklist? survey forms?).

4. What symptoms the medication will alleviate.

5. Permission to contact the physician if more information is desired.

# Miscellaneous Management Strategies

Parents may be tempted by strategies that offer a quick fix. Often advertisements lure parents with scare tactics or promises to get their children off Ritalin or to cure dyslexia.

Often these services or products can be expensive or require a lengthy commitment. It is important to be cautious and carefully scrutinize any product or service before you subject your child to it. Ask for scientific studies that show a correlation between the use of the product and a decrease in symptoms.

Once we see the "scientific proof," we must decide if the source and results are trustworthy. Mark Twain once wrote there are three kinds of lies: "lies, damn lies, and statistics." Studies can be slanted to produce results that endorse a product or service. Scientific studies need to meet several criteria before the results can be considered valid. As consumers, we may not have the ability, inclination, or access to information to determine if all claims are accurate. The best advice is to follow the motto of the state of Missouri: "Show me." Then, show me, show me, and show me again. If a product, therapy, or service has been studied, investigated, and endorsed by a variety of professionals or organizations, you can determine if there is at least a consensus regarding it's efficiency. Some questions to ask are:

- Was there a test and then a retest that proved the results were a result of the intervention?

- What kind of test was done? Is the only evidence from testimonials? Is the improvement real or a result of paying attention to the symptom?

- Who participated in the study? Were participants "creamed" to produce a favorable outcome?

- Can the results be reproduced by another study, independent of the original?

The last question is especially problematic in regard to treatments for attention deficit disorder. There have been claims that treating the child's allergies; changing his diet; giving him vitamins, minerals, and enzymes; vision therapy; or biofeedback can make the child nearly symptom free and at the very least remove the need for medication.

Often these claims have little or no scientific basis. Furthermore, such unproven strategies are rarely covered by insurance.

# Academic Remediation

Many students who experience difficulty in school have been identified as having a specific learning disability or a skill deficiency. These learners qualify for remediation within the school environment. Unfortunately, not all students who struggle with learning can rely on their school district to provide successful remediation.

Many parents find their child falls through the system's cracks (which many parents feel are about the size of the Grand Canyon). Qualifying for services often depends on measurable gaps in performance and ability or deficits in specific skills. A child who struggles may still fail to qualify for remediation through the school district. Or he may receive remediation, develop new skills, close the gap and find he no longer qualifies for services, though his withdrawal is bound to have a negative impact. Children do not magically stop being learning disabled when their scores improve.

As one parent frankly stated, "The harder you work to keep your child's head above water and close the gaps in learning the more likely it is you will find your child does not qualify for services. This often means parents must find other resources to help their child stay on the road to success.

## Community-Based Tutoring

Many parents choose to provide tutoring or remediation using private individuals or tutoring services to assist their children. One caution must be addressed. Often children with learning disabilities are not slow learners, but they learn differently and need to be taught differently. If tutoring only reinforces ineffective strategies, it won't be very helpful. Make sure the person or service you engage to assist your child understands your child's specific learning problems and knows how to teach to his strengths. Before you make your choice, ask the following questions.

1. Is the teacher state-certified, and does he or she have classroom experience?

2. Is the teacher certified to teach at your child's grade level and in the subject area in which he needs help?

3. Is the teacher or service highly recommended by other parents and professionals?

4. Does the teacher or service use a variety of learning materials that are adaptable to a broad range of learning styles?

5. Are parents given regular updates on their child's progress?

6. If you engage a service, does it provide testing and regularly retest to check progress?

7. How long has the teacher or service been in business? Does he have a proven track record? Will he be there six months from now?

8. How willing is the tutor to communicate with the classroom teacher about the child's progress and needs?

Finally, consider the child-teacher match. We cannot overemphasize how important this is. Even the most skilled teacher won't hit it off with every student. A teacher who connects with a child, on the other hand, can motivate and guide the child to incredible achievement. Darlene was amazed to see the A in American history on her son's interim report. His previous social studies grades had been mediocre at best. The secret? An interesting teacher who brought history to life.

# Social Skills

It is easy to underestimate the importance of social skills. They seem to just come naturally to many children. However, a closer look reveals what an awesome task it really is to develop them.

The book *Skill-Streaming the Adolescent* identifies fifty structured learning skills that constitute social success in adolescents functioning at school and at home, with peers and others. The skills are divided into six groups: beginning social skills, advanced social skills, skills for dealing with feelings, skill alternatives to aggression, skills for dealing with stress, and planning skills (see Figure 26.3). This list was developed for adolescents; younger children have not developed as many skills as have teens. These skills are very complex, and even adults struggle to acquire many of them, especially those dealing with stress, aggression, and feelings.

As you look at the following list, think about how well your child performs each task on a scale of 1 to 5, with 5 representing the highest level of competency. Problem areas can then be targeted for development, while helping your child identify his areas of strength can take some stress out of social situations.

## Social Skills and Communication

Interpersonal conflict and lack of social skills may interfere with learning. Realizing this, schools often design prevention/intervention programs that teach problem-solving skills to resolve conflict, raise awareness, and improve communication. The following are examples of programs and interventions that teach social skills and are integrated into school programs.

**Fig. 26.3. Skills for Social Behavior**

I. Beginning Social Skills
  1. Listening
  2. Starting a conversation
  3. Having a conversation
  4. Asking a question
  5. Saying thank you
  6. Introducing yourself
  7. Introducing other people
  8. Giving a compliment

II. Advanced Social Skills
  9. Asking for help
  10. Joining in
  11. Giving instructions
  12. Following instructions
  13. Apologizing
  14. Convincing others

III. Skills for Dealing with Feelings
  15. Knowing your feelings
  16. Expressing your feelings
  17. Understanding the feelings of others
  18. Dealing with someone else's anger
  19. Expressing affection
  20. Dealing with fear
  21. Rewarding yourself

IV. Skill Alternatives to Aggression
  22. Asking permission
  23. Sharing something
  24. Helping others
  25. Negotiation
  26. Standing up for your rights
  27. Responding to teasing
  28. Avoiding trouble with others
  29. Keeping out of fights

V. Skills for Dealing with Stress
  30. Making a complaint
  31. Answering a complaint
  32. Sportsmanship after the game
  33. Dealing with embarrassment
  34. Dealing with being left out
  35. Standing up for a friend
  36. Responding to persuasion
  37. Responding to failure
  38. Dealing with contradictory messages
  39. Dealing with an accusation
  40. Getting ready for difficult conversation
  41. Dealing with group pressure

VI. Planning Skills
  42. Deciding on something to do
  43. Deciding what caused a problem
  44. Setting a goal
  45. Deciding on your abilities
  46. Gathering information
  47. Arranging problems by importance
  48. Making a decision
  49. Concentrating on a task

## Giving It, Taking It, Working It Out

Students are taught to express themselves in an assertive and positive manner. They are taught to solve problems and communicate effectively. Teachers or counselors can help students define what they want and what they are willing to do to get it. Parents or a therapist can review the skills below and help brainstorm when things fall apart. They can help students analyze situations in which their behavior was not useful. The therapist can also help teens understand what they are good at now and what they need to work on. Reinforcing and accentuating the positive builds hope and encourages change.

**Giving it.** The student is taught to stay calm when there is a conflict and to ask to talk to the other person. The student must say something positive if he can and then tell the other person what is on his mind.

**Taking it.** Now the child must stay calm and listen to what the other person has to say. He must ask the person to explain if he doesn't understand, and then ask the person what he wants done. Finally, he must tell the person he understands and agrees and apologize, or he can ask to tell his side.

**Working it out.** The student must stay calm and tell the person what he wants. Next, he listens to the response. If there is still disagreement, he must ask if the person has another way to deal with the problem. Finally, he must propose a compromise. He repeats these steps until he reaches an agreement.

## BEST and VENT

These acronyms represent strategies designed to reinforce desired behaviors. Once again, the focus is on learning how to communicate. When students find it difficult to implement these models, they can be taught to use a defusing technique, the "keep calm" method. This is another form of self-talk. They breathe deeply through the nose as they count to five. Then they hold their breath for two counts and then count to five again. After they have calmed down, they can then use BEST or VENT to bring resolution to the problem.

Body posture. Be aware of your nonverbal forms of expression.
Eye contact. Be sure to maintain it, and speak with authority.
Stance. Watch your posture.
Think. Consider what you are going to say. Use "I" statements.

Voice. Monitor the tone of voice, stay calm.
Eye contact. Look at the person and use "I" statements.
Nice language. Do not accuse.
Talk in a confident manner. Stand up straight and maintain eye contact.

## Students' Creative Response to Conflict (SCRC)

This program began in 1972 in New York City public schools. The SCRC is now used internationally in twenty-one cities. Its themes are affirmation, cooperation, communication, conflict management, and appreciation of differences.

This program helps children develop social skills by creating an atmosphere among children and adults that is warm, affirming, and supportive. The program uses modeling and experiential learning to help students integrate the ideas into their own environment and experiences. Children learn to deal with conflict in humane and constructive ways. These are especially relevant goals for the child with a learning difference, as he may struggle with all of the core themes of the program.

SCRC was originally designed for children in kindergarten through eighth grade, but it has been modified and used with many different populations. The program may be presented as a workshop, integrated into the daily classroom activities, or included in the curriculum.

# Study Skills

As children progress to secondary education, they are required to be more detail oriented, more organized, and better able to interpret and comprehend information. Ideally, students should understand their learning style, have generalized study skills, and realize when it is appropriate to use each skill. This can be a challenge. Students with learning differences have often been characterized as poor in five areas: organizing themselves and their time, following directions, completing and turning in assignments, identifying main ideas in lectures and texts, and note taking.

## Study Suggestions

1. Two heads are better than one. Join a study group, or study one-on-one. Take turns quizzing each other, or work together as a fact-finding team.

2. Schedule time to study, preferably the same time each day.

3. Review material as soon as possible after the class.

4. Set small goals for each day.

5. Use a dictionary or a text glossary when you do not understand.

6. Try to link what you are studying to what you know.

7. Decide what environment works best. Can you concentrate better with background noise? Do you need complete quiet?

8. Clarify expectations. Students often report they studied everything but what was on the test. If this sounds like you, schedule a conference with the teacher and ask for assistance in setting up a study plan that will insure success.

## PQRST

The goal of this method of textbook study is to help you learn the information, remember what you have learned, concentrate as you study, and organize your materials into main ideas and supporting details.

**P is for "preview."** First, preview the assignment quickly. Read headings and subheadings. Review maps, graphs, charts, pictures. Read the introductory and summary paragraphs. This will alert you to what the chapter is about before you study.

**Q is for "question."** Ask, What is the author trying to tell me? Look over questions at the end of the chapter. What questions do you expect to find the answers to? This will give you something to hunt for.

R is for "read." Read the assignment carefully. Underline major points. Summarize the key idea in your own words in the page margins.

S is for "state." State in your own words what you have read. Restate major concepts at appropriate stopping places in the chapter.

T is for "test." Test yourself on your understanding of the assignment. Repeat a few days later and review as necessary.

## Tips for Note Taking

1.  Try to get the main idea and important facts down on paper. If the instructor repeats an idea or makes a statement several times, there is a good chance it is a main idea. Write it down.

2.  Write so you can read your notes.

3.  Ask for copies of transparencies if the instructor uses an overhead.

4.  Tape lectures and take notes later. Type these notes.

5.  Be aware of key words and phrases such as *finally, then, at last*.

6.  Get a note partner who takes clear notes, and copy these notes.

7.  Organize notes in outline form.

8.  Try to spend 80 percent of your time listening to the lecture and 20 percent writing notes.

9.  Write notes using your own words. Incorporate right-brain adaptations such as charts and cartoon pictures to link ideas together.

10. If outlining from a text, you may wish to purchase the text, highlight the main ideas, and write supporting ideas in the margin.

## Memory

The process of memorization begins when the senses receive information from the environment. Information fades quickly unless it is processed and stored in short-term memory. Poor attention, fatigue, or distractions may prohibit a sufficient depth of processing, resulting in superficial registration of information.

Before we can remember, we must package information into a usable form. This coding of information reduces the load of incoming information and allows us to relate it to previously stored information. Active working memory allows us to hold information in our minds while we work on it.

Short-term memory holds a remarkably small amount of information, only seven digits. This type of memory is tested by word and digit span tests, where students must repeat lists of words or numbers, whose length increases with each successful completion. Information stays in short-term memory for only up to a minute. From there it must be processed to register in long-term memory.

Once information makes it into long-term memory, it can remain indefinitely. The key to finding information in memory is the richness of our individual indexing systems.

One key to remembering well is knowing to what you should pay attention. Some students have difficulty determining what is important and what deserves their attention. Others do not pay attention to information long enough to get it into long-term memory.

Older children may benefit from mnemonic activities, such as rehearsal and chunking large amounts of information into more manageable sections. By the age of eleven, most children have learned how to use mnemonic devices such as those in the following list. Children with learning disabilities may fail to use strategies. They know what they are and how to apply them, but they don't understand when they will be beneficial.

### Techniques to aid memorization.

- Present information in a variety of ways. Use a multimedia or multisensory approach to present the same idea.
- Color code information to highlight key points.
- Use rhyme or music.
- Organize information by categories.
- When you think you know the information, practice it another ten times.

- Pace rote learning of items to 8- to 10-second intervals.
- Chunk information to be learned into smaller manageable amounts.
- Create mental pictures of what is to be remembered.
- Use of verbal rehearsal by whispering information as a way of reinforcing registration in memory.

# Parent Training Programs

You need a license to drive a car, cut hair, or sell a home, but there is no license required to be a parent. Most of us do a pretty good job, but we do get overwhelmed and need a motivational speech or a pat on the back now and then. Below is a brief summary of several popular parenting programs. This is not an inclusive list. These programs are not targeted for parents of children with learning differences. But good advice is good advice.

### Active Parenting and Active Parenting of Teens

This program focuses on parenting methods that increase a child's self-esteem, responsibility, and cooperation. For information: (800) 825-0060.

### Black Parenting Education Program

This program is designed for young black parents with young children. It is a competency-based, comprehensive, culturally relevant program designed to decrease infant mortality and meet the unique needs of young, at-risk African-American parents. It addresses issues of nurturing and raising children from an African-American perspective and helps reduce or eliminate child abuse and developmental deficiencies and increase the child's readiness to learn. For information: (703) 920-7006.

### Systematic Training for Effective Parenting (STEP)

This program has three levels geared to different ages. It is designed to teach parents about raising responsible, confident children. The topics are understanding children's behaviors, expressing ideas and needs, instilling discipline, building self-esteem, and learning how to communicate, including using "I" messages. Family meetings are also addressed. For information: (800) 328-2560.

### Confident Parenting: Survival Skills Training Program

There are two versions of this program. One is for parents of children ages two through twelve. This program teaches a variety of child-management skills designed to increase social behaviors and decrease problematic behaviors.

The second program is for black parents of children of any age. This program is a black-heritage and child-management skills program within an African-American frame of reference, using the behavior-modification concept to foster effective family communication, healthy black identity, extended family values, and child growth and development. For information: (808) 980-0903.

### Los Niños Bien Educados

This program is for Spanish-speaking and Hispanic-origin parents of children of all ages. It focuses on raising children to be well educated, using strategies and skills for promoting and maintaining children's behavior. For information: (808) 980-0903.

### Parenting Effectiveness Training (PET)

This program focuses on humanistic family relations and communication skills, using nonauthoritarian methods of problem identification and conflict resolution. Designed to be an economic alternative to psychotherapy for emotionally damaged children and stressed families. For information: (619) 481-8121.

### Parent Plus

This program is for parents of high-risk children in elementary and middle school. It is designed to teach parents how to provide "protective factors" for their children, such as expression of feelings, and healthy coping strategies. Qualities of a healthy family life, appropriate child development, and ways of building self-esteem are also themes of the program. For information: (313) 455-4343.

Parent to Parent

This program is designed to help parents of teens and preteens guide their children through the "high risk" years by using information, attitude formation, and skills development. For information: (404) 451-9689.

# Points to Ponder

1. **What's the presenting problem?** Children with learning difficulties may experience a myriad of difficulties and may require a multifaceted approach to remediation and strategy development. Prioritize your concern. It is more effective to work on one or two goals at a time.

2. **Who pays for the therapy?** Many health-care plans offer limited mental-health benefits. Academic testing and remediation are normally not covered, so parents of children who do not fall within bureaucratic guidelines are left to carry the full financial burden themselves. The school, however, is responsible for testing your child. You may also ask for a second opinion if you are not satisfied with the school's findings.

3. **Is therapy really necessary?** It often helps to have a mental-health professional who understands your child and your family and who can support and advocate for the child. Given time, the crisis may resolve itself. If you have a strong support system, you may be able to work through most problems together. But if what you are doing isn't working and you don't know what to do, get some help. Have a professional you can call in times of crisis or when you get stuck.

4. **How do we facilitate change?** The first step toward change is to accept the challenge to change. Realize that each new idea or technique must be repeated and practiced until it becomes

second nature. Realize that change takes time and there may be roadblocks. Be open to new ideas and new ways of doing things.

5. **What skills does our child need to acquire?** Social and academic problems are often manifestations of skill deficits. When problems arise, ask yourself if the child is able to comply, or whether this is a manifestation of the disability.

# 27

# Planning for Success

As students with learning disabilities prepare to graduate and leave home, parents worry: Will they be safe? Will they be able to take care of themselves? Will they find employment? Will they be taken advantage of? These worries are not completely unfounded. Students with disabilities often need ongoing support and services that are not readily available, and studies indicate they are less likely to find competitive employment. It follows that development of a plan for skill building is an important step toward success. One component of that plan is surviving standardized tests.

## Standardized Testing

Children with disabilities may request accommodations in standardized testing, such as untimed tests, the use of a calculator, braille or large-print test booklets, audiocassette editions, and the services of a reader. School guidance counselors can assist parents and students in obtaining the necessary registration material.

Scan sheets used with some standardized tests are a problem for many students. The student is supposed to fill in the space on the sheet that corresponds with the correct answer on the test. The sheets are then scanned and graded electronically. But errors made by the student in recording his answers often result in an inaccurate assessment of his abilities. Ron was so frustrated with his standardized test that he just made an attractive design on the scan sheet. It was so much easier than trying to keep track of which block to darken.

## SAT

To obtain specific details on special accommodations, contact the organization that develops and conducts the test: SAT Services for Students with Disabilities, P.O. Box 6226, Princeton, NJ 08541-6226.

## ACT

For students with physical or diagnosed learning disabilities who are able to test under standard conditions, call (319) 337-1510 for information about accommodations at national test centers. For students with physical or diagnosed learning disabilities who cannot test under standard conditions, call (317) 337-1448 for information about Universal Testing.

## Minimum Competency Testing

Minimum competency testing is an attempt to establish minimal acceptable levels for achievement. Thirty-six states now require some type of minimum competency testing (MCT). Some states tie the passage of these tests to graduation, testing children as freshman and again as seniors. There is considerable debate over minimum competency testing. One concern is that MCTs will shift blame for inadequate educational programs to the individual. While the goal of MCT—to improve overall achievement—is admirable, many are concerned that the testing will become an educational ceiling that depresses some students' achievement levels. The impact on minority groups is also debated. To study these questions, a random sample of

11,995 students from more than 1,000 schools was studied. Data for the study came from the High School and Beyond longitudinal study completed by the National Center for Educational Statistics. The results indicated that MCT does raise the academic floor but also decreases the likelihood of a student scoring in the highest academic categories. Remediation also has a dual effect on high and low achievers. Although findings are weak, there was an increased tendency toward dropping out of school associated with MCT implementation. A good question raised by the authors of the study is whether the higher test performance of all students attributable to MCT is worth the increased dropout rate.

If your child has difficulty in school, MCT may be a major concern. Children with identified learning disabilities can waive the MCT requirement. This sounds good at first, but suppose by the time your child is ready to graduate from high school he or she is no longer exempt? The student could then be in the anxiety-provoking situation of having to pass all sections of the test during her senior year.

Some schools are suggesting their students with learning disabilities take the tests without any modifications as freshmen, thus establishing a baseline. Many students with AD/HD or learning disabilities are surprised to discover they pass most or even all subtests of the test. This can be a great morale booster. If the students does not pass any portion of the test, he can then retake the test with any modification (such as oral or untimed testing) that is stipulated in his IEP. If your child is still exempt as a senior, you can stop worrying about passing and exercise your child's right to an exemption.

# Alternative Roads to Success

## Home Schooling

Some children are not successful even in the best of traditional school settings. What do you do when your school is not meeting the needs of your child? When faced with this dilemma, many parents today are choosing an old option, home schooling. The number of home-schooled children is now an estimated 1.2 million.

Regulations vary from state to state, but your home school district can inform you of the process you must comply with to home school in your state. The Home School Legal Defense Association in Paeonian Springs, Virginia (703) 882-3838, is a great resource for parents considering home schooling and will provide information about your state's laws.

Many communities have home-school support groups or networks. These networks often create social learning opportunities for the child who is home schooled. They also provide information regarding curricula and teaching supplies and help you with state compliance.

## Vocational Education

Vocational education has long been a viable choice for students. For generations, vocational education happened in the family. The family often taught the child a trade or skill that would enable the child to grow into a productive adult. In recent years, the changing needs of society created a greater demand for formal education and more specific skills.

Today vocational education occurs at the secondary, postsecondary, and university levels. Vocational education can assist students in obtaining relevant skills and job experience. Successful training begins with an assessment of the individual's vocational strengths and limitations. It identifies optimal vocational objectives and presents a plan for reaching those objectives. School counselors and counselors from the Vocational Rehabilitation Bureau can help students locate vocational education programs in your community.

# Preparing for College

Searching for a school that will support the student who needs accommodations can be a challenge. Parents and students are often surprised to find that many colleges have few resources to help students with disabilities.

Three college guides that are especially relevant for students with learning disabilities are:

- *The K & W Guide to Colleges for the Learning Disabled*, edited by Marybeth Kravets and Imy F. Wax. New York: Harper Collins, 1992.
- *Peterson's Guide to Colleges with Programs for Students with Learning Disabilities*, edited by Charles T. Mangrum III and Stephen S. Strichart. Princeton, N.J.: Peterson's Guides, 1992.
- *Unlocking the potential: College and Other Choices for Learning Disabled People—A Step-by- Step Guide,* by Barbara Scheilber and Jeanne Talpers. Chevy Chase, Md.: Adler and Adler, 1987.

These guides are a great starting place. Don't forget to check out local four-year and community colleges. Many schools have services for students with disabilities but do not advertise them. The other side of the coin is just because a school has a program, does not guarantee it will meet your child's needs. A thorough interview can give you a good sense of a school's ability and desire to work with your student.

Many colleges have student disabilities services, learning labs, and special students' services. These offices usually help students with disabilities acquire a special accommodation and even advocate for the student. They might include a resource center where students gather for tutoring, hook up with a support service, and test with accommodations.

It is important that college administrators understand the student's disability. When discussing enrollment, have documentation available regarding the student's condition, including testing, evaluations, and diagnoses. Make a written list of support services you believe your child needs. Discuss what is available and how easy these services are to access.

Things to look for in a college:

- An attitude of support and empowerment for the student with special needs.
- A staff of full-time specially trained professionals who are active in the admissions process.

- Easy-to-access services.

- Special classes, such as study-skills, remedial, and developmental classes.

- Comprehensive supports, such as tutors, computers, note takers, scribes, taped lectures, untimed tests, and counselors.

- Opportunity for a reduced course load, course waiver, or substitution.

- Arrangements for separate or alternative testing administration, with such accommodations as oral or untimed testing and readers or scribes.

## It Takes Two

The frustrating truth is that no matter how much we investigate and how committed the school is to educating students with disabilities, the program will only be successful if the student is willing to access these services. Late adolescence is a time when students strive to become independent and develop their own identity, separate from their parents. This is appropriate, but at times students who learn differently take the concept of independence to the extreme.

Students may mistakenly believe they no longer need accommodations. They may not want teachers and other students to know they have a disability. Even though colleges are sensitive to these feelings and protect confidentially regarding specific disabilities, students may fail to register with teachers and counselors or request needed accommodations.

As parents, we want and need our children to develop a sense of independence. This desire is tempered by our understanding of their need for ongoing support and assistance as they make the transition from children to young adults. As never before, parents must adopt the roles of partner, coach, and cheerleader for the student with a learning difference.

We must work to remove the stigma from learning differences and honor the child who marches to the beat of his own drum. Sometimes it's hard for the child to find his place in the world. With our support, love, and encouragement, that will happen. "I resist anything better than my own diversity," wrote the poet Walt Whitman. Let us celebrate our children's diversity. Let's resist attempts to label, sort, and mold them. Let's resist attempts to limit their options and optimism. Their song may be different from ours. It may not be the popular or approved melody and lyric. But it is uniquely theirs.

# Appendix

## Individualized Education Program (IEP) Form

# INDIVIDUALIZED EDUCATION PROGRAM

NAME _____ DATE OF BIRTH _____ / _____ / _____ GRADE LEVEL _____ ☐ MALE ☐ FEMALE

CHILD/STUDENT ADDRESS _____

PARENT ADDRESS _____ PARENT/GUARDIAN _____

_____ HOME TELEPHONE _____ WORK TELEPHONE _____

EFFECTIVE DATES From: _____ To: _____ MEETING DATE _____ ☐ INITIAL IEP ☐ PERIODIC REVIEW

## ADDITIONAL CONSIDERATIONS

Considerations for the IEP team as they complete the IEP process, steps 1–5. Refer to State of Ohio Model Policies and Procedures for the Education of Children with Disabilities and IEP *Tour Book* for specific information on procedures/process. If needed, use space provided or attach additional sheet.

| | Discussed and Not Applicable for This Child/Student | Discussed and Incorporated into IEP |
|---|---|---|
| 1. Testing and assessment programs, including proficiency tests [See IEEE Addendum 608a] | ☐ | ☐ |
| 2. Transition from early childhood (ages 3–5) to school-age programs | ☐ | ☐ |
| 3. Transition services statement, no later than age 16 [See IEP Addendum 608b] | ☐ | ☐ |
| 4. A plan to address behavior, if the IEP and MFE team have determined this to be a concern | ☐ | ☐ |
| 5. Physical education must be addressed for ALL children and incorporated into the IEP (MUST BE INCORPORATED) | | ☐ |
| 6. Extended school year services | ☐ | ☐ |
| 7. Children/students with visual impairments [See IEP Addendum 608c] | ☐ | ☐ |

Relevant Information/Suggestions (e.g., medical information, other information)

| Present Levels of Development/ Functioning/ Performance | Annual Goals | Objectives |
|---|---|---|
| [Refer to State of Ohio Model Policies and Procedures for the Education of Children with Disabilities or IEP Tour Book for specific information on procedures/process]<br><br>**Step 1**<br>Review the results of the evaluation team report or intervention-based multifactored evaluation or current IEP. In a narrative form, explain the child's/student's present levels of performance. Include progress, strengths, capabilities, interests, and needs displayed in school, at home, and in the community.<br><br>**Step 2**<br>Determine the area(s) of the child's/student's needs. | **Step 3**<br>Write goals and objectives in areas of need<br><br>(What will the child/student be able to do in one year?) | What are the intermediate/sequential steps leading to the goal? |

[This form can be used vertically or horizontally]

Name _____

| Evaluation of Each Objective | | | | | Services | Initiation/ Duration | LRE |
|---|---|---|---|---|---|---|---|
| Procedures | Criteria | Schedule | Who | Review of Progress | | | |
| *How?* | *What? How much?* | *When will we review?* | *Who is respon-sible?* | *Results?* | **Step 4** Determine special educa-tion services, including related services, needed to implement each goal, as well as the amount of services. *(e.g., modifica-tions, supple-mental aids, assistive tech-nology, providers)* | | **Step 5** Determine setting in which to deliver the service. *(Where will services be provided?)* |

Name _____

| | **IEP Meeting Participants' Signatures** |
|---|---|
| EXTENT OF PARTICIPATION IN REGULAR EDUCATIONAL ENVIRONMENT OR, FOR PRESCHOOL, PARTICIPATION WITH TYPICALLY DEVELOPING PEERS | 1. Parent(s): _____ |
| | 2. Child's/Student's Teacher: _____ |
| Additional modifications: | 3. District Representative: _____ |
| | 4. Child/Student: _____ |
| | 5. Other Titles: _____ |
| | 6. _____ |
| REASON FOR PLACEMENT IN SEPARATE FACILITY (if applicable) | 7. _____ |
| | 8. _____ |
| | 9. _____ |
| Having considered each of the service delivery options, this IEP team has decided that placement in a separate facility is appropriate because: | Chairperson of IEP Team: _____ |

**Consent**

(For initial placement or change in special education services and placement only)

❑ I give consent to initiate special education and related services specified in This IEP.

❑ I waive my right to notification of special education and related services by certified mail.

❑ I give consent to initiate special education and related services specified in this IEP except for _____

❑ I do not give consent for special education services at this time.

**Parent Signature:** _____ **Date:** _____

**PARENT NOTICE OF PROCEDURAL SAFEGUARDS:**

❑ I have received a copy of the parent notice of procedural safeguards, or

❑ I have a current copy of the parent notice of procedural safeguards.

**Parent Signature:** _____ **Date:** _____

State and federal rules and regulations mandate that every child/student with a disability be reevaluated at least every three years. THIS IS TO NOTIFY YOU that your child will be provided that mandated reevaluation prior to his/her next periodic review. Applicable if this box is checked ❑

| School district of residence: _____ |
|---|
| School district of service: _____ |
| Building: _____ |
| Date of Next IEP Review: _____ |
| Date of Last MFE: _____ |
| Next MFE to be Completed By: _____ |
| CHILD/STUDENT ID#: _____ |
| AGE AS OF NEXT DECEMBER 1 Specify age in years: _____ |

**Summary of Services for EMIS Purposes**

| LRE: | Related Services: (list all services to be received) |
|---|---|
| Attendance option for Preschool/kindergarten: | |

| Disability (circle the child's/student's primary disability) | | | | |
|---|---|---|---|---|
| MH | DB | HI | VI | SH | OH | OHI |
| SBH | DH | SLD | P/D | AU | TBI | |

Reprinted from *Ohio Tour Book.* Used with permission of the Ohio Department of Education.

# Glossary

**Achievement tests:** Tests measuring the amount a student has learned in one or more subject area.

**Acquired disability:** A condition that occurs as a result of an injury or illness.

**Active working memory:** One type of memory that enables a person to keep the parts of the task in mind while working on it.

**Adaptive response:** The appropriate and effective reaction to a stimulus. The reaction should be purposeful and goal-directed.

**American Sign Language (ASL):** The official language used by deaf and hearing-impaired individuals. It consists of hand gestures to represent words.

**Amniocentesis:** A method used to test the amniotic fluid for cells from the fetus that may indicate possible genetic disorders. This can be done between the sixteenth and eighteenth weeks of pregnancy.

**Annual goals:** What the child receiving special education services can accomplish within twelve months.

**Apraxia:** The lack of motor planning common in children with sensory integrative dysfunction (SID).

**Aptitude test:** Paper-and-pencil assessments of intellectual functioning that are supposed to predict how the child will do later. Examples include Standardized Aptitude Test (SAT).

**"At no cost":** The term used in PL 94-142 to assure parents that they do not have to pay for any special services provided for their child under the law.

**Attention-deficit/hyperactivity disorder:** A neurological disorder resulting from an imbalance in the release of the brain's neurotransmitters. It requires a medical evaluation and diagnosis. Subtypes include predominantly inattentive type, predominantly hyperactive/impulsive type, and combined type (meeting the criteria for both inattention and hyperactivity-impulsivity).

**Audiologist:** A trained, nonmedical professional who evaluates for a hearing loss. All audiologists have a minimum of a masters degree. Most have a Ph.D. or Au.D.

**Audiometry:** The tests given to determine a hearing loss. They vary according to the age of the individual. Some are sensitive enough to be used with newborns.

**Auditory discrimination:** The ability to differentiate between closely related sounds or spoken words.

**Autism:** A condition where the child appears not to prefer social interaction and has difficulty making his thoughts and feelings known.

**Automatic memory:** The ability to remember things quickly without thinking about it. Remembering math facts depends on this type of memory.

**Basal ganglia:** The area of the brain that consists of the caudate, putanem, and globus pallidus. This area can be thought of as a relay station that integrates a variety of inputs into motor activity.

**Blending or closure:** Putting together the sound units in a recognizable form of the word.

**Braille:** A system of dots or points that conveys a message through touch.

**Brain contusion:** A bruising of the brain.

**Central nervous system (CNS):** The part of the nervous system that consists of the brain and the spinal cord and which receives, organizes, and processes sensory information from all over the body.

**Cerebral palsy:** A condition characterized by a lack of muscular coordination, shaking, and often unclear speech.

**Chorionic villus sampling:** A method used during the ninth to eleventh weeks of pregnancy to test the chromosomes of cells for possible genetic disorders.

**Chromosomes:** The genetic material found in our cells.

**Closed head injury:** A type of brain injury that occurs when the brain undergoes a violent motion that results in the tearing of nerve fibers and blood vessels within the brain.

**Cochlea:** The part of the ear that converts sound into nerve pulses, making hearing possible.

**Cognition:** The process of knowing, thinking, reasoning, making judgments, and planning activities of the human mind.

**Communication:** The transfer of a message between the sender and a receiver.

**Communication delay:** Speech and language patterns appear to develop "normally" but at a slower rate than expected.

**Communication disorder:** Developmental patterns, rate of speech, and language are affected.

**Comorbid disorders:** Co-occurrence of two or more disorders, such as AD/HD and specific learning disability.

**Compulsion:** An irresistible urge to perform irrational actions over and over again.

**Concussion:** An injury to the brain that may result in loss of consciousness.

**Conduct disorder:** Extremely disobedient behaviors in young adults, including theft, vandalism, lying, and early drug use.

**Conductive hearing loss:** One type of hearing loss that may be restored with medication and/or surgery. This type of hearing loss occurs in the external or middle ear.

**Consent:** Indication that the party involved agrees with the arrangements made for the child. Signed consent is necessary before a child can be evaluated or initially receive services.

**Conservation:** The ability to recognize that shape and quantity are not affected when the environment or container is changed. Whether in a gallon jug or a bucket, a gallon of milk is still a gallon of milk.

**Content words:** Words that carry the main message by expanding and describing. Nouns, verbs, adjectives, and some adverbs are content words.

**Context clues:** Hints about word meanings that come from illustrations or other words in the sentence.

**Deafness:** Defined as a hearing loss of greater than 90 decibels.

**Decibel:** A measure of sound intensity.

**Decoding:** The mental process used to figure out word pronunciation and meaning.

**Demystification:** The removal of the mystery about a learning difference by learning the facts through education.

**Developmental delay:** Development of the child at a slower pace than normal.

**Developmental disability:** The term used to describe individuals who have a condition that prevents normal development. The condition appears before age eighteen.

**Directionality or tracking:** The ability to move from left to right and follow words across the page.

**Dopamine:** A chemical that acts as a neurotransmitter in the brain. Dopamine neurons are involved in the regulation of motor activity.

*DSM IV:* The manual compiled by the American Psychiatric Association that provides the criteria for the diagnosis of mental health disorders, including AD/HD.

**Down syndrome (Trisomy 21):** A developmental disability with a genetic predisposition. The individual is born with forty-seven chromosomes, rather than the normal forty-six. The extra chromosome results in very distinctive physical characteristics and significant developmental delays. This is the most common form of genetically determined mental retardation. The measurable IQ is usually less than 70.

**Due process:** Legal safeguards provided to protect the individual's rights.

**Dyscalculia:** The difficulty some encounter when learning math.

**Dyslexia:** A disorder commonly characterized by reversals and inversions that can seriously interfere with the reading process.

**Facilitated communication:** A controversial technique used to help those with autism and other severe communication disorders communicate with the assistance of a facilitator.

**Family therapy:** A group of therapies in which members of families are helped to relate better to one another.

**Fetal Alcohol Syndrome (FAS):** Retarded growth of the developing fetus and infant caused by heavy consumption of alcohol by the mother during pregnancy.

**Figurative language:** Language used to add interest to the reading selection. This includes idioms, metaphors, and similes. They are not meant to be taken literally (for example, "He blew up!" meaning he was angry).

**504 Plan:** The plan of action written by parents and teachers under the guidance of the school's 504 coordinator. Provisions for the writing of this management plan are made in Section 504 of the Rehabilitation Act of 1973.

**FM amplification system:** Sound is transmitted to the child's hearing aid via a wireless FM microphone. This microphone can be worn by the teacher to assist the child in the classroom.

**Fragile X syndrome:** The second most common form of mental retardation, found most often in males. This genetic disorder results in a defect found at a fragile site on the X chromosome. It causes a severe form of mental retardation in males and a milder one in females. Like Down syndrome, it has distinctive physical characteristics.

**Free appropriate public education (FAPE):** Provides for all children with disabilities, from age three to twenty-one (for those who've not received a diploma), the right to an education at public expense.

**Function words:** Words that support content words (*see separate entry*). Pronouns, prepositions, articles, and auxiliary verbs are function words.

**Genes:** The heredity material found in chromosomes that determines our specific traits.

**Grapheme:** A visual symbol, such as a letter, number, or word.

**Hearing impaired:** Defined as a hearing loss between 15 and 90 decibels.

**Hyperactivity:** The excessive high-energy level and perpetual motion of one's body. It is like being driven by a motor.

**Impulsivity:** Leaping before you look. Rushing into something without considering the consequences.

**Inattention:** A hallmark characteristic of AD/HD referring to the inability to selectively attend to the task at hand. It is not the inability to pay attention but rather paying attention to everything.

**Inclusion:** The policy of providing special services within the general education classroom. This concept recognizes the general education classroom as the "least restrictive environment" for all learners.

**Individualized education plan (IEP):** A written plan for students with disabilities in accordance with state and federal guidelines.

**Intelligence quotient (IQ):** A measure of the individual's cognitive abilities based on scores from specific standardized tests. It is expressed as a standard score with the mean of 100 and the standard deviation of 15. (An average IQ measures around 100.)

**Invisible disorder:** Another way to view AD/HD. Referring to the lack of visible signs of a disorder, which often leads to misunderstanding. It is not the lack of desire to conform, but the inability because of the brain's functioning. Without eye glasses or crutches to signal a disability, we often forget it is there.

**Involuntary:** A function beyond the control of the individual. Motor and vocal tics are involuntary responses.

**Language:** An organized system of symbols, shared among a group of people, which represents objects, actions, feelings, processes, and relationships. Each language has a set of rules governed by the content, use, and form of that language.

**Least restrictive environment (LRE):** The placement of a child with a disability with other learners who are not disabled, usually the general education classroom.

**Legally blind:** A legal term used to determine eligibility for services. Many individuals with this diagnosis have, and use, their remaining vision.

**Lexicon:** The dictionary of a language. This is how we figure out the words used in language.

**Linguistics:** Anything pertaining to language or the study of language.

**Low vision:** A visual impairment that is severe enough to require special education services.

**Math facts:** Basic addition, subtraction, and multiplication tables. Automatic recall of these facts facilitates computation.

**Math manipulatives:** Objects that can be used to help students learn math. Counters, pattern blocks, geoboards, coins, and raisins and buttons are examples of math manipulatives.

**Math operations:** The processes used to solve math problems. Addition, double-digit multiplication, and finding the area of a triangle are math operations.

**Math phobia:** The fear and anxiety that can accompany learning math.

**Mean:** The average score on standardized tests. In most cases, the mean is 100. A score of 100 would be average.

**Mental retardation:** Cognitive functioning below what is considered average. There are three ranges: mild (55 to 70), moderate (40 to 55), and severe (25 to 40). Mental retardation does not refer to the level of dysfunction but rather to the fact that children with this disability learn and develop more slowly than peers the same age.

**Metalinguistic awareness:** Developing an "ear" for what sounds correct in language usage. It is the ability to make judgments about what makes sense. Jokes, puns, synonyms, or words with multiple meanings make sense to the person who is metalinguistically aware. This skill develops and becomes more acute as the knowledge of language increases.

**Modality:** The vehicle through which a message is communicated.

**Morphology:** The study of how words are constructed. There are two types of morphemes. The ones that stand alone and have meaning by themselves, such as *farm, make, sing*, are called free morphemes. Bound morphemes are the prefixes, suffixes, and other "add-ons" that do not have meaning as independent words.

**Motor tics:** Movements beyond the control of the individual. Eye blinking, grimacing, rolling eyes upward, and shrugging the shoulders are examples of motor tics.

**Multidisciplinary team:** A group that works together to meet the needs of the students.

**Multifactored evaluation (MFE):** An evaluation conducted in more than one area of the child's functioning so that no one criterion is used that may result in a misdiagnosis or labeling of the child.

**Multiple sclerosis:** An incurable, progressive disease of the central nervous system.

**Neuron:** A single nerve cell.

**Neurotransmitters:** Chemicals released into the synapses in the brain to carry messages from one nerve ending to another.

**Noncompliance:** Refusal to cooperate and follow rules.

**Norepinephrine:** A chemical that acts like a neurotransmitter in the brain. Norepinephrine acts as a modulator of other neurotransmitters, especially dopamine.

**Obsessions:** Meaningless and intrusive thoughts, ideas, images, and impulses.

**Obsessive-compulsive disorder:** A neurological disorder resulting in uncontrollable obsessive thoughts and/or compulsive behaviors, causing significant distress and interference with everyday functioning.

**Open head injury:** Another type of brain injury that occurs when the head hits a stationary surface or is hit by a moving object. The injury is usually localized to a specific area of the brain, resulting in the loss of specific skills or functions.

**Ophthalmologist:** A physician specializing in the care and treatment of the eye.

**Oppositional defiant disorder:** An antisocial condition, often a precursor to conduct disorder, that results in hostile and deviant behavior, usually directed toward adults and peers the child knows well.

**Optic nerve:** The nerve along which information from the retina is transported to the brain.

**Otitis media:** A chronic infection of the middle ear that often results in a hearing loss.

**Paraprofessionals:** Support personnel who offer special services to children with learning differences. They might include speech-and-language pathologists, physical and occupational therapists, tutors, reading specialists, etc.

**Performance intelligence quotient:** The standard score with a mean of 100 and a standard deviation of 15. Involves visual-spatial and visual-motor abilities to measure nonverbal reasoning.

**Phoneme:** The sound assigned to a symbol that may be used in different ways.

**Phonics:** A reading technique used to relate sounds to symbols (letters). Being able to discriminate between sounds is an essential element in reading and communicating effectively.

**Phonology:** The range of sounds within a language. *Phonics* comes from this word.

**Poliomyelitis:** A disease, commonly called polio, caused by a virus attacking the nervous system.

**Positron emission tomography (PET):** Computer-assisted scans used in brain imaging. Created by analysis of radioactive particles from isotopes injected into the bloodstream.

**Pragmatic language:** Verbal and nonverbal language, such as gestures, facial expression, tone of voice, posture, and the intent of the message, that is used in social interaction.

**Praxis:** The ability to integrate sensory input and to formulate, organize, and execute a sequence of unfamiliar actions. Also known as motor planning.

**Proprioceptive system:** A sensory system that uses receptors in the muscles, joints, and tendons to make us aware of our body's position in space.

**Reading comprehension:** The ability to understand messages related through the printed word.

**Reticular activating system:** The area where the brain filters extraneous stimuli and helps us stay focused.

**Retina:** Located at the back of the eye. It consists of light-sensitive receptors that send impulses to the occipital lobe of the brain via the optic nerve.

**Rituals:** Patterns of behavior that reduce the anxiety caused by obsessions.

**Scoliosis:** A curvature of the spine.

**Self-monitoring:** The strategy of going back over your work to check for errors.

**Semantics:** The study of words and their meanings. It can include words in isolation, as in a vocabulary list, or combined in sentences to express a thought.

**Sensorineural hearing loss:** A serious impairment that results from a malformation in the cochlea or auditory nerve.

**Sensory diet:** A management plan that the child and occupational therapist develop to help the child learn skills and adaptive activities that lessen the effects of sensory integrative dysfunction.

**Sensory integrative dysfunction (SID):** Dysfunction that occurs when the central nervous system can neither make sense of the information being sent by the sensory systems nor make the appropriate adaptive responses.

**Serotonin:** A neurotransmitter in the brain that inhibits behavior. A deficiency in brain serotonin is thought to be linked to increased susceptibility to a complex of related behaviors, including impulsivity, obsessive-compulsive behavior, aggression, and depression.

**Sight words:** Words that are either memorized or learned through repetition and recognized on sight. The larger the sight-word vocabulary, the more fluent the reading process.

**Social-skills training:** Procedures for teaching individuals how to perform social skills, such as meeting others, giving and receiving criticism, offering compliments, making requests, and expressing feelings.

**Sound/symbol association:** The knowledge that specific sounds go with specific symbols.

**Spatial ability:** The ability to imagine objects or symbols in space and their relationships to other objects.

**Specific learning disability (SLD):** A disorder that interferes with the ability to use and understand language. Listening, reading, mathematics, spelling, speaking, thinking, and writing are all areas that may be affected.

**Spina bifida:** A condition that occurs prenatally, in which part of the spine fails to close. Sometimes the spinal cord is exposed through an opening occurring anywhere along the spine.

**Splinter skills:** Specific areas in which the child with autism displays a unique talent. Unfortunately, seldom is the child aware of or able to use his or her special skills and talents.

**Standard deviation:** The most commonly used measurement of the variability in a set of scores.

**STAR:** An acronym for "Stop, think, act responsibly." Used to help manage impulsivity.

**Strengths:** The hobbies, interests, skills, or talents a person possesses and uses to compensate in problematic areas.

**Summarization:** Putting into your own words a shortened version of what you've heard or read.

**Sydenham's chorea:** A movement disorder related to obsessive-compulsive disorder.

**Synapse:** A small gap between two neurons where the nerve impulse passes from one neuron to another.

**Syndrome:** A group of symptoms that tend to appear together in particular diseases or disorders.

**Syntax:** The way words are combined into sentences. The order of the words and use of grammar rules determine the clarity of the meaning expressed.

**Tactile defensiveness:** A sensory integrative dysfunction in which the individual is extremely sensitive to touch, temperature, and textures.

**Teacher place:** The spot where most teachers stand to present important information. Some children need to learn to recognize this cue to listen.

**Teacher talk:** The jargon and terms used by teachers that may need to be translated for parents.

**Telecommunication device for the deaf (TDD):** A way for the deaf to communicate by phone. They can receive messages and make calls. The messages are typed on the TDD and translated into human speech.

**Thalidomide:** A fertility drug given to women in the 1960s that resulted in birth defects and deformities.

**Tics:** Involuntary functions associated with Tourette syndrome. Tics may be motor, vocal, or mental.

**Time out:** A quiet place to calm down and regain control. May be used by parent or child or in an academic setting.

**Token economy:** A behavior-therapy procedure whereby tokens such as poker chips are given for desired behaviors. These tokens can then be turned in for predetermined rewards, such as privileges or treats.

**Tourette syndrome:** A neurological disorder named after a French neurologist. It is characterized by the demonstration of both motor and vocal tics.

**Traumatic brain injury:** A preventable form of injury that often results in major neurological changes that can influence motor, language, self-care, sensory, and cognitive skills.

**Trichotillomania:** The compelling need to pull out one's own hair to relieve anxiety.

**Verbal intelligence quotient:** A measure of reasoning that involves words and language, with a mean of 100 and a standard deviation of 15.

**Vestibular system:** The sensory system located in the inner ear that determines head position, changes in speed and direction of movement, and gives us a sense of balance.

**Visual acuity:** Sharpness of sight, especially in the discernment of fine details.

**Vocal tics:** Involuntary sounds such as grunts, clicks, or smacking of the lips. Sometimes called phonic tics.

**Visualization:** The making of mental pictures.

**Waxing and waning:** The coming and going of tics. The range of flux can include one tic being replaced by another, a new tic overlapping an existing one, to the complete cessation of the symptoms for varying periods of time. The degree of severity is often determined by the amount of stress.

**Word calling:** The ability to recognize a word without understanding the meaning.

# Bibliography

Almeida, David. "Behavior Management and the Five C's." *Teaching K-8* (September 1995): 88–89.

Amen, Daniel, M.D., *Images of the Mind.* Fairfield, Calif.: Mind Works Press, 1995.

*American Family Physician*, 51, no. 1: 139.

*American Family Physician*, 52, no. 3: 1022.

American Psychiatric Association. *Diagnostic and Statistical Manual of Mental Disorders IV.* Washington, D.C.: American Psychiatric Association, 1994.

Anderson, Elizabeth, and Pauline Emmons. *Unlocking the Mysteries of Sensory Dysfunction.* Arlington, Tex.: Future Horizons, 1996.

Ayers, Jean A., Ph.D. *Sensory Integration and the Child.* Los Angeles: Western Psychological Services, 1979.

Baker Anne M., and Ellen M. Lynch, eds. *Children Who Challenge the System.* Norwood, N.J.: Ablex, 1993.

Barkley, Russell A., Ph.D. *Attention Deficit Hyperactivity Disorder: A Handbook for Diagnosis and Treatment.* New York: Guilford Press, 1990.

——. *Defiant Children: A Clinician's Manual for Parent Training.* New York: Guilford Press, 1987.

Barkley, R., and J. Murphy. "Treating Attention-Deficit/Hyperactivity Disorder: Medication and Behavior Management Training." *Pediatric Annals* 20, no. 5: 256–266.

Barraga, Natalie, Ed.D. *Increased Visual Behavior in Low Vision Children.* New York: American Foundation for the Blind, 1964.

Baton Rouge TS Support Group. *Toughing Out Tourette's.* Baton Rouge: Baton Rouge TS Support Group, 1989.

Batshaw, Mark L., M.D., and Yvonne M. Perret, MA, MSW, LISW. *Children with Disabilities: A Medical Primer.* Atlanta: Paul L. Brookes, 1992.

Begley, Sharon. "Your Child's Brain." *Newsweek.* February 19, 1996.

Benjamin, Arthur, Ph.D., and Michael Brant Shermer, Ph.D. *Teach Your Child Math.* Los Angeles: Lowell House, 1991.

Benz, Carolyn, Marilyn Fabian, and Wilson Nelson. "Assessing Study Skills of Students with Learning Disabilities." *Clearing House.* 69, no. 6.

Berger, Robert, James McBreen, and Marilyn Rifkin. *Human Behavior: A Perspective for the Helping Professions.* White Plains, N.Y.: Longman, 1996.

Bergman, Thomas. *On Their Own Terms: Children Living With Physical Disabilities.* Milwaukee: Gareth Stevens Children's Books, 1989.

Bilken, Douglas. *Communication Unbound.* New York: Teachers College Press, 1993.

Bishop, Jerry E. "Scientists Isolate Gene Causing Mental Disorder." *The Wall Street Journal,* May 30, 1991.

Borba, Michele. *Esteem Builders.* Torrance, Calif.: Jalmar Press, 1989.

Boyles, Nancy S., and Darlene Contadino. *Parenting a Child With Attention Deficit/Hyperactivity Disorder.* Los Angeles: Lowell House, 1996.

Briggs, Dorothy Corkille. *Your Child's Self-Esteem.* Garden City, N.Y.: Doubleday, 1970.

Bruetsch, Anne. *Multiple Intelligences Lesson Plan Book.* Port Chester, N.Y.: National Professional Resource, 1995.

Buehrens, Adam. *Hi, I'm Adam.* Duarte, Calif.: Hope Press, 1991.

———. *Adam and the Magic Marble.* Duarte, Calif.: Hope Press, 1991.

Buzan, Tony. *Use Both Sides of Your Brain.* New York: Plume Books, 1990.

Cahall, Jeanne S. *Stages of Reading Development,* 2nd ed. New York: Harcourt Brace College Publishers, 1996.

Campbell, Linda. *Teaching and Learning Through Multiple Intelligences,* rev. ed. Needham Heights, Mass: Allyn & Bacon, 1996.

Canino, Ian A., and Jeanne Spurlock. *Culturally Diverse Children and Adolescents.* New York: Guilford Press, 1994.

Canter, Lee. *Homework Without Tears.* New York: Harper & Row, 1987.

Coates, Rodney D., and Karen R. Wilson-Sadberry. "Minimum Competency Testing: Assessing the Effects of Assessment." *Sociological Focus,* 27, no. 2.

Coling, Marcia Cain, M.A. *Developing Integrated Programs.* Tucson: Therapy Skill Builders, 1991.

Comings, David E., M.D. *Tourette Syndrome and Human Behavior.* Duarte, Calif.: Hope Press, 1990.

Cook, David L., O.D. *When Your Child Struggles.* Atlanta: Invision Press, 1992.

Copps, Stephen. *The Attending Physician.* Atlanta: SPI Press, 1993.

Crary, Elizabeth. *Pick Up Your Socks and Other Skills Growing Children Need.* Seattle: Parenting Press, 1990.

Cummings, Rhoda, Ed.D., and Gary Fisher, Ph.D. *The School Survival Guide for Kids with LD.* Minneapolis: Free Spirit, 1991.

Ferrel, Kay Alicyn. *Parenting Preschoolers: Suggestions for Raising Young Blind and Visually Impaired Children.* New York: American Foundation for the Blind, 1984.

First, Patricia F., and Joan L. Curcio. *Individuals with Disabilities: Implementing the Newest Laws.* Newbury Park, Calif.: Corwin Press, 1993.

Flavell, John H. *The Developmental Psychology of Jean Piaget.* Princeton, N.J.: D. Van Nostrand, 1963.

Flesch, Rudolf. *Why Johnny Still Can't Read.* New York: Harper & Row, 1981.

Flodin, Mickey. *Signing for Kids.* New York: Putnam, 1991.

Fontenelle, Don H. *How to Live with Your Children.* Tucson: Fisher Books, 1989.

Fowler, Mary. *C. H. A. D. D. Educator's Manual.* Plantation, Fla.: C.H.A.D.D., 1993.

Friedland, Bruce. *Personality Disorders.* New York: Chelsea House, 1991.

Fry, Edward, Ph.D. *How to Teach Reading.* Laguna Beach, Calif.: Laguna Beach Educational Books, 1995.

Gardner, Howard. *Multiple Intelligences.* New York: Basic Books, 1993.

———. *Frames of Mind: The Theory of Multiple Intelligences.* New York: Basic Books, 1983.

———. *Leading Minds: Anatomy of Success.* New York: Basic Books, 1995.

"Girls in the Middle, Working to Succeed in School." American Association of University Women Education Foundation, 1996.

Goldstein, A., Robert Sprafkin, Jane Gershaw, and Paul Klein. *Skill-Streaming the Adolescent: a Structured Learning Approach to Teaching Prosocial Skills.* Champaign, Ill.: Research Press, 1980.

Gordon, Michael, Ph.D. *Jumpin' Johnny Get Back to Work.* New York: GSI, 1991.

———. *My Brother's a World-Class Pain.* New York: GSI, 1992.

———. *I Would If I Could.* New York: GSI, 1993.

Gould, Toni S. *Get Ready to Read: A Practical Guide for Teaching Young Children at Home and in School.* New York: Walker, 1988.

Greene, Lawrence J. *1001 Ways to Improve Your Child's Schoolwork.* New York: Dell, 1991.

Haerle, Tracy. *Children with Tourette Syndrome: A Parents' Guide.* Rockville, Md.: Woodbine House, 1992.

Hallowell, Edward M., M.D., and John J. Ratey, M.D. *Driven to Distraction.* New York: Pantheon, 1994.

———. *Answers to Distraction.* New York: Pantheon, 1995.

Hasenstab, M. S. *Language Learning and Otitis Media.* Boston: College Hill Press, 1987.

Healy-Romanell, Mary Ann. "The Invisible Griever: Support Groups for Bereaved Children." *Promoting Student Success Through Group Intervention.*: 67–89.

Himber, Charlotte. *How to Survive Hearing Loss.* Washington, D.C.: Gallaudet University Press, 1989.

Hinshaw, S., and S. Milnick. "Self-Management Therapies and Attention-Deficit Hyperactivity Disorder. *Behavior Modification* 162, no. 2: 253–273.

Howard, Barbara J., and Karen J. O'Donnell. "What is important about a study of within-group differences of 'cocaine babies'?" *Archives of Pediatric and Adolescent Medicine* 149, no. 6: 663.

Ingersoll, Barbara, Ph.D. *Your Hyperactive Child.* New York: Doubleday, 1988.

Kelley, Mary Lou. *School-Home Notes Promoting Children's Classroom Success.* New York: Guilford Press, 1990.

Kellner, Millicent, and Judith Tutin. "A School-Based Anger Management Program for Developmentally and Emotionally Disabled High School Students." *Adolescence* 30, no. 120: 813–825.

Kleinfeld, J., and S. Wescott, eds. *Fantastic Antone Succeeds!* Fairbanks: University of Alaska Press, 1993.

Kotulak, Ronald. *Inside the Brain.* Kansas City, Mo.: Andrews & McMeel, 1996.

Krevisky, J., and J. Linfield. *Bad Speller's Dictionary.* New York: Random House, 1974.

Lakein, Alan. *How to Get Control of Your Time and Your Life.* New York: New American Library, 1974.

Lawton, Millicent. "States move to toughen exit exams." *Educational Week* 15, no. 22: 1.23.

Levine, Melvin, M.D. *Educational Care.* Cambridge, Mass.: Educators Publishing Service, 1994.

————. *Keeping a Head in School*. Cambridge, Mass.: Educators Publishing Service, 1990.

————. *Developmental Variations and Learning Disorders*. Cambridge, Mass.: Educators Publishing Service, 1987.

McEwan, Elaine K. *The Parent's Guide to Solving School Problems, Kindergarten Through Middle School*. Wheaton, Ill.: Harold Shaw Publishers, 1992.

McGuinness, Diane. *When Children Don't Learn*. New York: Basic Books, 1985.

Meltzer, Lynn, Ph.D., and Bethany Solomon, M.A. *Educational Prescriptions for the Classroom for Children with Learning Problems*. Cambridge, Mass.: Educators Publishing Service, 1988.

Meyer, Carol, and Mark Mattaini. *The Foundations of Social Work Practice*. Washington, D.C.: NASW Press, 1995.

Moser, H. M. *Prenatal/perinatal factors associated with brain disorders*. Washington, D.C.: U.S. Government Printing Office, 1985.

Mueller, H. G., and M. C. Killion. "An easy method for calculating the articulation index." *The Hearing Journal* 43, no. 9: 14–22.

Nardo, Don. *The Physically Challenged*. New York: Chelsea House, 1994.

National Association for Children with Learning Disabilities. *What Every Parent Should Know About Learning Disabilities*. South Deerfield, Mass.: Channing L. Bete, 1976.

National Information Center for Children and Youth with Disabilities. *News Digest*.

New City Schools. *Succeeding with Multiple Intelligences: Teaching Through the Personal Intelligences*. Port Chester, N.Y.: National Professional Resource, 1996.

Nia-Azariah, Kinshash Kern-Crotty, Frances Bangel, and Louis Gomer. *Year of SCRC: 35 Experiential Workshops for the Classroom*. Cincinnati: Ohio Center for Peace Education, 1992.

Nicholas, Michael, and Richard Schwartz. *Family Therapy Concepts and Methods.* Needham Heights, Mass.: Allyn and Bacon, 1990.

Ohio Department of Education Language Task Force. *Ohio Handbook for the Identification, Evaluation, and Placement of Children with Language Problems.* Columbus: Ohio Department of Education, 1991.

Oldham, John M., M.D., and Lois B. Morris. *Personality Self-Portrait.* New York: Bantam, 1990.

Olsen, W. O., D. B. Hawkins, and D. J. Van Tassell, representatives of the Longterm Spectrum of Speech. *Ear & Hearing,* Suppl. 8: 100–108.

Piaget, Jean. *The Child's Conception of Numbers.* New York: Norton, 1965.

Quinn, Patricia, M.D. *ADD and the College Student.* New York: Magination Press, 1994.

Quinn, Patricia, M.D., and Judith Stern. *Putting on the Brakes.* New York: Magination Press, 1991. (An activity book is available under the same title.)

Radencich, Marguerite C., and Jeanne Shay Schumm. *How to Help Your Child with Homework.* Minneapolis: Free Spirit, 1988.

Rapoport, Judith L., M.D. *The Boy Who Couldn't Stop Washing.* New York: E. P. Dutton, 1989.

Reinecke, Mark, Frank Dattilio, Arthur Freeman, eds. *Cognitive Therapy with Children and Adolescents.* New York: Guilford Press, 1996.

Rezen, Susan V., Ph.D., and Carl Hausman. *Coping with Hearing Loss: A Guide for Adults and Their Families.* Fort Lee, N.J.: Barricade Books, 1993.

Rief, Sandra. *How To Reach and Teach ADD/ADHD Children.* New York: The Center for Applied Research in Education, 1993.

Ring, Elizabeth. *Assistance Dogs.* Brookfield, Conn.: Millbrook Press, 1993.

Robins, Lee N. *Deviant Children Grown Up.* Baltimore, Md.: Williams & Wilkins, 1966.

Rogers, Fred. *Dear Mister Rogers.* New York: Penguin Books, 1996.

Ross, Bette M. *Our Special Child: A Guide to Successful Parenting of Handicapped Children.* Old Tappan, N.J.: Fleming H. Revell, 1984.

Sanders, Matthew R., and Mark R. Dadds. *Behavioral Family Intervention.* Boston, Mass.: Allyn and Bacon, 1993.

Sattler, Jerome M. *Assessment of Children,* rev. 3rd. ed. San Diego: Jerome M. Sattler, 1992.

Schliechkorn, Jay, Ph.D, P.T. *Coping with Cerebral Palsy: Answers to Questions Parents Often Ask.* Austin, Tex.: PRO-ED, 1993.

Schwartz, Jeffery, M.D. *Brain Lock.* New York: Regan, 1996.

Sebastian, Richard. *Compulsive Behavior.* New York: Chelsea House, 1993.

Selekman, Matthew. *Pathways to Change: Brief Therapy Solutions with Difficult Adolescents.* New York: Guilford Press, 1990.

Sensory Integration International. *A Parent's Guide to Understanding Sensory Integration.* Torrance, Calif.: Sensory Integration International, 1991.

Simon, Charlann S., ed. *Communication Skills and Classroom Success.* Eau Claire, Wis.: Thinking Publications, 1991.

Smith, Carl B., Ph.D. *Help Your Child Read and Succeed.* Bloomington, Ind.: Grayson Bernard, 1991.

State of Ohio. *Model Policies and Procedures for the Education of Children with Disabilities.* Columbus: Ohio Department of Education, 1995.

———. *Whose IDEA Is This?* Columbus: Ohio Department of Education, 1995.

———. *Individualized Education Program: A Tour Book for the Journey.* Columbus: Ohio Department of Education, 1995.

Stray-Gundersen, Karen. *Babies with Down Syndrome: A New Parents Guide.* Rockville, Md.: Woodbine House, 1986.

Streissguth, Ann P. "A Long-Term Perspective of FAS." *Alcohol Health and Research World* 18, no.1: 74–81.

Sunderland, Ron. *Getting Through Grief Caregiving by Congregations.*: Abingdon Press, 1993.

Susman, Ed. "Cocaine's role in drug-exposed babies' problems questioned." *The Brown University Child and Adolescent Behavior Letter* 12, no. 9: 1.

Teele, Sue, Ph.D. *The Multiple Intelligences School—A Place for All Students to Succeed.* Port Chester, N.Y.: National Professional Resource, 1995.

Torres, Iris, and Anne L. Corn. *When You Have a Visually Handicapped Child in Your Classroom: Suggestions for Teachers.* New York: National Association for the Blind, 1990.

Trott, Maryann Colby. *Sensibilities Understanding Sensory Integration.* Tucson: Therapy Skill Builders, 1993.

Turecki, Stanley, M.D. *The Difficult Child.* New York: Bantam, 1989.

Tuthil, Robert W. "Hair lead levels related to children's classroom attention-deficit behavior." *Archives of Environmental Health* 51, no. 3: 214.

Tuttle, Cheryl Gerson, M.Ed., and Penny Paquette. *Parenting a Child with a Learning Disability.* Los Angeles: Lowell House, 1993.

Vail, Priscilla. *Common Ground: Whole Language and Phonics Working Together.* Rosemont, N.J.: Modern Leaning, 1991.

Vander Schaaf, Rachelle, and Maija Johnson. "Alert: Imported Vinyl Miniblinds" *Parents Magazine* 71, no. 8: 29.

Vergason, Glenn. *Dictionary of Special Education.* Denver: Love, 1996.

Vivigen Corporation. "Fragile X Syndrome." Santa Fe: Vivigen, 1991.

Wadsworth, Barry J. *Piaget for the Classroom Teacher.* New York: Longman, 1978.

Walker, Lou Ann. *Amy: The Story of a Deaf Child*. New York: E. P. Dutton, 1985.

Waltman-Greenwood, Cynthia, Ph.D. *Solve Your Child's School-Related Problems*. New York: Harper Collins, 1995.

Ward, Brian R. *Overcoming Disability*. New York: Franklin Watts, 1988.

Weiner, Lyn, and Barbara Morse. "Intervention and the Child with FAS." *Alcohol Health and Research World* 18, no. 1: 67–72.

Whitney-Thomas, Jean, and Cheryl Hanley-Maxwell. "Packing the Parachute: Parents' Experiences as Their Children Prepare to Leave High School." *Exceptional Children* 63, no.1: 75–87.

Wigginton, Eliot, eds., and his students. *Foxfire: 25 Years*. New York: Doubleday, 1991.Wilbarger, Patricia, and Julia Leigh Wilbarger. *Sensory Defensiveness in Children Aged 2-12*. Santa Barbara: Avanti Educational Programs, 1991.

"Winners All: A Call for Inclusive Schools." The Report of the NASBE Study Group on Special Education. The National Association of State Boards of Education, 1012 Cameron Street, Alexandria, VA 22314. (703) 684-4000.

# Index